Teaching
Foreign Languages
in the Primary School

Also available from Continuum

Getting the Buggers into Languages 2nd Edition, Amanda Barton
100 + Ideas for Teaching Languages, Nia Griffith
Teaching Art and Design 3–11, Sue Cox and Robert Watts
Teaching Physical Education in the Primary School, Ian Pickup and Lawry Price
Teaching 3–8 3rd Edition, Mark O'Hara
Reflective Teaching 3rd Edition, Andrew Pollard
Reflective Language Teaching, Thomas S.C. Farrell
Bilinguality and Literacy, Manjula Datta

Teaching Foreign Languages in the Primary School

Claudine Kirsch

continuum

Continuum International Publishing Group

The Tower Building   80 Maiden Lane
11 York Road   Suite 704 New York
London SE1 7NX   NY 10038

www.continuumbooks.com

British Library Cataloguing-in-Publication Data
A catalogue record for this book is available from the British Library.

ISBN: 978082689494 (paperback)

Library of Congress Cataloging-in-Publication Data
A catalog record for this book is available from the Library of
Congress.

Typeset by Newgen Imaging Systems Pvt Ltd, Chennai, India
Printed and bound in Great Britain by Cromwell Press, Wiltshire

To Michael

Contents

List of Figures and Tables

Figures

Tables

Preface

'*Coupez, s'il-vous-plaît*' ('Could you please cut') were among the first French words I was able to speak and I actually remember asking nurses at hospital to cut my meat. Many nurses spoke French in multilingual Luxembourg, a fact that considerably complicated communication for me, a monolingual Luxembourgish child whose mother tongue is 'Lëtzebuergesch' (Luxembourgish). As a three-year-old I could barely understand the nurses, and tended to answer most utterances with smiles and shrugs of the shoulders. My father taught me some 'important' words such as *merci* and, *bonjour*, but for me, '*Coupez, s'il-vous-plaît*' were certainly the most important. They guaranteed that my meals were presented in child-friendly portions.

A song contest on holidays in Belgium similarly marked my early foreign language learning experience. I sang 'Chevaliers de la Table Ronde', a French song which seemed long and difficult for a six-year-old. I won the first prize – probably because I was a little girl from Luxembourg who could sing in French. A Belgian lady asked me a number of questions of which I was able to answer only a few. I knew when to say my name and coped by repeating 'Luxembourg' and 'six' from time to time. The hostess smiled and showed me a selection of what I considered babyish toys. I understood that one of these was to be my prize. But I had selected a different present for myself: an orange T-shirt displaying a big blue camera, the prize for the adolescents. While the hostess tried to persuade me to choose a toy, I kept on smiling and repeating the few words I knew, '*Je veux T-shirt*' ('I want T-shirt'). I eventually got it and was very pleased with this special prize I had won for my linguistic competence in a language other than my mother tongue.

Looking back, I can see how important communicating in additional languages was for me at that early stage and how much pleasure I took in doing so. Like most children I was curious and eager to make sense of the world around me and therefore willing to put considerable effort into learning a few words. This positive attitude was important in primary school where I was confronted with German in Year 1, aged six, and French in Year 2. Language learning occupied almost half of the timetable. The same emphasis on languages continued at secondary school although I studied science. In addition to German and French, which were taught as a discrete subject and used as a language of instruction, I learned Latin and English.

It was only at Teachers' College where I trained as a primary teacher that I began to reflect on the process of learning languages. I noticed that the four languages I had studied had been taught entirely differently and that the methods (Immersion, Audiolingualism, Grammar-Translation and Communicative Language Teaching) had a different impact on my oral and written competence, my knowledge about language and my attitudes. Nevertheless, the overall focus lay on form: we were expected to write accurately and fluently. Little emphasis was put on our intercultural competence or understanding of the language learning process.

When it came to teaching Luxembourgish, German and French in my own class, I intended to provide the children with a productive and safe environment that took account of their sociocultural backgrounds and allowed them to take control of their learning. I used a 'whole language approach' (an approach that considers language as an entity rather than an assemblage of rules and patterns) and involves listening, speaking, reading and writing. I helped pupils to explore a wide range of genres, texts and styles, and to engage in authentic situations of communication with a wide range of people in and outside the classroom. My teaching was guided by my understanding of language learning as a dynamic social process in which children develop language skills and learn how to use languages when they participate in meaningful activities with more knowledgeable people.

In order to develop my knowledge and understanding of how children learn, and particularly learn languages, I enrolled in an MA and carried out a PhD in London. At the time of writing this book I lecture at Goldsmiths College, University of London. I teach, among other subjects, methodology of foreign languages to trainee teachers. I aim to help them develop the knowledge, understanding and skills to teach foreign languages competently and confidently.

I wrote this book on foreign language teaching from different perspectives and drawing on different experiences: learning foreign languages at an early age, teaching languages at primary school, delivering continuous professional development on language learning and researching how children learn languages in Luxembourg and England. As a learner, practitioner and researcher, the topic is very close to me. The book is intended both for tutors who are new to language teaching and experienced teachers. The former might particularly be interested in the case-studies and the practical parts, the latter in the theoretical sections.

I begin this book with a rationale for an early start and an overview of the provision of foreign language learning throughout the world (Chapter 1). I hope that the many case-studies in chapters 2, 5 and 11 illustrate the pleasure children derive from learning languages and the extraordinary wealth of knowledge and understanding that both learners and teachers bring to the subject. The two theoretical chapters on second language acquisition (Chapter 3) and teaching methods (Chapter 4) build the backbone of the book. I present different theories with different takes on learning and teaching and draw some implications for teaching languages. These theoretical parts will help you understand and contextualize your own methods.

Most chapters are of a practical nature: they offer some background information on how children develop listening, speaking, reading and writing skills (chapters 7 and 8); knowledge about language (Chapter 9); intercultural competence (chapter 10) and language learning strategies (Chapter 11), and provide some practical activities that you can carry out to develop these skills. The examples fit into a structured and a transactional approach. Chapter 6 gives some suggestions on how to use games, songs and stories effectively. Throughout these chapters, I pay attention to error correction and planning. The final chapter is on assessment and ways to facilitate transition between primary and secondary schools (Chapter 12).

The introduction of each chapter includes a section called 'Food for thought'. My aim is to activate your background knowledge and to make you reflect on your own experience of learning or teaching a language – in the same way as I did at the beginning of this book. I hope that I can sometimes challenge your beliefs and open you up to new ideas. Apart from Chapter 5 each chapter ends with a section called 'Main points to remember'. It provides a summary of the chapter in the form of implications for practitioners. Throughout the book I refer to many books, articles and reports which may be useful further reading. All references can be found in the Bibliography.

I finish this preface with some acknowledgements. I would like to express my thanks to all the children who participated in my studies. Thanks to their commitment, the book can provide a real insight into what it means for children to learn foreign languages. Further thanks go to some head teachers and teachers in England, Germany and Spain: Pauline Hindle, Carol Smith, Maggie Van Loan, Marion Jones, Sam Smyth, Marta Saez, Katrin Harder and Montse de Loa Fuente. I would like to thank them for their collaboration, support and time. Further thanks go to the following colleagues for helping me gain access to information about the provision of early language learning throughout the world: Dr Tony Liddicoat, Angela Scarino, Dr Lixian Jin, Dr Eduardo Garcia Villada and Dr Rod Case. I am deeply grateful to my French colleagues Prof Françoise Haramboure and Dr Michèle Catroux for their professional advice and critical insights. They made many suggestions which helped me make the book more reader-friendly. I would also like to thank John Simopoulos, Emeritus Fellow at St Catherine's College, Oxford, for proofreading the book. Other thanks go to my colleagues Dr Anna Traianou and Dr Sarah Pearce for their advice. Special thanks to Jo Allcock, my publisher, and Sue Cope, copy-editor for their professional support and perceptive and constructive critiques. My final thanks go to my partner Antony Warde-Jones who kept me in a good mood and gave me the necessary time to write.

Teaching Foreign Languages in the Primary School: An Overview

Chapter Outline

1.1 Introduction

Most people would agree today that the ability to speak more than one language is highly beneficial. Research has shown that multilingualism contributes to a learner's personal fulfilment and cognitive growth. Among the gains listed are creativity and originality; divergent thinking and cognitive flexibility; problem-solving; enhanced performance in literacy and numeracy; improved ability to reorganize information and to form concepts; higher metalinguistic ability; greater facility for learning further languages and augmented sensitivity to the communicative needs of interlocutors (Baker, 1997; Armstrong and Rogers, 1997). On a societal level, the benefits have been primarily described in economic, political and social terms. A multilingual workforce enhances a country's national and international development and its economic competitiveness in global markets. Multilingualism contributes also to the cultural and linguistic richness of a society, promotes tolerance and intercultural awareness, and furthers communication, mutual understanding and global citizenship.

David Blunkett, a former Education and Employment Secretary in the UK, drew on the above ideas when he stated:

> Learning a language is vital for international trade, communication and understanding, and for the insights it provides into the languages and cultures of our own country.
>
> (Blunkett quoted in CiLT, 1999)

Similar ideas have been stated throughout the world. In the United States, language programmes have been couched in terms of enhancing national security through a better understanding of the world (Holt, 2003; US Department of State, 2006). In Australia the rationale is based on the need for intercultural competence. The aim is to help residents cope with changes in relation to globalization and internationalization (Liddicoat *et al.*, 2007). In China, English is perceived as the gatekeeper to higher education, employment, economic prosperity and social status. This world language gives the Chinese access to modern scientific and technological advances, promotes commerce and fosters understanding and good relationships with other people speaking English (IATEFL, 2005).

These paragraphs make it clear that language learning programmes do not exist in a vacuum. Rather, they are influenced by political, economic and societal factors. A great momentum was created in Europe in 2000 when the European Council set itself the target to become the most competitive and dynamic knowledge-based economy in the world. In order to realize this, the European Council recommended in 2002 that all citizens needed to become proficient in two languages other than their mother tongue. Statistics show that 56 per cent of citizens in all EU Member States are able to hold a conversation in one foreign language but there are huge disparities between countries. While more than two thirds of the residents in Luxembourg, the Netherlands and Slovenia are fluent in one foreign language, the majority of people in six Member States, among them England, are not (Eurydice, 2005). The Council of Europe, like other organizations throughout the world, continues to work on the provision of foreign language learning in primary, secondary and adult education.

The pressure to make citizens fluent speakers of more than one language led to the implementation of foreign languages in primary schools. Foreign language learning is both a precious experience and an essential part of children's education. The majority of parents and the general public do not consider it to be superfluous or overburdening pupils (Eurydice, 2006). Young children are eager to learn languages and to find out about children in other countries.

In this chapter, I outline some advantages of an early start to language learning and give a brief overview of the provision of language teaching in the United Kingdom, Europe, the United States, Australia and China. I focus on the situation in England and describe the changes that led the government to make language learning compulsory from January 2010.

> **Food for thought**
> - Imagine that you are a head teacher and want to convince staff, parents and pupils of the benefits of language learning. What do you say?
> - Analyse the provision for foreign language learning in a primary school. What foreign language(s) is(are) taught? What is the rationale for modern foreign languages (MFL)? Who are the learners? Who are the teachers? What resources are used?

1.2 Advantages of an early start

People often assume that an early start is 'better' and results in higher achievements at secondary school. The question of the advantage of an early start has to be seen in relation to the Critical Period Hypothesis (CPH) suggesting that the brains of young children are particularly adaptable to acquiring languages before puberty. Language acquisition after puberty is said to be of a different nature and less successful (Penfield and Roberts, 1959; Lenneberg, 1967). Such an approach is consistent with other developmental theories of learning such as Piaget's theory of stages. However, this theoretical model and the concept of an 'optimum age' have been much criticized (Ausubel, 1964). While some researchers dispute the idea of a 'cut-off point' others provide evidence for the CPH. But proponents of the CPH disagree on the age at which children lose their inborn language learning ability (Horwitz, 2006). I refer readers to Lightbown and Spada (2003) and Hyltenstam and Abrahamsson (2001) for a presentation of arguments for and against the CPH.

Research studies that tested the Critical Period Hypothesis particularly in relation to the acquisition of native-like pronunciation in a second or foreign language have provided contradictory findings. Some indicate that young children are more efficient than older learners in both oral and aural performance (Vilke, 1988; Singleton, 1989; Long, 1990; Garajova, 2001 and Bagaric, 2003 mentioned in Edelenbos *et al.*, 2006). Others suggest that older learners have better phonetic perception and production; superior grammatical understanding; greater cognitive maturity; better general learning strategies and skills; and improved facilities for concept development (Ausubel, 1964; Snow and Hofnagel-Höhle, 1978; Hawkins, 1987; Collier, 1989; Johnstone, 1994; Garcia and Gallardo, 2003 mentioned in Edelenbos *et al.*, 2006). Children's age may play a key factor in these improved skills and increased knowledge, but the type of instruction and the teachers' competence in the target language play a role as well.

Though research into the optimum age for language learning is inconclusive, many neuroscientists still hold that age affects areas such as phonology and syntax. The latest studies have shown that there is a growth of the area responsible in the brain for language development from the age of six to puberty.

After reviewing a range of research studies carried out in schools in Europe, Blondin *et al.* (1998) and Edelenbos *et al.* (2006) conclude that 'younger' is not necessary 'better'. If the amount of teaching time is held constant, there are few differences in the speed of acquisition between younger and older learners. It seems that the only advantage of an early start is the total amount of time spent actively on learning a language (Edelenbos and Johnstone, 1996). Research has shown that there is a direct correlation between the time on task and the language proficiency that learners can be expected to attain (Curtain and Pesola, 1994).

While researchers have debated the extent to which an early start is beneficial for linguistic achievements, they all agree on its impact on attitudes. Blondin *et al.* (1998) point out that an early start promotes the development of positive attitudes towards language learning which in turn foster confidence, enthusiasm, motivation, openness to pronunciation and a greater willingness to take risks. It also furthers the development of positive attitudes towards other cultures and reduces ethnocentric thinking, racism and stereotyping.

To conclude, educationalists agree that an early start can result in early achievements such as improved communication skills, positive attitudes towards languages and cultures and heightened metalinguistic and metacognitive awareness provided that the learners are well taught and that there is continuity within primary schools and between primary and secondary schools (Martin, 2000; Edelenbos *et al.*, 2006).

The next sections look at the provision of foreign language learning throughout the world.

1.3 Language learning in the United Kingdom

1.3.1 Early language learning in England

As in many European countries, foreign languages have traditionally been taught in secondary schools. It was as recent as March 2007 that the government decided to make early language learning compulsory for children aged seven to eleven from January 2010 (DfES, 2007).

History of early language learning

From 1964 to 1974, the government funded a pilot project to test the implementation of French in 35 per cent of primary schools in England and Wales. The participating schools agreed to have all children learn French from the age of eight until at least 13. The National Foundation for Education Research (NFER) funded an extensive longitudinal study of pupils' attitudes and performances. Burstall, who spearheaded the project, concluded that further expansion was neither advisable nor appropriate. Apart from listening comprehension, the researchers did not find any significant differences between the achievements in French of secondary school pupils who had learned French from the age of eight from those who started at secondary school. They reported:

> Learning French in the primary does not seem to confer a lasting advantage from the point of view of achievement in spoken French, but it does seem to exert a lasting influence on the pupils' attitudes towards speaking French.
>
> (Burstall *et al.*, 1974: 169)

The authors did not consider the more sustained and favourable attitudes to French of the younger learners to be a strong enough reason to continue the project. As a consequence, most local authorities (LA) and state-maintained primary schools cut back their provision of foreign language (FL) teaching. A few selected state schools and most of the public schools responded to parental demands and continued to provide foreign language learning in one form or another.

The findings of the NFER project and the recommendation to stop provision have subsequently been challenged on the grounds of the research methodology and the failure to acknowledge the lack of differentiated provision for the young learners at secondary school. However, it was too late to change the perception that the project had been a failure.

It was only between 1980 and 1990 that the early study of FL received more positive notice from official authorities and the situation began to turn in favour of the implementation of languages at primary school. Many factors contributed to this change, among them being England's multilingual and multicultural population, global markets, enhanced and cheaper travel opportunities and pressure from the European Union.

At the turn of the century, guidelines for the introduction of modern foreign languages (DfEE, 1999b), non-statutory schemes of work (QCA, 2000) and the revised National Curriculum for England (DfEE, 1999a) including guidance for teaching languages in KS2 were published. At roughly the same time, the findings of two major research studies commissioned by the British government were published. The Nuffield Foundation (2000) heavily criticized the nation's 'deplorable monolingualism' (pp. 3 and 4) and blamed the ineffective educational system and the lack of national strategic responsibility of the government for the general linguistic incapacity. The researchers urged the government to establish a long-term strategy for the development of capability in languages and recommended the teaching of FL at primary school. This strong statement was, however, not echoed by the report of the Qualification and Curriculum Authority (Powell *et al.*, 2001). Their research concluded that it would be inappropriate to extend the statutory requirements for MFL into Key Stage 2 (KS2).

Influenced by the reports, the government recommended a mere 'entitlement' to foreign language learning for all children in KS2. At the same time as promoting languages at primary school, it asked to take languages off the National Curriculum at KS4 (Green Paper, 14–19, DfES, 2002a).[1] The 'National Languages Strategy: Languages for All: Languages for Life' (DfES, 2002b) describes the entitlement in the following words:

> Every child should have the opportunity throughout KS2 to study a foreign language and develop their interest in the culture of other nations. They should have access to high quality teaching and learning opportunities, making use of native speakers and e-learning. By age 11, they should have

> the opportunity to reach a recognized level of competence on the common European Framework
> and for that achievement to be recognized through a National scheme.
>
> (DfES, 2002b: 15)

Though the document does not make language learning compulsory, it raises the profile of the subject, gives some indications about resources and states expectations as to possible outcomes. The National Languages Strategy promotes a range of initiatives to help implement the entitlement and guarantee its success. Among them are the creation of networks and partnerships between LAs, schools and Specialist Language Colleges (SLC); the Languages Ladder (a recognition system complementing existing qualifications) (DfES, 2005b) and the development of primary teacher training courses (TDA, 2007).

In 2005, the Department for Education and Skills (DfES) published the *Key Stage 2 Framework for Languages* (DfES, 2005a). The document is broad and flexible, provides for a single-language or a multilingual approach and is skills-based. It does not prescribe a language or specific topics. The framework has three parts: learning objectives and sample teaching materials; targeted advice for different users of the framework and support for whole school planning. The learning objectives are listed within five strands: oracy, literacy, intercultural understanding, knowledge about language and language learning strategies. The first three are designed to be linear and progressive, the last two as transversal, arising from and supportive of the core teaching and learning strands. Lessons ideally include elements from three to five strands. The sample activities should act as prompts to help teachers develop their own programmes suited to their own circumstances and needs. It gives teachers the freedom to be creative and innovative and develop their own MFL course.

The publication of documents such as the framework, schemes of work (QCA, 2007) and the Languages Ladder (see Chapter 12), and the encouraging results of pilot projects made it possible for the government to make language learning compulsory in KS2 from January 2010. Lord Dearing, who recommended to make languages statutory, hopes that seven years of study will enable children to build up a 'critical mass of knowledge', a 'love of languages', confidence and experience (BBC News, 2007a; Andalo, 2007; Garner, 2007). His report did not suggest reversing the decision to make languages optional for students over 14. This decision has been criticized by teachers and the British Chambers of Commerce.

The Dearing Report has been received with some scepticism. Many point out that the primary curriculum is overloaded. Others warn that there are currently not enough foreign language graduates going into teaching and that it will take years to get the necessary workforce into place (BBC News, 2007a, 2007b). The Dearing Report tackles this issue by indicating that an extra £50 million a year is needed to help primary and secondary teachers deliver foreign languages. Some of this money will be spent on resources and training.

Provision of early language learning

Several studies describe the situation regarding language learning in primary schools in the period from 1998 to 2005. Below I present the picture at a national level in relation to the amount of provision, choice of language, staffing, language programmes, allocated teaching time and assessment.

Findings in 2004 (Driscoll *et al.*) reveal that 35 per cent of the approximately 3,000 primary schools responding to their survey taught 'some languages' in KS2 in curricular time in 2002 (from 5 to 120 minutes a week). This is about three times the figure found some years earlier by Powell *et al.* (2000). However, a closer look reveals that, generally, not more than 30 minutes was spent on language teaching and that only 3 per cent of the responding schools provided foreign languages to all children in KS2 (Driscoll *et al.*, 2004). These numbers contrast with more recent studies published in 2005 and 2007 where allegedly 56 per cent and 70 per cent of primary schools had implemented foreign language teaching or had planned to do so (BBC News, 2007b). In 2002, provision depended from LA to LA and school to school: Twice as many schools offered FL in the south-east as in the north-east. Schools offering provision tended to be in more favoured socio-economic areas and were slightly more successful academically.

The choice of language is influenced by a number of factors: the availability of staff, resources, the expectations of parents and children, the provision of languages at the local secondary schools, contacts with other countries, the language policies of the LA and the writing system. French was taught most. Few schools offered more than one language. If that was the case they offered generally German, Italian or Spanish.

The language programmes varied in their staffing, aims and lesson organization. In 2002, 41 per cent of all foreign language lessons were delivered by primary school generalists, 16 per cent by secondary specialists and 43 per cent by language advisers, advanced skills teachers, FL assistants or parents (Driscoll *et al.*, 2004). Driscoll (1999a) points out that children achieved higher results in the regime of primary school generalists than secondary specialists. She attributes this result to their good relationships with pupils, their pedagogy, classroom management skills and the rich opportunities for continuous language use. There is now a general agreement that children should be taught by language specialists according to the principle of 'primary pedagogy' (Driscoll and Frost, 1999; Nuffield Foundation, 2000; Sharpe, 2001). In 2007/08, 38 teacher-training institutions address this need by offering primary courses with a specialism in foreign languages to almost 950 students.

Half of the primary teachers surveyed by Driscoll's team perceived attitudinal outcomes as the most important benefits of foreign language teaching and a mere 10 per cent, generally the secondary specialists, aimed at the development of linguistic competence (Driscoll *et al.*, 2004).

Powell *et al.* (2000), Driscoll *et al.* (2004) and Muijs *et al.* (2005) found three different models of delivery in their data: the *competence model*, a *language awareness approach* and a *sensitization approach*.

The aim of the *competence approach* is to enhance children's four language skills (listening, speaking, reading, writing) in one (or possibly two) European language(s). The emphasis lies on performance and progression. This requires intense language teaching of at least one to two hours weekly. Programmes generally start at the end of primary school. Teachers need to have good subject knowledge to plan successfully for linguistic progression, to assess children's skills and to guarantee continuity within primary and between primary and secondary school. This requires careful planning and monitoring as well as efficient working relationships with secondary schools.

The researchers found few instances of the competence model in England. Because of the high linguistic requirements, it tended to be used by secondary specialists teaching French to pupils in Years 5 and 6. Teaching time lasted approximately half an hour a week.

The researchers seldom found the *language awareness* model in England (see Chapter 9, section 9.2.3). The aim of a language awareness programme is typically to sensitize learners to the nature, purposes and structure of languages. Teachers who chose this approach in England worked predominantly with older pupils. They developed children's knowledge about language predominantly by making links between English and the target language.

The dominant model found in England was a *sensitization approach*, but it differed slightly from the way one generally defines this model. A sensitization approach can comprise one or both of the following elements: language awareness and cultural awareness (Doyé and Hurrell, 1997: 100). Cultural awareness is an important aspect of language learning because it visualizes the link between language and culture. According to Hawkins (1987) cultural awareness furthers children's understanding of other cultures and ways of life in multi-lingual and multicultural societies and fosters the development of a critical perspective of their own cultural 'norms'. The approach is particularly beneficial in classrooms with children from different linguistic and cultural backgrounds who can share their experiences.

Sensitization approaches have been used in many European countries to develop positive attitudes to languages and cultures, basic language skills, knowledge about language and cultural awareness. The very broad aims and the minimal language requirements make it possible for primary teachers, hence generalists, to teach the subject to children of all ages. Apart from short lessons, five to 15 minutes a day, they tend to integrate language learning into the daily happenings at school. They choose active and enjoyable methods such as songs or games, make links with countries abroad and compare languages. Continuity with secondary school is less of an issue than with a competence model, but assessment can be more problematic because it is difficult to assess children's change of attitudes to languages and cultural awareness.

Sensitization approaches have been successful to some extent but there seems to be some general agreement that sensitization approaches are not enough (Doyé and Hurrell, 1997). Practitioners agree that the objectives are too vague and global, and better suited to multicultural education than to foreign language learning (Sauer, 1992; Felberbauer and Heindler, 1995). The evaluation of the programme Evlang (éveil aux langues) which had been piloted in 160 primary schools in France, Réunion, Austria, Italy and Spain from 1999–2001, did not win over public opinion. After reviewing the results Candelier *et al.* (2003) concluded that the programme did not show an absolute efficiency.

As indicated above, the most dominant model found in England at the turn of the last century was a sensitization approach, with a focus on the development of affective rather than cognitive factors. Teachers fostered the development of positive attitudes to languages and cultures by familiarizing children with one or more languages and cultures. Apart from short sessions (roughly 10 minutes) they used a foreign language throughout the day, generally in daily routines (e.g. weather) and for basic routine interactions (e.g. organizing children). More rarely, they used it when revisiting topics already covered in other subjects, for example reciting the times tables in French (Driscoll, 1999b). Some teachers made cross-curricular links with English (literacy), Mathematics (mental calculation), PE (physical education), Music and Dance.

Having observed and analysed language lessons and interviewed teachers and children, Driscoll *et al.* (2004) and Muijs *et al.* (2005) reported that pupils lacked opportunities to use the language creatively such as producing imaginative utterances, making jokes or expressing personal thoughts. Lessons were heavily teacher-led and teachers worked on a limited range of vocabulary and structures which they reinforced through rote learning, intensive oral question-and-answer work and extensive repetition in games, songs and rhymes (Powell, 2000; Muijs *et al.* 2005). There were occasional instances of pair work or group work including ICT (Information and Communication Technology). The OFSTED (2005) report of the Pathfinder areas, funded to develop good practice, indicates that most children had developed very good listening skills and were confident speakers. However, their reading and writing skills were underdeveloped. Teachers very rarely asked pupils to read or to look up words in dictionaries, reference books or word lists. In addition, the inspectors reported that only a minority of children had developed good intercultural awareness or knowledge about language. They found some examples of good practice where teachers made links with other countries via email or video-conferencing and exchanged typical artefacts.

Interviews with pupils showed that they were generally enthusiastic about language learning (Driscoll *et al.*, 2004; Muijs *et al.*, 2005). They liked songs, games, oral activities in pairs and groups and activities where they learned about a foreign country. Most perceived language learning as a 'fun' subject and distinguished it from those where they had to work hard. They seemed to 'play along' with the lessons (Muijs *et al.*, 2005: 13). Pupils commented negatively on the amount of repetition and memorization and the lack of differentiation. Some explained that their class teacher relied too heavily on games. Though they generally liked games, the enthusiasm faded in many Year 6 classes. The researchers recommended that teachers increase the variety of lessons; plan contents appropriate for children's cognitive development; change the status of foreign languages, ensure progression and continuity within primary and between primary and secondary school and work on assessment to ensure that children keep their enthusiasm.

Generally, children's performance was not measured. Many practitioners resisted the idea of formal feedback (such as error correction) and testing because they feared this could threaten the 'fun' element, undermine children's confidence and change the nature of the language learning experience (Jones and Coffey, 2006: 103). As a result, many primary schools could not adequately communicate the pupils' achievements and progress on entry to secondary school. In addition, many secondary schools did not use information (when it was received) to plan for Year 7 and beyond. Only a small minority of secondary schools, usually specialist language colleges (SLC), modified their provision in Year 7 to assist young linguists particularly through differentiation, setting and fast-tracking. Many Year 7 students spoke of their frustration at repeating earlier learning at secondary school (OFSTED, 2005).

These studies were carried out at a time when early language learning was not compulsory. It will be interesting to see how the situation changes after January 2010.

1.3.2 Early language learning in Scotland

During the 1960s the Scottish government funded projects to implement French in the upper primary but as in England, they were considered unsuccessful (Johnstone *et al.*, 2000). Foreign languages more or less disappeared from primary schools until 1989 when new projects were carried out at national and regional level. The success of the projects led the government to recommend an entitlement for language learning and to launch the National 5–14 Guidelines on Modern Languages (the equivalent of a national curriculum). The aim of language learning is the development of competence. The policy was supported with costly national programmes involving extensive professional training to ensure there was one qualified language teacher in 95 per cent of schools by 2000.

The entitlement, outlined in *Citizens of a Multilingual World* (Scottish Executive, 2000), stipulates that pupils begin to learn foreign languages in the last two years of primary school (Years 6 and 7, known as P6 and P7) and cover a minimum of six years or the equivalent of 500 hours. While the document gives some indication on teaching time and learning experiences, it does not define a minimum level of proficiency, nor does it clarify what percentage of pupils should have attained a particular level at a particular stage.

The report of Her Majesty's inspectors (HMIE, 2005) reveals that 96 per cent of pupils in P6 and 98 per cent in P7 study a foreign language. The inspectors found that the 5–14 National Guidelines on Modern Languages, the equivalent of the National Curriculum in England, had assisted in the development of more suitable learning programmes and improved teaching approaches. They reported that in the best examples pupils had developed good listening skills, could produce extended pieces of oral and written language and were able to read short texts with expression. However, they reported that not enough consideration had been given to improving learning, teaching and achievements from P6 to S2 (second year of secondary school). As a result, the learning experiences of many pupils lacked coherence and challenge in the first years of secondary school. Transition is one of the main issues of language programmes throughout Europe.

1.3.3 Early language learning in Wales

Wales has formulated its own National Curriculum that gives due recognition to the importance of Welsh, spoken by 26 per cent of the population (Welsh Language Board, 2003). The curriculum requires all pupils to study English and Welsh from the age of five to 16. This, for many, means studying Welsh as a second language.

Primary education through the medium of Welsh is available everywhere in the country. In Welsh-medium schools pupils are taught exclusively in Welsh up to the age of seven. Thereafter, English is introduced as a subject and may be used as a language of instruction for some parts of the curriculum.

Generally, foreign languages are compulsory from KS3. However, a pilot project to promote foreign languages (other than Welsh) at primary school runs from 2003 to 2008 in 118 schools involving mainly Years 5 and 6. Most schools have chosen French but there are also instances of Spanish, German and Italian. The aim of the project is the development of oracy, literacy, communicative skills and language awareness. Teachers use a wide range of models of delivery.

As in England, the government in Wales is committed to providing pupils in primary schools with an entitlement to learn foreign languages by January 2010.

1.3.4 Early language learning in Northern Ireland

In Northern Ireland, there is currently no statutory requirement to teach MFL at primary schools but there are a number of pilot projects aiming to implement this subject. Currently 25 per cent of schools are involved in some form of teaching foreign languages (Irish, French, German, Spanish and Italian) (www.rewardinglearning.com/development/new/latest/childsplay.html). A research team is currently working on a language strategy to promote and develop the provision and quality of language teaching and learning at primary school. It will report to the government in March 2008. It is hoped that children will have an opportunity to learn a foreign language in curricular time by 2013.

Provision of Irish is guaranteed in Irish-medium nursery and primary schools. Pupils learn Irish as a first or second language and learn content through Irish.

1.4 Factors influencing provision for foreign languages

Before I provide details on the situation of early foreign language learning in other parts of the world, it is useful to remember that provision is influenced by a number of factors, including:

- geographical and societal factors (e.g. degree of exposure to the target language, attitudes to language learning)
- economic factors (e.g. a country's economic needs)
- political factors (e.g. policies to promote language learning, funding)
- linguistic factors (e.g. closeness of the target language to the first language, teachers' proficiency in the target language).

The following example illustrates the impact of economics, politics and geography on language provision.

> Luxembourg, a small country in the heart of Europe bordering France, Germany and Belgium, has three official languages: Lëtzebuergesch (Luxembourgish), French and German. French is the language of 'integration'. Most people use it with non-Luxembourgish speaking residents or commuters. Forty per cent of the population are not Luxembourgers by nationality and 40 per cent of the active population commute daily from the three neighbouring countries (Kollwelter, 2007). These figures help explain the importance and status of French, which is reflected in the provision of foreign language teaching. Children learn German from Year 1, aged 6 to 7, and French from Year 2. Both languages are compulsory subjects. In addition, they are used as the languages of instruction in most subjects in primary and secondary school. The immersion situation both in and outside school provides pupils (and their teachers) with many opportunities to use the target languages and become fluent speakers.

1.5 Language learning in Continental Europe

At the turn of the twenty-first century many European countries have adapted language teaching to the overall framework articulated by the Council of Europe's language policy (Council of Europe and Council of Cultural Co-operation, 1996). However, there are huge discrepancies within and across Member States with respect to starting age, language(s) taught, time allocation, staff and policies on language learning.

The Eurydice study published in 2005 provides insights into the provision of early language teaching in the EU Member States. It reveals that approximately 50 per cent of primary pupils in the Member States learned at least one foreign language in 2003/04 (the time most data were collected). The subject was statutory in almost all EU Member States. In Luxembourg, Estonia, Sweden and Iceland the study of two languages is compulsory.

The starting age for language teaching has tended to fall. In some countries (e.g. Malta, Norway, Luxembourg) provision starts in Year 1 (children aged 5/6) and in some autonomous communities in Spain and France it even starts before primary school. However, the majority of pupils are introduced to foreign languages at the ages of 8/9 or 10/11. English is taught most widely followed by German or French. Children's proficiency in the target language is assessed in some countries at the end of primary school (i.e. Scotland; Spain; Italy; Greece and the Netherlands).

Where language teaching is compulsory, lessons generally last from 30 to 50 minutes. This is less than 10 per cent of the overall teaching time. The majority of language teachers are primary teachers, thus generalists. The situation is different in Belgium and France where languages are taught by either specialists or generalists, and in Malta where semi-specialists do the job.

Most countries would agree that the aims of foreign language learning are to help learners to develop competence in the target language, to acquire a sense of belonging to a wider community and to develop a good understanding of their opportunities, rights and responsi-bilities as European citizens. However, the emphasis of language programmes depends on each country. Edelenbos *et al.* (2006) described four different models of provision across Europe:

1. Language competence models based on a particular syllabus or textbook.
2. More flexible programmes aiming at language competence. The foreign language is taught as a separate subject and links are made between the language and other subjects.
3. Language awareness models with the aim to develop both metalinguistic awareness and intercultural sensitivity.
4. Bilingual education or partial immersion programmes. In immersion programmes children are taught some or all the subjects through the target language. The amount of time the first and second languages are used depends on the programmes and the schools. This is a very effective model and pupils generally attain high levels of proficiency because the target language is used as a vehicle for communication and the language of instruction.

According to this description, the provision in English primary schools falls into the third category. Very similar models are used in the United States as will become clear in the next section.

1.6 Language learning in the United States

Foreign language learning is not a statutory subject in primary or secondary schools in the United States. During the 1950s and 1960s the teaching of foreign languages was popular in elementary schools, and numerous early language learning programmes were set up. However, they soon disappeared for the following reasons: lack of trained and proficient teachers; unrealistic programmes; inappropriate teaching methods; insufficient materials; problems with continuity and lack of appropriate assessment procedures. The problems encountered in the United States were not different from those in Europe.

The provision of language learning has increased by nearly 10 per cent over 10 years and 31 per cent of schools offered foreign languages during the school day in 1997 (Branaman and Rhodes, 1999). Nevertheless, only 7 per cent of the 50 States required schools to teach a foreign language to students between the ages of 6 and 12 in 2004 (Steinbach, 2004). The majority of students start foreign language tuition only at age 14 (Pufahl *et al.*, 2000).

According to Stewart (2005) three models are currently used to teach languages:

- FLEX programmes (Foreign Language Exploratory)
- FLES programmes (Foreign Languages in Elementary Schools)
- Immersion.

The vast majority of teachers use *FLEX programmes*. They are similar to the language awareness or sensitization approaches found in Europe. (This would correspond to category 3 in Edelenbos *et al.* (2006).) The aim of the programme is to develop a foundation for foreign language study and an appreciation of other cultures. Children explore one or more languages once or twice a week. They learn about languages and cultures through typical songs, games, greetings and traditions. They also learn some basic phrases but language competence is not the aim.

In *FLES programmes*, the second language is taught as a separate subject once or twice a week depending on the school. Pupils learn basic classroom vocabulary and are able to hold simple conversations. There are huge variations among different FLES programmes (Curtain and Pesola, 1994) and therefore children's proficiency varies a lot. Only 7 per cent of all schools focus on language competence as required by the National Standards. The FLES programmes correspond to categories 1 and 2 of Edelenbos *et al.* (2006).

Table 1.1 summarizes the situation in the United States. In that table I refer once again to the National Security Language Act, 2003 and the National Security Education Initiative (2006) (US Department of State, 2006; Bush, 2006).

Table 1.1 Foreign language teaching in the United States

Factors influencing the provision	• growing awareness of the benefits of an early start • non-statutory standards for foreign language learning from kindergarden to Grade 12 (K-12) in 1996 • 'Goals 2000' • the Education Act 'No Child Left Behind' (2001) • National Security Education Program (1999), National Security Language Act (2003), National Security Language Initiative (2006)
Languages taught	• Spanish • followed by French, Japanese and Italian
Teachers	• Predominantly native speakers
Models used	• FLEX programmes • FLES programmes • immersion
Frequently used resources	• audiovisuals • textbooks • materials from the target country • computer-based materials • home-made resources
Frequently used assessment strategies	• selected-response tests (e.g. multiple choice) • short-answer tests • student presentations • portfolios • self-assessment Nevertheless, continuity with secondary school remains a problem and generally no extra provision is made at secondary level for young beginners.

1.7 Language learning in Australia

Language education for all students is a relatively new concept in the history of Australian schooling. The importance of language learning has been recognized in the 1989 National Goals and reaffirmed in the *National Goals for Schooling* (MCEETYA, 1999) where languages other than English were identified as one of eight key areas of learning. There is no centralized curriculum: it is up to the State and Territory governments, education authorities (and schools) to decide how they implement the National Goals. Some states and territories make language teaching compulsory at primary school, others leave it optional. Some decide on the language to be studied and the allocated teaching time, others leave that decision to individual schools.

Since the 1990s, the number of language programmes, learners and languages taught has increased. Research published by the Ministerial Council of Education, Employment, Training and Youth Affairs (MCEETYA, 2003) indicates that 50 per cent of students were learning a language in mainstream schools. Chinese, Japanese, French, German, Indonesian and Italian were the most commonly taught languages, but all in all 103 languages were taught in both mainstream and non-mainstream schools (MCEETYA, 2005). Primary schools figured predominantly high in terms of numbers and range of languages taught. The review pointed to major challenges such as inappropriately trained teachers, lack of continuity between primary and secondary and inadequate time allocation, and called for a renewed national effort. All Ministers of Education agreed to the development of a *National Statement for Languages Education in Australian Schools 2005–08* (MCEETYA, 2005) which describes the purpose and nature of the learning activities. It promotes the teaching and learning of Asian, European, Auslan and Australian indigenous languages, and fosters community language programmes in ethnic schools. To support the implementation of the National Plan, the Australian government asked the University of South Australia to carry out a survey in primary and secondary schools in all states. The aim was to describe the current state and nature of provision, to identify key issues and to develop strategies to improve the quality of language teaching.

Liddicoat and his team report (2007) that the bulk of language learning was concentrated in primary schools. Fewer students studied languages at secondary level and participation decreased with each grade. Enrolment in Year 12 has tended to stabilize around 13 per cent recently, which is a long way from the 25 per cent set as a target by the government.

The researchers found it impossible to describe 'the' situation of early language learning in Australia. They pointed to large variations in terms of starting age, allocated teaching time and continuity of language study. In some schools, foreign language study started in Year 1 and lasted until Year 6; in others it started in the last years of primary school. Some schools offered language lessons, others integrated languages into the general curriculum. Allocated teaching time varied from 35 to 150 minutes and most pupils studied languages for only part of a school year. Some schools offered programmes with a focus on language competence;

others offered taster-courses that familiarize pupils with a range of languages. Though curricula varied greatly, they all included a communicative and cultural dimension. Languages were generally taught by special language teachers with the class teacher not being present in the classroom. The lack of qualified teachers made the languages programmes highly vulnerable.

Liddicoat *et al.* (2007) point out that the concentration of language learning in primary schools is problematic since pupils study languages on average for 45 minutes for several years which is not enough to develop real competence. In addition, such programmes did not help to increase the very low enrolment of secondary school students in foreign language classes.

1.8 Language learning in China

Education in China has improved tremendously and experienced great achievements since the foundation of the People's Republic of China in 1949. In 2002, 99 per cent of pupils attended primary school and 95 per cent attended the full six years. At present the main objectives of the government are the generalization of nine years of compulsory education, the eradication of illiteracy and further developments for vocational and adult education by January 2010.

The study of English is another priority. Many Chinese perceive this world language as a necessary tool to achieve scientific and economic developments, to develop intercultural understanding, to boost relationships with other English-speaking countries and to further commerce. More than one million Chinese teachers teach English to more than 600 million Chinese, more than twice the population of the United States (Qiang and Wolff, 2005).

English has not always been popular in China. (I refer to Cortazzi and Jin (1996), Lin (2002), and Kramer (2002) for an historic overview of the teaching of English as a foreign language (EFL) in China.) The language was banned from the curriculum and replaced by Russian in 1949. It resurfaced in secondary schools and primary schools in big cities in the mid-1950s when the relations between China and the Soviet Union became tense. English was again dropped during the Cultural Revolution. It has been the most widely taught foreign language since the end of the Cultural Revolution in 1977.

In the early 1980s, English became a compulsory subject in college entrance and post-graduate entrance examinations. Foreign language learning became compulsory in 2001. To support the provision, the Ministry of Education released the Basic Requirement for Primary School English. It requires schools to start the study of the foreign language in Year 3 and recommends a time allocation of 80 minutes a week (Qiang, 2002). The curriculum aims at the development of communication skills, thinking skills and knowledge of the culture of English-speaking people through the means of games, project work, portfolios and history lessons. Children's competence and skills are assessed at the end of primary school with a 'band system'. Band 2 is the level expected to be reached by primary children in Years 3 to 6 (8–11), Band 5 by junior middle school students (12–14) and Band 7 by middle school students (15–17).

Since China is a vast territory characterized by economic disparities, the provision of English teaching in primary schools still differs in big cities from rural areas. This was also illustrated by Lam (2005) who visited four primary schools in different areas offering two semesters of English. She found variations in the starting age (e.g. from Year 1 to Year 6) and in the number of lessons taught per week (generally from one to three). Teachers used textbooks which stemmed from different sources such as the Education Commission of the City, the Ministry of Education or commercial publishers. Assessment depended on the area. District and city examinations were held at the end of primary in two schools whereas the other two schools did not formally evaluate the pupils' achievements.

With the plan to generalize and improve primary education in the coming years, the teaching of English will also become more uniform across the country.

1.9 Main points to remember

The younger the better?

- Research into the optimum age for language learning is inconclusive.
- An early start has a positive impact on children's attitudes.
- The only advantage of an early start is the total amount of time spent actively on learning a language.

Provision of foreign language learning in primary schools

- Early language learning has been promoted around the world and is increasingly common in primary schools.
- Language programmes differ within Europe, the United States, Australia and China and between these areas in relation to:
    o the status of the language(s) taught
    o allocated teaching time
    o continuity
    o type of teacher
    o type of curriculum
    o teaching methods
    o procedures for assessment.
- The problems identified are similar:
    o teacher shortage
    o inadequate training
    o lack of continuity within primary and between primary and secondary school
    o lack of appropriate assessment procedures

o lack of materials and funding shortages.

- Language programmes seem to be least well established and sustained in countries where the majority of residents speak English. These countries express concerns in relation to enrolment at the level of secondary school.

Successful provision seems to depend on the following factors:

- An early start
- Sufficient amount and distribution of teaching time (at least one hour a week)
- Coherent and age-appropriate programmes and methodologies
- Well-trained teachers (successful teacher training programmes and programmes for professional development)
- Authentic materials (including the use of Information and Communication Technology)
- Continuity of programmes within and between schools of different levels
- Appropriate assessment procedures
- Strong local and national policies.

Note

1. The recommendation to take language off the compulsory curriculum for 14- to 16-year-olds led to a rapid decline in students studying a language up to GCSE. From 2004 to 2006, the number of exam entries for French and German at GCSE dropped each year by 14 per cent (Smithers and Whitford, 2006). Interest in Spanish remained more stable. Findings of surveys carried out by CiLT show that less than 50 per cent of students studied a language in KS4 in the majority of state schools (BBC News, 01.11.2006).

Case Studies of Two Successful Schools **2**

2.1 Introduction

When speaking to teachers about FL teaching in England I often came across comments such as 'We have a large number of non-native English speakers in our school. We focus on making them competent in English rather than introducing them to yet another language.' In this chapter, I present two success stories that show that it is possible to provide effective and enjoyable foreign language teaching even in 'tough' schools. I present two London schools with a large intake of children from ethnic minority backgrounds. Both schools began to teach foreign languages in 2002. Since then they have developed their provision considerably. Languages are currently timetabled throughout KS2 but younger children have opportunities to learn some languages as well.

I hope that these case-studies and the pupils' comments which testify to their enjoyment of the subject and the success of the language learning provision, encourage practitioners to introduce languages and give them some practical ideas. Examples of good practice from both schools are used throughout the book.

Food for thought

- Think about schools you have visited. Did they teach foreign languages? What was the rationale behind the decision to teach/not to teach foreign languages?
- What were the aims of foreign language teaching and what methods were used?
- Can you think of possible reasons why young learners enjoy the subject?

2.2 Foreign language learning at Portway Primary School

Portway Primary School is a popular, large, mixed community school in East London. It was attended by almost 600 pupils in 2006/07 aged three to 11 (see Figure 2.1). Eighty-seven per cent came from a minority ethnic background, the largest proportion being Bangladeshi.

Around 70 per cent spoke English as an additional language. About 50 different languages were spoken in the school. The number of children with special educational needs was about 15 per cent in 2006, which was below the national average. About a third of the children were eligible for free meals, which was above the national average.

Pupils' SATs (Standard Attainment Tests) results in 2006 were above the local and national average. OFSTED (2007) qualified Portway Primary school as an 'outstanding school'.

Figure 2.1 Welcome poster.

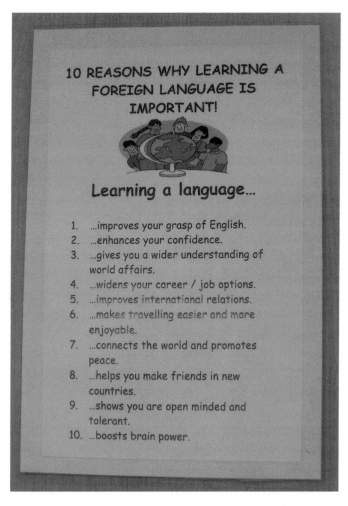

Figure 2.2 Ten reasons why learning a foreign language is important.

The children's attitudes, behaviour and moral, social, language and cultural development were assessed as outstanding. The school was awarded the e-Twinning Label for the Performing Arts project in November 2006. It was also awarded the International School Award at Intermediate Level in November 2006 and the full International School Award in July 2007, presented by the British Council on behalf of the DCSF.

The large proportion of children speaking English as an additional language has not deterred the school from introducing foreign languages. In 2002, some classes learned Spanish and French for short periods. The situation was very different in the academic year 2006/07. The head teacher and the FL coordinator had ensured that children had an opportunity to be involved in a range of international projects and to learn Spanish, French or German in curricular time.

The reasons for learning languages were openly discussed in class and were also displayed in a poster hanging in a main corridor (see Figure 2.2).

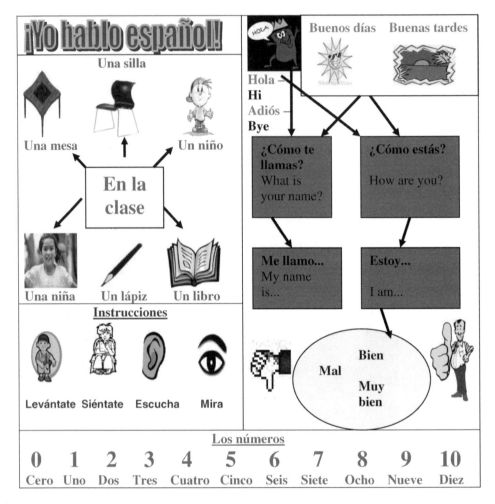

Figure 2.3 Spanish learning mat.

Children in Reception learnt a foreign language for 30 minutes. The time allocation rose to 45 minutes in KS1 and an hour in KS2. Apart from the timetabled lessons, teachers and children used basic vocabulary in the foreign language on a daily basis. Each classroom had labels for some classroom objects, a list of simple instructions, cards for the date and the daily timetable, learning mats and posters in the relevant language. The learning mat is displayed in Figure 2.3.

Most members of staff taught FL. They used the scheme of work written by the language coordinator. It was built around a range of topics (e.g. animals, family members, clothes, body parts) and did not impose a particular teaching style. However, it recommended an 'active' methodology and enjoyable methods such as games, role-plays, songs and the use of

Figure 2.4 Traditional clothes.

mime and physical actions. A range of material was available to all teachers (e.g. reference books, books, big books, CD-ROMs, realia and audio/visual material).

The language coordinator supported teachers, invited them to INSET training, organized informal weekly 'drop-in FL' sessions and updated the scheme of work and the new Language Policy (2006). This document described the aims for the teaching of FL as follows:

- to increase children's linguistic competence
- to prepare them for a multicultural and multilingual world
- to raise awareness that languages have a structure which might differ from each other
- to develop positive attitudes to learning languages
- to build up language learning skills that serve as a foundation for future learning.

In order to achieve progress in one of the three foreign languages over time, the head teacher and language coordinator planned to have pupils learn the same language for at least three years. Children learned increasingly demanding grammatical structures based around simple verbs. An example of progression is given in the policy:

single nouns and adjectives	*perro/grande*	dog/big
nouns with appropriate adjective	*un perro grande*	a big dog
verbs in the first person	*yo tengo un perro*	I have a dog
verbs in the third person	*él/ella tiene un perro*	he/she has a dog
verbs with nouns and adjectives	*él/ella tiene un grande perro*	he/she has a big dog

In Reception and KS1 teachers focused on listening and speaking skills and presented the written word only occasionally. Apart from developing oral skills, the KS2 pupils engaged in some reading for pleasure and did some writing such as copy-writing high-frequency words, basic expressions and simple sentences. All written work was marked.

Developing language competence in Spanish, French or German was only one of many aims; opening pupils up to other languages and cultures was equally important (see Chapter 10).

Figure 2.5 Signposts in community languages.

Figure 2.6 Language of the month.

Pictures of children wearing traditional costumes and displays of costumes were used to promote the diversity of society and to make pupils knowledgeable about aspects of different cultures (see Figure 2.4). Signposts in community languages can be found anywhere in the school (see Figure 2.5).

Teachers highlighted the heritage languages used in children's homes. The aim was to make them proud of their mother tongue and realize how many languages they could already speak. Some of these languages became the 'language of the month'.

Bengali was the language of the month in January 2007, Lithuanian assumed this role in February (see Figure 2.6). All classrooms had a display with greetings and numbers in the target language so that children could familiarize themselves with some words. The teachers took the register in the language of the month and invited children with the heritage language to act as role models.

Developing intercultural understanding was also a main aim of projects with other countries. In 2006/7, the Year 4 and Year 5 classes had a pen-pal link with a French and Spanish class respectively. They learned, for example, about the traditions of celebrating Christmas in

France and Carnival in Spain. Years 1, 2 and 3 worked on a Performing Arts project with a school in Spain. The idea was to celebrate the British cultural heritage (e.g. paintings, dances and songs) and to learn about Spanish artists, traditional songs and dance. Classes exchanged ideas and resources.

Knowledge about language was taught implicitly, for example when teachers compared numbers in different languages or spoke about word order (see Chapter 9). In fact, many children spontaneously made links between languages. For example, when pupils in Year 5 spoke about the German sentence 'Wir wollen nach Dakhar fahren' (we want to drive to Dakhar), some Bangladeshi children noticed that the verb fahren was at the end of the sentence in both Bengali and German. This comparison helped them remember the word order. On other occasions, some children were intrigued to see the similarities between, on the one hand, Bengali and Punjabi and, on the other, Spanish and French. The discussions following their discovery taught them something about language families. The language coordinator explained that some children had developed a feeling for languages over the years and now implicitly knew when something sounded wrong. The sentence 'Wir wollen spielen Fußball' (We want to play football), for example, left many with a feeling that something was wrong.

Assessment, mostly formative, was a regular feature of language lessons. Teachers observed and recorded pupils' progress. They used this information to support their planning and teaching and to group pupils according to levels of ability.

Apart from observation, teachers used self-assessment sheets as well as formal tests with KS2 classes. The self-assessment sheets encouraged pupils to reflect on their learning and to acknowledge their progress. Younger learners identified what they had learned, wrote down the topics covered and colour-coded their achievements according to the 'traffic-light' system. Green meant 'mastery', yellow 'okay' and red 'to be developed'. Pupils in KS2 were given a blank sheet of paper and asked to reflect on their achievements and level of understanding. Pupils also commented on aspects of work they particularly enjoyed or found difficult and set themselves targets for future development. In previous years, assessment was done with 'I can do' statements which children colour-coded in red, yellow and green. The captions for the section on reading, for example, read as follows:

> I can read:
> - some words or labels
> - sentences
> - simple conversations
> - a simple description
> - a short story
> - a poem.

Tests are another means of assessing progress. After three or four topics, teachers checked children's knowledge of vocabulary, their spelling and composition skills. Year 5 and Year 6 pupils were also assessed on their grammar (e.g. singulars and plurals). While instructions in tests were given in English in Year 3, they were presented in the target language with older learners. Pupils generally did well and were proud of their progress. Examples of self-assessment sheets and tests can be found in Chapter 12. Children who did very well in their language lessons were awarded a Certificate of Merit. Generally, four or five certificates per class were distributed each term.

Teachers assessed the level of achievement of each pupil at the end of each term according to the descriptors of the Languages Ladder (see Chapter 12). In Year 6 pupils tended to be at the levels B1 or B2. In the Summer term, teachers wrote a formal report which they handed to parents and teachers of the next class. FL had the same status as other curriculum subjects in the report. Apart from this formal information, parents had the opportunity to get informal feedback on their children at parents' evenings.

2.3 Foreign language learning at Cardwell Primary School

Cardwell Primary school is an average-sized, mixed school located in South London. In 2006/7 about 500 children aged from 3 to 11 were enrolled. The school catered for children with a range of different ethnic backgrounds, African being the most dominant. Most of these children spoke Ibo, Yoruba or other African languages. More than 30 languages were spoken and about 66 per cent of pupils spoke English as an additional language. About 25 per cent were registered as having special educational needs (SEN), a number well above the national average. More than half were eligible for free meals, again more than the national average.

In 2007 OFSTED praised the head teacher and deputy head for their outstanding leadership and the staff for their good teaching and the rapidly improving standards. Inspectors commended the school's impressive degree of racial harmony and integration, and the pupils' good attitudes and behaviour. Achievements were good overall, but below the local and national average in English.

Given the high intake of non-native speakers, it might come as a surprise that Cardwell Primary School decided in Spring 2002 to open an optional French afternoon-club for Years 5 and 6. The aim was to teach simple phrases and dialogues to enable children to speak to each other and to other French speakers in the community. The main target group were the English children for whom learning an additional language was completely new.

The success of the well-attended club encouraged the head teacher to introduce French in the curriculum. This was not an easy task since only two members of staff were confident users of French: the head teacher herself and the teacher who ran the afternoon-club. The head teacher decided to release the 'French teacher' for some hours so that she could teach the language for half an hour a week in each KS2 class. The class teachers were present in the lessons so that they could pick up both some French and some teaching strategies. Initially, the new language coordinator loosely followed the QCA non-statutory schemes of work

(QCA, 2000). She introduced pupils to a range of topics and encouraged plenty of oral work. Children had many opportunities to listen to, repeat and practise these words with the teacher, with classmates and on their own. The lessons proved highly enjoyable for pupils and promoted the value of language learning and multilingualism. In addition, they raised the self-esteem of bilingual children and increased children's confidence in their ability to learn a new language. This was particularly true of children who were academically less able or had special educational needs.

In order to move the teaching of French forward, five teachers attended continuous professional development courses in 2003/04. In the following years, the language coordinator supported more and more staff and helped them teach French. She began to work with a small number of enthusiastic teachers who soon acted as role-models for others. The school joined language centres which gave them access to further courses, expertise and resources. French was timetabled in each KS2 class. The school began to develop its stock of resources so that teachers in 2007 had the opportunity to work with several published schemes of work and a variety of audio and video material. In addition, they used the BBC website, made good use of the interactive whiteboard and drew on the KS2 framework to support their planning.

The school was fortunate to work with a foreign language adviser from the borough. In the past years, he regularly taught French, observed teachers and gave feedback. In addition, he offered resources and organized staff meetings and INSET training on FL methodology. He even delivered one session entirely in Spanish to allow staff to experience learning a completely new language from the beginning.

The support and training of the language coordinator and the borough adviser had a huge impact. In 2006/07, children in Foundation Stage and KS1 (Key Stage 1) enjoyed five minutes of French on a regular basis. Like the older children, they used French during registration and for classroom instructions. Nursery children had some opportunities to listen to French stories told by the language coordinator. All pupils in KS2 learned French for half an hour weekly. The main aims were to make them confident language users and learners. The head teacher hoped that this gave pupils a headstart at secondary school. In KS2 teachers introduced new vocabulary or sentence structures and offered pupils many opportunities to practise the new language in enjoyable, motivating and relevant activities in groups, in pairs or on their own. The vocabulary was reinforced through games at the whiteboard and recycled in a range of contexts. For example, pupils did not only learn numbers and the sentence structure '*J'ai . . . ans*', they also learned the questions '*Quel âge as-tu?*' and '*Quel âge a-t-il/elle*'? Similarly, when they spoke about the weather, they learned sentences like '*Il fait beau/mauvais/il neige*', as well as relevant questions such as '*Quel temps fait-il aujourd'hui/à Pâques?*' The new vocabulary and structures were practised in oral exercises and on written worksheets. Some of the work was displayed in posters in the corridors. Children proudly showed me their books where they had copied lists of words with translations or pictures on a range of topics. They had also copied simple sentences and dialogues such as questions and answers about their age, siblings or the weather.

Teachers introduced pupils to the written word because pupils were keen to copy words and sentences. Children felt that they did not 'own' the new vocabulary until they had transferred it from the board to their books. They soon realized that their books were good records which allowed them to go back to things learned previously. Some noticed that writing in a foreign language made them aware of spellings and pronunciation which were sometimes very different from those in their mother tongue. Writing helped them spot patterns which facilitated reading in the foreign language.

In line with the KS2 framework, the teachers found a place for the development of pupils' knowledge about language and intercultural awareness. Developing knowledge about language is a developing part of the language lessons, especially in the upper years of KS2. The language coordinator explained that frequently either the teacher or a pupil spotted some similarities or differences between English and French and commented on vocabulary, syntax, gender, articles and agreements. Children saw, for example, that the French words for colours are placed after the noun unlike in English (e.g. *un chapeau rouge* rather than '*un rouge chapeau*'). They also understood that sentences cannot be translated word for word (e.g. *je m'appelle* would be 'I call myself/I myself call').

Intercultural understanding was promoted through curriculum areas such as Religious Education (RE) and Personal, Social and Health Education (PSHE) and special daily, weekly and annual events. All classes contributed to the yearly 'French Day'. Activities in previous years had included learning French songs and rhymes, learning about French customs and food and telling stories in French using puppets. Nursery and Reception classes enjoyed storytelling sessions with the language coordinator. Several days later the children recited the songs and rhymes learned on the special occasion in a 'French' assembly. The Year 6 class performed the story 'Les Trois Petits Cochons' to the younger children.

The staff chose a theme that ran through the whole year as well as themes for several weeks (e.g. the 'French Week' or the 'China Week'). Each class was named after a particular theme, for example, authors, artists or designers. This allowed pupils to learn about the sociocultural and geographic background of well-known people.

The language coordinator listed the next steps to be taken: teachers were to revise the school policy for FL and set up a monitoring programme to ensure continuity and progression across all year groups. The plan was to use the Languages Ladder to assess pupils' achievements in French.

Apart from the language coordinators I interviewed pupils in order to see what they had to say about their language learning experience.

2.4 What children had to say about language learning

I interviewed 18 pupils from Year 3 to Year 6 in both schools. They were native speakers of English, Bengali, Punjabi, Lithuanian and Nepalese. All were proud of their mother tongue and the 'little bit' of French, Spanish or German they knew. My aim was to find out why children wanted to learn foreign languages, what they enjoyed and what tips they could give to children who might feel less confident about learning a foreign language.

The desire to communicate on holiday was a catalyst for learning languages for most children. While abroad, for example in Spain and France, some children had learned some basic greetings and expressions because their parents wanted them to speak at least some words as a matter of politeness. These chunks of language were not enough to enable children to play with other children, to buy themselves food or gadgets or to understand labels and signposts. Some were lucky enough to have parents or siblings who were able to translate some words but all wished to be independent rather than to rely on relatives.

Most pupils stated that they wanted to learn a language to become part of a language community at school or at home. This was a strong integrative motive. Many had developed friendships with non-English speaking children who had recently arrived in the UK. They tried to teach these pupils some English and to pick up some words in their native language.

Parents or siblings of many pupils I interviewed learned a foreign language informally or formally. The children sometimes felt like 'outsiders' when they heard family members use a language they did not understand. They often asked the 'experts' to teach them some words or to show them books and CD-ROMs.

Several children mentioned the advantage of mastering a language before going to secondary school. They believed that early language learning is a good foundation for secondary. One boy commented that he would hate to 'feel weak and unprepared' or even 'risk getting bullied' if he did not know some basics.

Learning a language for employment was only mentioned by a few children. This extrinsic motive seems to lie too far ahead to be a real catalyst for language learning (Deci and Ryan, 1985; Crookes and Schmidt, 1991; Brumfit, 1995). Pupils' positive inclinations and their strong intrinsic goals are likely to influence their motivation, task engagement and mindset, and to result in success (Gardner and Lambert, 1972; Gardner, 1988; Skehan, 1989; Gillette, 1994; Long, 1997; Pufahl *et al.*, 2000).

Children enjoyed a range of activities in their language lessons. They spoke favourably of songs, games, role-plays, the use of mime and gesture and the use of the interactive whiteboard. Since they liked to be challenged and to meet high expectations many also enjoyed practising vocabulary; completing worksheets; rearranging scrambled sentences and copying words.

Apart from the 'fun activities' almost all children mentioned that they liked 'learning' and 'making progress'. One boy explained that he had felt almost lost in the first weeks in Year 3 when the teacher spoke French. Now in Year 4, he was able to understand her which made him feel very proud. Another boy expressed the same idea as follows:

> At the beginning, you don't get it and you don't feel good. Then the teacher helps you and you get it right. You feel proud and warm inside.

The challenging content prepared pupils well for learning languages outside primary school. Since their needs were met, their interests were likely to further expand and their motivation to improve (Dewey, 1916; Graham, 1997).

A monolingual English girl commented that she enjoyed learning how to express ideas in a different language and becoming bilingual like her friends. Another girl explained that coming to terms with pronunciation in French provided her with a real feeling of success and joy. Several children announced proudly that they were able to do some basic additions and subtractions in French.

The comments of these pupils, representative of many others, show that progress and success gave rise to a great source of pleasure, increased children's confidence in their own abilities and raised their motivation.

Apart from commenting favourably on their language lessons and their learning progress, pupils were pleased to have developed some knowledge of other countries. A girl remembered every detail of how the Eiffel Tower was built, a sign that the subject captivated her. One boy enjoyed discovering new towns, another finding something out about traditions. Making contact with children in France and Spain through a pen-pal link and the Performing Arts projects were mentioned as highly enjoyable, stimulating and interesting activities by most of the children at Portway Primary School.

A final positive factor mentioned in the interview was the class teacher. Some children at Cardwell liked their language lessons because their teacher visibly enjoyed French and was 'often carried away'. This good role-model had a clear effect on children's feelings and motivation.

These few comments show that the teachers in both schools have instilled a love for languages in children and lit the fire for further learning. The beginners even knew how to encourage children who were less confident to learn foreign languages. Here is some of their advice:

'Have a go. Keep on trying. Don't feel discouraged.'

'Ask somebody for help. This can be a parent, a brother, a teacher, a tutor in a club. Tell them to say something to you and repeat after them. Ask them to correct you.'

'Meet people who speak other languages and listen to them. Take any opportunity offered to you [to learn].'

'Repeat what people say to you. Keep on saying things aloud so that you don't forget them.'

'Get some language materials. My brother's books and CD-ROMs are really helpful.'

'Write things down so that you remember them. When I write down French words, I sometimes write down how I would pronounce them in English. I also find it helpful to write translations or to draw pictures of the words.'

'You need to put your mind to it so that you can remember.'

'Practice makes perfect!'

These comments show that the children interviewed had developed some language learning strategies which they were able to share. Most importantly, they wanted to share their knowledge that language learning, though not always easy, was achievable and definitively worth it.

2.5 Main points to remember

In this chapter I have presented success stories of two London schools with a high intake of non-native speakers of English. Below are the factors that contributed to the efficient implementation of FL into the timetable and the effective teaching:

- a highly committed head teacher
- an experienced and enthusiastic language coordinator who provided training for staff, developed resources and liaised with secondary schools, the LA and CiLT (National Centre for Language Learning)
- the gradual introduction of the new subject which gave class teachers time to become confident about teaching the subject
- appropriate content of language lessons
- active teaching methods
- the integration of both 'modern' and 'heritage' languages into the life of the school
- embedding languages in the curriculum and making cross-curricular links
- projects with other countries.

Many of these factors have been described as examples of good practice by Rumley and Sharpe (1999) and CiLT (2002a, 20002b). The next steps in both schools were to further develop schemes of work and assessment procedures to ensure continuity and progression.

The teaching of foreign and community languages led to many positive results:

- the propagation of multilingualism and multiculturalism across the school
- the development of positive attitudes towards language learning in both staff and pupils
- the teachers' improved ability to teach languages
- the pupils' enhanced skill in learning languages, their improved competence and their desire to interact purposefully with native and non-native speakers.

I hope that this chapter full of practical ideas and activities acts as a catalyst and results in a feeling of 'I can do it'. Details of how to develop pupils' oral and written skills, intercultural competence, knowledge about language and language learning strategies are presented in the respective chapters of this book. Rather than continuing with these 'practical' chapters I now present theories of second language acquisition and methodology. They will help you develop the knowledge that informs your choice of appropriate methods and guides your reflections on teaching and learning.

Theories of Second Language Acquisition 3

3.1 Introduction

Over the years, different disciplinary traditions have examined the ways in which people learn their first and any additional languages. Each tradition is associated with a particular philosophy, examines the question of learning from a particular perspective and uses a particular research methodology. They are therefore poised to explain different phenomena.

In this chapter I present three different traditions of theories: *behaviourist, cognitive* and *sociocultural*. The *behaviourist* perspective focuses on the learners' environment (i.e. external factors), the mainstream *cognitive* approach concentrates on their mental processes (i.e. internal factors) and the more recent *sociocultural* perspective takes account of both mental and social processes.

Albeit being termed theories of 'second' language acquisition (SLA), researchers do not always distinguish between *second* and *foreign* languages. They mean one or the other or indeed both without making this clear. It is generally agreed that a *foreign* language is generally not spoken by the main population of the country the learner lives in. People might learn it for communication purposes on holiday or for job opportunities. An example is an English student learning French at school in England. By contrast, one speaks of a *second* language when people learn a language subsequently to their mother tongue which is generally spoken in their home country. An example of this would be an English child learning French as a result of having moved to France.

In my presentation I pay some attention to errors because this is particularly important for language teachers.

> ## Food for thought
>
> - Compare the ways in which you learned your mother tongue and additional languages. What are the differences and similarities?
> - How do the following statements concur with your experience:
>   - I learn best when I can speak to people and try out my skills.
>   - I learn best when I am on holiday and can listen to people speaking.
>   - In order to learn, I need to be in a quiet room, read and practise the new skills over and over again.
>   - My foreign language developed almost automatically.

3.2 A behaviourist perspective on SLA

From the 1930s to the 1960s, behaviourism was the most prominent theory used to explain learning in general and language learning in particular. Behaviourists understood learning largely in terms of habit formation brought about through imitation, repetition, practice and reinforcement (Thorndike, 1932; Skinner, 1957). Habits are formed when learners repeatedly respond to a particular stimulus in the same way.

Structural linguistics, the dominant theory of language at the time, influenced the views on language acquisition considerably. Structural linguists are interested in the structure of language and study observable features of speech. From the perspective of behaviourism and structural linguistics children learn their first language through imitation and repetition. As Bloomfield (1933), an influential linguist, explained:

> His (the child's) more perfect attempts at speech are likely to be fortified by repetition, and his failures to be wiped out by confusion. This process never stops. At a much later stage, if he says *Daddy bringed it*, he merely gets a disappointing answer such as No! You must say 'Daddy brought it'; but if he says *Daddy brought it*, he is likely to hear the form over again: *Yes, Daddy brought it*, and get a favourable practical response.
>
> (p. 31)

Behaviourists further believe that learners acquire a second language through transfer of the rules and habits formed in the mother tongue to the second language. If these two languages have different grammatical structures, the transfer of the old habits can interfere with the acquisition of the new language. If the structures are similar, transfer may be positive and facilitate the acquisition process. Some examples clarify the point. Chinese does not have markers for the formation of plurals. One could therefore expect that Chinese learners face problems when they learn that (most) nouns in English take an –s in the plural. On the other hand, Spanish speakers learning French might find it relatively easy to understand the position of an adjective because both languages require the adjective to be placed after the noun.

The idea that the comparison of two languages helps explain (or even predict) a learner's progress is known under *Contrastive Analysis Hypothesis* (Lado, 1957; Wardhaugh, 1970). Linguists claimed that the differences between languages can explain the learner's difficulties or mistakes.

The *Contrastive Analysis Hypothesis* has been criticized on both theoretical and empirical grounds. Research findings showed that the majority of mistakes in the second language could not be explained through interference with the mother tongue. In addition, learners worked error-free when errors were to be expected and made mistakes although features of the languages were similar.

At the end of the 1970s, errors gained a new status in research. While behaviourists believed that they had to be avoided since they become permanent, linguists such as Corder (1967) argued that they are both inevitable and essential parts of the learners' internal system and offer important insights into the learning process. While Contrastive Analysis examined the learners' mistakes by comparing them to the learner's first language, Corder examined them in relation to the target language. He stated that errors represented a transitional stage between the first and the second language. Selinker (1972) called this stage *interlanguage*. It is 'an autonomous system dependent on its own rules which is developmental or dynamic and moves along a continuum of proficiency' (Klapper, 2006: 50).

The interlanguage changes constantly as learners integrate new structures into their system.

Shortcomings

Chomsky's (1959) review of Skinner's book *Verbal Behaviour* (1957) and Corder's seminal work on errors were a body blow to behaviourism and hastened the decline of Contrastive Analysis. Today theorists largely agree that learning is a more complex process which cannot be explained by behaviourism. Learners play an active role and cannot be considered as mere empty and receptive vessels to be filled.

Main ideas to remember

- A second language is learned through imitation, repetition, practice and reinforcement.
- Learners transfer habits from their mother tongue to the second language.
- Errors need to be avoided since they become permanent.

Implications for practitioners

- Compare the first and the target language.
- Give students practice to help them overcome interference problems.
- Reinforce correct productions.
- Correct errors.

While behaviourism focuses on observable features and avoids tackling mental processes, the cognitive approach, presented next, concentrates on internal mental processes.

3.3 The cognitive tradition

The mainstream cognitive tradition explains human behaviour and language learning through thought processes. Below I present the linguistic origin of the Cognitive Theory and a computational movement which understands the mind as a general, purpose-built computer.

3.3.1 The linguistic origin of SLA theory

The linguistic approach to first language acquisition was largely influenced by Chomsky (1965). Chomsky was fascinated by children's creative language use and the ease with which they acquire grammar. He claimed that children do not learn language through copying. Rather, they analyse the language they hear, infer rules and apply them to produce new language. When they overgeneralize rules, they make mistakes such as 'he goed' (for 'he went') or 'she bringed' (for 'she brought'). These creative constructions indicate that language is rule-governed and that language learning is an active and creative process.

Chomsky further claimed that children cannot infer all the grammatical rules they need to apply in order to speak correctly as a result of listening to the utterances they are exposed to. He described the language children hear as messy, incomplete and erroneous. (This is known as the *poverty of stimulus* argument.) Since the *degenerate* linguistic data can neither explain the speed of language acquisition nor children's creative productions, Chomsky hypothesized that children have an innate capacity to generate grammatical structures. They are born with a blueprint of how grammar works. He labelled this blueprint *Universal Grammar* (UG).

The principle of UG goes back to the assumption that all world languages, though different, share many universal underlying similarities. Chomsky explained that all languages had universal *principles* and language-specific *parameters* (Chomsky, 1981). *Principles* are unvarying components common to all language. For example, one principle holds that all languages have subjects. However, different languages express the subject in different ways. Speakers of English need to use a special term to characterize the subject (the pronoun in the example below). In Italian, by contrast, the verb ending indicates the subject and there is no need for a special term.

> I am going to Rome.
> *Vado a Roma.*

The way in which the subject is expressed is defined by the *parameter*. This particular parameter is the *pro-drop* parameter. It determines whether or not the subject of a sentence must be overtly pronounced. A parameter characterizes a language and distinguishes it from others.

Chomsky further posited that people are born with a special language organ or *language acquisition device* (LAD). It enables children to produce language that is consistent with the rules of the Universal Grammar. Cook (1997: 262) describes it as

> the mechanism in the mind which allows children to construct a grammar out of the raw language materials supplied by their parents.
>
> (quoted in Mitchell and Myles, 1998: 42)

The LAD has often been compared to a station button on a radio. At first, it gives access to many different channels, but once it is set one can only listen to a particular station. In the same way, the linguistic input of the environment 'triggers' the LAD and the brain selects the parameters for the specific language. The language then develops almost 'automatically', with the child not needing a more mature speaker to instruct or correct errors.

Chomsky has made no specific claims about the impact of the LAD on the acquisition of additional languages. There is no agreement as to whether or to what extent the LAD is still accessible to additional languages and whether and to what extent the UG has been altered through the acquisition of the first language. Some researchers claim that second language learners can access the UG and, as a result, that the process of learning a first and a second language are very similar. By contrast, others hold that the UG cannot be accessed in a second language. In order to learn a second language, people have to apply general problem-solving skills. Others maintain that learners can only access the UG to a limited extent. Strong defenders of all positions can be found and the continuing debate has not been concluded. However, the direction of research seems to have shifted from the question of availability or non-availability of the UG towards a modular view of language ability. Today there is a general acceptance of learners' innate predispositions to first language acquisition and an agreement of a modular view of language acquisition. However, there is no consensus on the number of these modules and on their impact on SLA (Mitchell and Myles, 1998).

Further reading

In recent years, neurolinguistics has provided some insights into lateralization and modularity of the brain. Neurolinguists research brain circuitry to determine what processes are engaged in the production, comprehension and learning of languages. Modern technology like PET (Positron Emission Tomography) and MRI (Magnetic Resonance Imaging) give neurologists direct insights into how the brain works.

Early studies detected that language is lateralized in the left part of the brain in right-handed people and in the right part in left-handed people. Researchers also found that various parts of the brain are responsible for various language skills. For example, the so-called Broca's area controls fluency and proficiency and the Wernicke's area is responsible for language comprehension.

Shortcomings

Chomsky's theory has been criticized for limiting its explanations to the acquisition of grammatical *competence* at the expense of *performance*. Competence is concerned with the abstract and hidden representation of language knowledge held inside the head of the learner. Performance is the ability to use this competence in real-life situations.

A second criticism is concerned with the role of the learner. Although children are seen as active learners able to construct a grammar out of the raw material provided by competent speakers, the learner as such still has no place. They seem to function as a kind of container from which the LAD can work. Their needs, attitudes, memory and other social and psychological variables which influence the language learning process have been ignored.

These criticisms made it clear that the area of study needed to be widened. The emphasis on grammar was slowly replaced with a concern for 'language in use'. Rather than understanding language exclusively as a rule-bound system, it was argued that language was a resource that children acquire in order to communicate.

Research into second language learning

From an empirical point of view, the linguistic approach has been particularly beneficial in offering explanations of the learner's *competence* (limited to their grammatical knowledge) and in providing precise descriptions of the learner's language. Studies have shown that people pass through the same stages when learning languages. Dulay and Burt (1974), for example, have demonstrated that French and Chinese learners acquire grammatical morphemes in the same order. Language development is thus considered as systematic, rule-governed and developing in stages. The fact that learners acquire morphemes in a similar way suggests that they are guided by internal principles which are independent of the language.

The notion of step-by-step progression ever upwards has been heavily criticized. Mitchell (2003) claims that second language learning is a complex and recursive process with multiple interconnections, backslidings and complex trade-offs between advances in fluency, accuracy and complexity.

Other critiques argue that research into the acquisition of *all* morphemes in *all* languages is necessary to prove that aspects of language learning are innate. In their eyes, the sequential order can be explained by *perceptual saliency*: speakers learn some features first because they notice them first.

Saying that language is *developmental* has several implications.

1. Teachers need to concentrate on grammatical points that the learners are ready for. They cannot make learners jump ahead of a stage. However, Pienemann *et al.* (2006) maintain that a method like task-based learning can accelerate learning (see Chapter 4).
2. Errors have to be considered as a normal step in the acquisition process. They are common to all learners and not permanent.
3. The usefulness of correcting mistakes (i.e. *negative feedback*) has been investigated in many studies, particularly in *recasts*. These are 'utterances that rephrase a child's utterance by changing one or more sentence components (subject, verb, or object) while still referring to its central meaning' (Long, 1996: 434).
   Lyster and Ranta (1997) found that this popular way of correcting mistakes does not influence the ability to use grammatically correct language. Ellis (1984) reported that the correction of grammatical errors does not have long-term effects. After reviewing many studies, Johnson (2004) claimed that there is still not enough evidence for a positive impact of recasts.

Main ideas to remember

Language learning is innate, creative, systematic and rule-bound.

- Children are born with a *language acquisition device* that has evolved over time to acqu.. *Grammar.*
- All languages share common features (principles). Parameters distinguish languages from each other.
- The language used in the environment triggers the LAD of a young child. The brain sets the parameters for the acquisition of their first language.
- There is no agreement if and to what extent second language learners can still access the LAD.
- Making errors is a normal part of the process of learning a language.

Implications for practitioners

- Present second language learners with rich and varied opportunities for language input.
- Encourage language use.
- There is no need to correct mistakes or to focus on grammar. Pupils will acquire the forms and structures for which they are developmentally ready.

3.3.2 The information-processing paradigm on SLA

Cognitive models of learning focus on the mental processes that the learner uses to acquire language and to transform the 'input' into 'output'. Below I describe a computational view of learning, the 'Input Hypothesis' and the 'Interaction Hypothesis'.

Learning through automatization and restructuring

Unlike Chomskyan linguists, many cognitivists deny the existence of a specialized module responsible for language acquisition. They maintain that learning in general and language learning in particular, proceed through internal mental operations. Learning is seen as a constructive process in which the active learner selects from incoming information, relates it to prior knowledge, encodes the information into long-term memory, retains what is important and reflects on the learning outcomes (Gagné *et al.*, 1993).

The cognitive model is underpinned by a view of the human mind as a computer with a limited amount of memory. Expressed more technically, the mind is understood as a general-purpose, symbol-processing system with limited *channel capacity* (Gagné, 1985). This implies that novice learners can only pay a certain 'amount' of conscious attention to information. Because they need to pay attention to every single bit they can only hold a limited amount in their memory and thus do not have much 'space' to focus on other areas. When they practise a low-level skill they will eventually automatize it. The automatized sub-skill frees up some space which enables the mind to concentrate on other aspects which need more attention. For example, pupils who have just learned how to construct the past tense need to pay a lot of attention to tenses in order to get them right. They might therefore not have enough channel capacity to focus at the same time on producing accurate grammatical sentences and getting the meaning across. Experience and practice enable them to automatize the procedure (e.g. construction of tenses) so that they can concentrate on fluency and accuracy at the same time. Learning a language is therefore considered as a movement from controlled processing, where the learner focuses much attention to a variety of information and procedures, to automatic processing, where many sequences have been automatized and can therefore happen quickly and without much of the learner's attention (McLaughlin, 1978, McLaughlin *et al.*, 1983).

Like the behaviourists, cognitivists emphasize the importance of practice in the learning process, but unlike them they insist that practice is meaningful and that learners need to develop knowledge of how language works. For example, behaviourists make learners practise 'I went' to avoid the error 'I goed'. Cognitivists, on the other hand, believe that learners are more likely to produce the correct form if they have some explicit knowledge of past tense formation and know that they deal with an irregular past tense.

In order to explain how knowledge is stored and retrieved, many cognitivists distinguish between *declarative knowledge* (conceptual knowledge such as facts and rules) and *procedural knowledge* ('know how', unanalysed, automatic knowledge such as grammatical competence or learning strategies). Anderson (1983, 1985) conceptualizes language learning as a shift from declarative to procedural knowledge. Knowledge is first *declared* to learners (e.g. the teaching of grammatical rules) and subsequently becomes *proceduralized* in the course of using them. Language learning is therefore a progression from the initial active manipulation of information to full automaticity of language use.

Other than *automatization through practice*, learning involves the construction and *restructuring* of mental representations. As learners incorporate new information into existing schemata (mental representation of knowledge), they simplify, relate and unify representations. In doing so, they gain increasing control over the new information and improve their performance (McLaughlin, 1987). While automatization takes time, restructuring which is a new way of seeing things, often occurs suddenly. It can explain brusque changes in the learner's competence as well as backsliding which happens when learners incorporate too much or the wrong information into the old structures.

Shortcomings

The information-processing view has been criticized for its perception of mind as a computer (Searle, 1984) and for the mere reformulation of old theories (i.e. behaviourist) into a new way (Bruner, 1996). Since the mind was not a topic of study of the behaviourists, the idea of the cognitive revolution was to put the mind back into psychology. However, the computational model ended up by being rather close to the behaviourist model. Although both approaches start with a different focus (e.g. internal versus external), they insist that practice leads to the automatization of knowledge and skills.

The questions of the role and the importance of practice have been much debated without leading to clear conclusions. Applied linguists such as Ellis (1994) claim that exercises that raise the learner's awareness of particular linguistic structures or grammar points are more efficient than drills. He also maintains that the value of practice might not appear immediately.

Main ideas to remember

- Repeated practice of structures leads to automatization. Automatized skills put less demand on cognitive processes. As a result, production accelerates, performance improves and errors are reduced.
- Language learning is a shift from declarative to procedural knowledge.

Implications for practitioners

- Activate the learners' background knowledge to facilitate the incorporation of new information into existing schemata.
- Provide many opportunities for practice so that students can gain automatic control.
- Make practice meaningful.
- Help pupils understand what they are learning. Explanations about grammatical structures are helpful.
- Give feedback and correct errors. Pupils are likely to learn incorrect forms if these are not corrected.

Whilst Anderson (1983, 1985) and McLaughlin *et al.* (1983), McLaughlin (1987) described the internal processes involved in language acquisition, the theoreticians presented below highlight the importance of interactions with the linguistic environment. However, the focus remains on the learner's mental processes. The environment only plays a secondary role as the provider of input. Interaction is understood as a cognitive matter that takes place inside the learner's head rather than being seen as a social issue.

The Input Hypothesis

Krashen (1982) was influenced by Chomsky and the research findings on the systematic and rule-governed nature of second language learning. He believed that all second learners can access their LAD regardless of their age and that language acquisition follows a predictable order. He considered *acquisition* rather than *learning* to be the basis of all language development. *Acquisition* is a natural, subconscious process similar to the way children acquire their first language. It enables learners to produce utterances and become fluent. *Learning*, on the other hand, is a conscious process. It includes activities such as memorizing vocabulary and rules, and practising grammar. As a result, learners develop knowledge *about* language. Krashen disagreed with Anderson (1983, 1985) and McLaughlin (1987) that conscious learning and explicit knowledge of formal rules can become automatic and be turned into acquisition. In his eyes, learning has only one function: the creation of a monitor. The *monitor* is an accumulation of knowledge about the language. Monitoring is a conscious process in which learners apply grammatical rules before or after language is spoken or written in order to check and possibly change the output. Learners can only use the monitor under particular conditions: they need to have enough time, know grammatical rules and focus on form rather than meaning. The use of the monitor explains learner differences. While monitor over-users produce hesitant and non-fluent speech, under-users speak fluently but with many

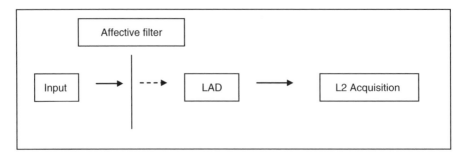

Figure 3.1 The affective filter.
Source: Krashen and Terrell, 1983: 39.

grammatical errors. Optimum-users use their learned competence as a supplement to their acquired one. According to Krashen, grammar does not need to be taught and can even be detrimental to the acquisition of language.

All individuals need in order to acquire new language is *optimal input*, in other words, input that is comprehensible, relevant and interesting, sufficient in quantity and not grammatically sequenced. In Krashen's words: 'Learners acquire language by understanding language that contains structure that is a bit beyond our current level of competence ($i + 1$). This is done with the help of context or extra-linguistic information' (1982: 21).

If communication is successful, that is, if the input is understood, $i + 1$ will be provided automatically. Input is the main condition for language acquisition but whether it develops into intake depends on the *affective filter*. This is an emotional barrier created by enthusiasm, interest, fear, anxiety, tension, etc. If an individual's *affective filter* is high, the input will not reach the LAD and hence will not be acquired. Learners with positive attitudes have a lower and weaker filter and their input strikes deeper (see Figure 3.1).

Shortcomings

Krashen's model had an enormous impact on further research even though it was strongly criticized as soon as it was published. For an overview of some of the criticisms see Johnson (2004: 46–51).

Krashen's belief that comprehensible input *caused* acquisition was strongly criticized. It has been argued that understanding input is a necessary but not sufficient condition for acquisition to take place. Some researchers argued for the recognition of other factors that *influenced* acquisition such as 'incomprehensible input' (White, 1987), 'comprehensible output' (Swain, 1985) or 'comprehended input' (Gass, 1988, 1997). Swain emphasized the importance of speaking for the learning process, as 'output' allows for the following procedures:

• notice the gap between what they know and want to say
• test hypotheses
• practise more varied and complex forms
• think about particular forms and structures
• revise structures they have internalized.

Gass moved away from comprehensible input, which puts the focus on the speaker, to 'comprehended' input, which focuses on the processes that the learner uses to understand the input. Her linear model (1997) has five major stages. *Apperceived input*, once understood, becomes *comprehended input* and then *intake*. After the intake has been *integrated* into the learner's grammar, it can be used as *output*.

The argument that grammar does not need to be taught and that formal practice is not necessary had major implications for teaching. As seen in section 3.3.2 the question of the importance of practice has not yet led to clear conclusions.

Main ideas to remember

Language is acquired in a predictable order.

- Language acquisition requires comprehensible input.
- Individuals acquire grammatical rules.
- Learning a language leads to the creation of a monitor that can be used to edit productions.
- Affective factors facilitate or impede the acquisition process.

Implications for practitioners

- Provide learners with listening and reading opportunities that offer comprehensible input. The input needs to be relevant, interesting, sufficient in quantity, not grammatically sequenced and just above the learner's level of proficiency.
- Speak slowly, use simple and short sentences, repeat and/or rephrase sentences, make pauses and use gestures, mime and context.
- Create a friendly and non-threatening learning environment and ensure that learners have positive attitudes.
- There is no need to focus on errors. Error correction could possibly increase the learner's affective filter.
- There is no need to teach grammar.

The Interaction Hypothesis

Long (1982, 1983) was one of the first to argue that it is necessary to pay greater attention to interactions in order to understand the nature and usefulness of input for the acquisition process. Researchers started to pay closer attention to the ways in which learners negotiate meaning to communicate and achieve an acceptable level of understanding. Ellis (1997) defines this negotiation as 'the interactive work that takes place between speakers when some misunderstanding occurs' (p. 141).

Long (1982, 1983) described four different ways in which people adapt their speech and change the structure of conversations. The most important modifications are 'modified speech' (e.g. motherese, foreigner talk, teacher talk) and 'interactional modification'. The following two examples from Long (1983) clarify the difference between these two types of modification:

Example 3.1 Modified speech and interactional modification

NS stands for native speaker and NNS for non-native speaker

Modified speech		*Interactional modification*	
NS:	What time you finish?	NS:	When did you finish?
NNS:	Ten o'clock.	NNS:	Um?
		NS:	When did you finish?
		NNS:	Ten clock.
		NS:	Ten o' clock.
		NNS:	Yeah.

In the first example, the native speaker (NS) modifies the input by leaving out the auxiliary to make the sentence easier to understand. In the second, the NS does not change the input but uses two other strategies to make communication successful: repeating the question and checking the answer by repeating it in the correct form (i.e recast). Long (1983) maintained that the second type of modification is especially important for learners. It provides them with necessary linguistic information that they can process and acquire. This 'negotiated interaction' came to be known as the 'Interaction Hypothesis'. In 1996, Long introduced the notion of selective attention to clarify how input becomes intake.

Shortcomings

Many researchers have provided empirical evidence that modified speech and interactional modification improve the learners' *understanding* (Pica *et al.* 1987; Loschky 1994), but only Ellis (1994) and Mackey (1999) have successfully demonstrated that comprehension of a number of lexical and syntactical features actually leads to the *acquisition* of these structures. Gass (1997) concludes that interaction and input play some role in second language acquisition but that their precise role has yet to be determined. As seen in section 3.3.1 there is not enough evidence for the usefulness of negative feedback.

While the interactionist approach acknowledges the central role of both person and environment, it still views them as two independent variables and treats them in isolation. The focus of the model remains on mental processes. Interactions (the context for learning) are considered as the mere source for input that propels acquisition. Recently, the strict demarcation between the learner's mental and social processes has been widely criticized.

Main ideas to remember

Getting input through listening and reading is not enough to acquire a second language. Speaking is necessary as well.

- Speakers negotiate meaning in conversations.
- Speakers modify their speech to make the input comprehensible.
- Modified interactions facilitate understanding.

It has been made clear so far that the behaviourist and cognitive ap
focus: the first one looks at external factors (behaviour, environment) and
internal, mental processes. Both traditions hold that behaviour and mental pr
tively, are rule-governed. The aim of both is to explain and predict these rules al
patterns. In addition, both traditions favour quantitative, experimental methods whi
take place in laboratories.

These traditions sharply contrast with the sociocultural tradition. Rather than predicting
processes and behaviours, this approach attempts to understand and interpret phenomena.
Research is based on qualitative methods (e.g. interviews, life histories, diaries) and the
research methods are associated with hermeneutics (literally the art of interpretation).

3.4 A sociocultural approach to SLA

Until recently, many SLA scholars have continued to locate language learning exclusively in the
mind of the learner and to attribute a minimal role to the environment. However, more and
more theorists were unsatisfied with the distinction between the learner's mental and social
processes and their competence and performance. There has been a growing recognition that
language learning is more than the acquisition of mere linguistic structures and that language
learning and its use are shaped by sociocultural processes (Block, 1996; Lantolf, 1996). In
a symposium, Firth and Wagner (1997) attacked mainstream, cognitive SLA studies for failing
to study language in context. They argued for a focus on the contextual and interactional
elements of language use and for the adoption of an insider's perspective. Although mainstream
researchers (Long, 1997; Kasper, 1997) criticized this view, theorists who worked from sociocultural perspectives saw an opportunity for the development of an approach to SLA that draws
on language socialization, social participatory and sociocultural frameworks (Markee, 2000).

This symposium has eventually led to a split between mainstream cognitive SLA and
emergent sociocultural approaches that take account of both cognitive and social factors
(Lantolf and Appel, 1994; Larsen-Freeman, 2004; Johnson, 2004; Seedhouse, 2005). This
transactional approach to SLA is based on sociocultural theory, also referred to as sociohistorical, cultural-historical or sociocultural historical approach. The origins go back to
the 1920s and 1930s when Vygotsky, Leont'ev, Luria and other scholars tried to restructure
psychology on Marxist lines.

Sociocultural theory holds that the origin of language competence in a first, second or foreign language lies in the social reality and therefore in language use occurring in a discernible

.ck, 1994; Donato, 2000;
Mondada and Pekarek
iage, individuals need to
inguage learning is there-
embedded in a particular

experienced participants
of thinking and behaviours
itsky's (1962, 1978) concept
ial processes turn into inner
inctions that individuals can
of an expert. The following
a procedure.
his level of competence, thus
m of the goal, advises him on
talk that supports the child in
et al., 1976). Language plays a
the mother and the child. With

The mo.. .
intra-mental processes resulting from ..
the child has learned some strategies such as paying attention to colour and shapes and con-
sulting the picture on the cover of his puzzle. He might also have learned to persist and focus.
He can internalize these processes which will enable him to control his behaviour and mental
processes in the future.

In a similar way, participation in second language learning activities with more experienced others enables learners to acquire more than the mere language. They also come to
understand the values and beliefs attached to learning a language, develop learning strategies
and learn how to participate in the target culture.

Children (or any novices) do not only acquire the particular beliefs, values and ways
of thinking of their community. Rather, they also shape them and can thereby influence or
transform the community. One only has to think of text messages or emails. Many children
have learned that they can encode messages in a particular form on their mobile phones
(e.g. '4u' instead of 'for you') and are allowed to use an informal register in emails. This particular way and style of writing quick messages has influenced the way people interact and
communicate. This is an example of the transactional nature of learning: the external
environment transforms inner mental processes which in turn transform activities in social,
cultural and institutional settings. The relationship between learners and context is dialecti-
cal, dynamic and constantly changing. Vygotskyan theorists are therefore critical of transmission models and interactional approaches in which learners and contexts are treated in
isolation.

The sociocultural approach to SLA investigates the ways in which participation in a variety of sociocultural contexts affects the learner's language ability. It provides accounts of the social processes of second language learning, portrays the personal qualities of the learners and examines the processes that enable second language learners to become active participants in the target culture (Johnson, 2004). This model has moved away from seeing language learning as 'acquiring' and 'possessing' linguistic structures, to conceptualizing it as 'doing' and 'increasing' one's participation in the language practices of a social group.

Shortcomings

The sociocultural approach to SLA has been criticized by mainstream cognitivists for failing to provide insights into the cognitive processes involved in the acquisition process and to give detailed descriptions of the language learners acquire.

Main ideas to remember

- Both the cognitive and social factors involved in learning a second language need to be taken into account.
- Learners acquire a second language when they participate in meaningful interactions with more experienced members of their community.
- Language plays a crucial role in mediating the processes between novice and expert.
- Novices internalize the values, beliefs, behaviours and ways of thinking of their community while interacting with more experienced people.

Implications for practitioners

- Learning a language means using a language. Involve learners in the language practices of the social group.
- Encourage meaningful and authentic interactions with a range of people and provide opportunities where learners can negotiate meanings.
- Use authentic materials.
- Correct errors in an appropriate way.
- Design tasks that are just beyond the learners' competence.
- Monitor learners and adjust the amount of assistance they need to carry out a task.
- Use scaffolding techniques like the following:
  - o simplify the task by breaking it down into smaller steps
  - o remind the learners of the whole task and the goal
  - o point out what is significant
  - o model other ways of doing the task
  - o control the learners' emotions during the task.
  (Wood, 1998; Cameron, 2001)

3.5 Main points to remember

Theories of SLA differ in their philosophy, focus, research questions, methodology and therefore also in their findings.

- No theory on its own can explain second language learning as 'a whole'.
- Findings are sometimes contradictory. For example, behaviourists insist on practice, while the linguistic tradition holds that language learning is developmental and, thus, that practice is not necessarily efficient. The information-processing approach calls for a focus on form while adherents of the Input Hypothesis are less inclined towards error correction and the teaching of grammar. Behaviourists would not encourage learners to engage in conversations with native-speakers since they could make mistakes which become permanent. By contrast, followers of interactionist and sociocultural approaches make interactions the key to learning.
- The role of error correction and practice has been much researched but evidence seems to be inconclusive.

Rather than summarizing the differences between the theories, I would like to conclude this chapter with some points that most theorists agree upon and that offer you some guidance when planning lessons and curricula:

- Pay attention to learners. Take account of their linguistic and cultural backgrounds, their needs, background knowledge, attitudes towards the new language and culture, confidence and, finally, their motivation to learn the language.
- Encourage as much contact with the target language and culture as possible.
- Provide meaningful activities where learners can develop listening and speaking and possibly all four language learning skills.
- Scaffold learners' use of language in class.
- Offer meaningful and relevant opportunities for practice. Focus on language areas that are age-appropriate and relevant.
- Give sensitive and appropriate feedback.
- Remember that learning is not a linear, but a complex and recursive process with many ups and downs.

Approaches to Language Teaching

Chapter Outline

4.1 Introduction

Chapter 3 has shown that the findings of SLA research are not sufficiently clear and uncontested to provide straightforward answers to how children learn additional languages. They can therefore not be used to draw conclusions on the 'best' method to teach foreign languages. Let's be clear from the beginning: there is no one best method. Each teacher needs to make informed decisions based on the learners' needs about what methods work best with particular pupils in a particular context at a particular moment. As Mitchell and Miles (1998) explain:

> teaching is an art as well as a science . . . There can be no 'one best method', however much research evidence supports it, which applies at all times and in all situations, with every type of learner. Instead, teachers 'read' and 'interpret' the changing dynamics of the learning context from moment to moment, and take what seem to them to be appropriate contingent actions, in the light of largely implicit, proceduralized pedagogic knowledge.
>
> (p. 195)

Over the last 100 years, educationalists have experienced many changes in teaching methods. These latter were informed, among others, by advances in information technology (e.g. internet); economy (e.g. global markets); linguistics (e.g. Chomsky); psychology (e.g. learning theories) and research into second language acquisition and the effectiveness of teaching. Each new approach has brought with it some important insights.

This chapter gives a brief historical overview of several methods of teaching foreign languages: Grammar-Translation, Direct Method, Audiolingualism, Total Physical Response, Communicative Language Teaching, Form-focused Instruction and Task-based Instruction. Note that these methods do not exist in a 'pure form' in the classroom. Teachers adapt them to suit the needs of their students.

Food for thought

- Reflect on your own experience of learning foreign languages. How did your teachers teach languages? Can you associate these methods with a name? Try to find some advantages and disadvantages of each method you experienced.
- Observe language lessons with children of different ages and in different schools. What teaching methods do you notice being used? Can you identify on which theory of language or language learning they are based?
- What methods would you like to apply?
- Can you think of ways in which social, economic and political factors influence your teaching?

4.2 Methods of language teaching

A method for teaching languages is a comprehensive approach that helps teachers decide what language skill(s) to develop, what activities and resources to choose and how to plan for progression.

4.2.1 Grammar-Translation

At the end of the nineteenth and the beginning of the twentieth century people did not have the same facilities for travel and the same access to media as today. Therefore, they did not have the same opportunities to encounter a range of languages as we have. People who learned Latin and Greek, the so-called classical languages, studied them to 'discipline the mind' rather than develop linguistic competence. Grammar-Translation (GT) was the most dominant teaching method. This mentalist method focused on the teaching of grammar and the translation of classical texts. Grammatical accuracy was the aim and little, if any, emphasis was put on producing the language. While the teaching of grammar was expected to develop the learners' analytical and logical skills, a strict canon of classical literature aimed to produce cultivated minds. The aim of the interpretation and translation of texts was not the learners' development of knowledge of a particular target culture. Rather, the learners were expected to develop 'general culture' and to discover universal values such as Truth, Beauty and Good.

Towards the end of the nineteenth century universities introduced 'modern' as opposed to 'classical' languages into the curriculum (e.g. French, German or Spanish). Teachers continued to draw on Grammar-Translation until the 1960s, but even today the method is still used although it is now considered old-fashioned.

In today's classes, teachers present readings that illustrate particular grammatical features or literary concepts. They draw learners' attention to grammar points or vocabulary items, explain grammatical rules and present bilingual lists of vocabulary. They encourage practice consisting largely of rote-learning and translations from and into the target language (TL).

Shortcomings

Since learners focus largely on reading, translating and writing it is understandable that research studies have shown that the method does not result in the development of good pronunciation and communicative skills. They have also illustrated that it guarantees neither greater accuracy nor linguistic knowledge (Savignon,1972; Lightbown, 1983; Montgomery and Eisenstein, 1985). In addition, the teacher-centred focus leaves learners little room for developing autonomy (Klapper, 2006).

Main ideas

Table 4.1 Summarizing table of Grammar-Translation
L1 stands for mother tongue (or main language) and FL for Foreign Language

Grammar-Translation (GT)	
Time span	Early to mid-nineteenth century
Big idea	Learners develop a foreign language by acquiring vocabulary and grammatical rules and by applying their knowledge
Engagement of the mind	Mentalist (i.e. learners construct knowledge)
Deductive/inductive	Deductive learning (i.e. learners are first given a rule which is later on exemplified and practised)
Use of L1/FL	Extensive use of the L1 (the teacher explains rules in the L1)
Authenticity of language	Texts used for translation are often constructed by the teachers
Language skills	Reading and writing skills; 'knowledge about language'
Main activities	Translation, comprehension tests based on set questions, précis writing
Technology/resources	Minimal use of technology
Theoretical underpinning	Atheoretical

Towards the end of the nineteenth century, a group of linguists dissatisfied with the Grammar-Translation method reformed language teaching. A range of methods emerged, one of the most important being the Direct Method, associated with Berlitz, a German who lived in America.

4.2.2 Direct Method

Berlitz intended to give grammar a more subordinate role, to avoid the use of the mother tongue and to give more emphasis to the spoken (foreign) language. The Direct Method drew on the emerging discipline of phonetics (science of speech sounds). The spread of phonetics went in parallel with the increased use of the new method.

The aim of the Direct Method is to enable learners to make direct associations between a concept and the word in a foreign language. Teachers would label the object that people live in, with doors, windows and a roof, a *Haus*. To make themselves understood, they would also use props, pictures, gestures and mime. As a result, the learners make a direct link between the object and the new word, rather like children learning their mother tongue. By contrast, a teacher following GT is likely to present the German word through the translation of the English word 'house'. Grammar-Translation and the Direct Method further differ in their focus on particular skills and their emphasis on grammar. GT emphasizes the written word and the teaching of grammar. The Direct Method, on the other hand, focuses on speaking skills. Teachers are even advised to withhold writing for as long as possible. Grammar is taught inductively. In other words, teachers present grammatical features to learners and expect them to discover the rules for themselves.

One important contribution of the Direct Method is the move away from the exclusive focus on grammar and the clarification that a language is a means for communication.

The Direct Method enjoyed great popularity at the end of the nineteenth century and is still used in schools today.

Shortcomings

The method's major shortcoming is related to the dogmatic focus on the target language. Since it requires the use of the target language only, teachers and learners have to concentrate on the 'here and now' in mundane conversations. They encounter difficulties when they speak about features beyond the immediate surroundings or abstract topics. In addition, teachers sometimes go to great lengths to express something in the target language when an explanation in the mother tongue would communicate the information faster and more effectively. The focus on the TL also means that the success of the method greatly depends on the teacher's proficiency in the foreign language and their communicative skills. Other criticisms address the lack of literary or cultural content and the teacher-centred nature of the method.

Main ideas

Table 4.2 Summarizing table of the Direct Method

Direct Method	
Time span	End of nineteenth century until today
Big idea	The learners make direct association between the object and the word in the target language
Engagement of the mind	Mentalist
Deductive/inductive	Inductive
Use of L1/FL	Extensive use of the foreign language
Authenticity of language	Authentic and real (used in context)
Language skills	Listening and speaking skills
Main activities	Communication in the 'here and now'
Technology/resources	Minimal use of technology, props, classroom objects, events
Theoretical underpinning	Phonetics

4.2.3 Audiolingualism

The Second World War and the intervention of Morse code, radar and the computer form the background for the development of Audiolingualism. After the end of the war, American soldiers were sent to different parts of the world, especially to South-East Asia. They needed to become competent in a number of languages as quickly as possible. In the absence of a method deemed appropriate to learn these 'new' languages, the Army developed a programme called the Army Specialized Training Program (ASTP).

The audiolingual approach, based on ASTP, is underpinned by the behaviourist theory of learning (which holds that language is a form of behaviour) and on structural linguistics, a movement that focused on the phonemic, morphological and syntactic systems underlying a language. The approach is therefore based on two premises:

- language learning involves knowing how to combine the building blocks of a language
- learning happens through habit formation.

As seen in Chapter 3, learners form habits when they repeatedly respond to stimuli in predictable ways and when these responses are reinforced. Errors need to be avoided since they might become engrained.

In a typical language lesson, the teacher introduces learners to a limited amount of vocabulary, often in the context of a dialogue. They then encourage practice of the new vocabulary and simplified, graded sentence structures in the form of dialogues and drills.

The dialogues are often set in the target language and are supposed to present language that native speakers would use in a particular situation. In fact, the sentence structures are learned for their grammatical content rather than for functional purposes. Memorization and the acting out of the dialogues enable learners to work on their pronunciation and to memorize the conversational phrases.

The aim of the drills is error-free production. Learners practise patterns until they recall them automatically. Drills can take the form of repetition (e.g. of a word), substitution (e.g. of a word or word phrase) or transformation (e.g. of an affirmative sentence into a negative one). In the example below, learners practise the structure 'Do you like?'. In each question they substitute a noun with the noun the teacher offers.

Teacher:	Coffee.
Child:	Do you like coffee?
Teacher:	Tea.
Child:	Do you like tea?
Teacher:	Wine.
Child:	Do you like wine?

Further examples of exercises are given in chapters 7 and 8.

Grammar is taught inductively. Textbooks tend to focus on a narrow range of grammatical points determined by Contrastive Analysis. Teachers exemplify the rules in sentences and ask pupils to practise them. They spend a minimum amount of time on the rules themselves and give relevant explanations once the learners have mastered the new structures.

The method dictates a particular sequence of learning skills by emphasizing the principle of primacy of speech (oral language before writing) and the development of receptive skills (listening and reading) before productive ones (speaking and writing). As a result, listening, speaking, reading and writing are learned in that order.

During the 1960s and early 1970s, the development of technology had a direct influence on language teaching, and tapes and videos became regular resources in the classroom and language laboratories. These materials enabled the learners to play units on tape recorders and films over and over again to help them practise and memorize structures. The resources had the further advantage of presenting language 'in context'. Learners saw how language is used in a particular situation and understood that the meaning of an utterance depends on the situation in which it is used. Audiolingualism developed into audiovisualism which made language memorable by presenting it in context and by bringing the context alive through the use of visual aids.

Shortcomings

Audiolingualism has been criticized on a number of accounts. First, it does not prepare learners for spontaneous talk in authentic situations of communication. The language used in real life is different from the sentences practised in isolation in the classroom. Consequently, there is little chance that learners automatically transfer the knowledge gained in the classroom to real-life situations.

Second, critics have raised issues about mechanistic drilling. Although drills can help the learner memorize simple patterns, Johnson (2001: 247) lists five shortcomings:

- repetitiveness
- meaninglessness
- lack of context (structures are practised in isolation)
- indirect contribution to communication (drills are not the 'real thing')
- control (learners do not have any freedom to be creative and to choose what to say).

Audiolingual drills can easily be improved in order to become more meaningful and effective by adding a problem-solving element. For example, the teacher could ask learners to do a mini-survey and find out some information about classmates.

Third, the form-focused nature of the lesson and the artificiality of the situations proposed fail to provide learners with meaningful and interesting opportunities to communicate. The great pressure to produce language correctly and the dependency on teacher input leave little room for learner-initiated questions, interactions between students and independent learning. Rather, they tend to discourage learners from producing (creating) and using language to express personal meanings. By avoiding learner errors and favouring drills, Audiolingualism does not take account of research findings that show that errors are a natural part of language learning, that language proficiency is developmental and that pupils learn both consciously (what Krashen terms 'learning') and unconsciously ('acquisition'). In addition, the form-focused nature of the lesson can also result in a decline of learners' motivation and attention (Long, 1997).

Research findings have shown that this prescriptive and mechanistic approach does not result in the development of either fluency or competence (Krashen, 1982; Lightbown and Spada, 2003). These findings together with Chomskyan linguistics and cognitive psychology accelerated the decline of Audiolingualism. Though less influential than in the 1960s, the method is still used in language classrooms today.

Main ideas

Table 4.3 Summarizing table of Audiolingualism

Audiolingualism

Time span	Widespread throughout the world up to the 1960s, still used in classrooms today
Big idea	Language is divided into structures and sentence patterns which are drilled and practised until learners recall them automatically. Errors need to be avoided.
Engagement of the mind	Behaviourist
Deductive/inductive	Inductive
Use of L1/FL	More FL than L1. The L1 is used during the presentation of new linguistic items
Authenticity of language	The sentence patterns drilled are produced for their grammatical point. Used in isolation, they are often useless.
Language skills	Listening, speaking, reading and writing in this order
Main activities	Substitution drills, multiple-choice tests, comprehension exercises, role-plays
Technology/resources	Tape recordings, film strips, work in language laboratories
Theoretical underpinning	Structuralism and behaviourism.

The Chomskyan revolution initially led to eclecticism in language teaching but then two major branches developed, humanistic approaches and communicative approaches. Both put the learner and communication at the heart of language learning. Humanism in applied linguistics also influenced the notional/functional syllabus, the Natural Approach and Communicative Language Teaching (CLT) (see section 4.2.5).

4.2.4 Total Physical Response

Developed in the 1970s and 1980s, humanistic approaches were a reaction against the mechanistic approaches of language learning. They are based on the belief that language learning should respect and be about the 'whole' learner. Educationalists adopting a humanistic approach recognize the importance of emotions. They attempt to respect the integrity of the learner, to enhance personal growth, to take account of psychological and affective factors and to make language learning meaningful to the learners (Roberts, 1998). Among the well-known humanistic approaches are Silent Way (Gattegno, 1972), Suggestopedia (Lozanov, 1978) and Total Physical Response (Asher, 1972, 1979). I will give more details on the latter since it is often used in primary school.

Total Physical Response (TPR) encourages listening and a 'silent period'. It is based on the belief that listening comprehension is the key to language development (e.g. Input

Hypothesis). The teacher produces language and asks learners to perform related actions that show that they have understood the input. This can take the form of acting out orders, enacting stories, drawing pictures in response to instructions or accompanying songs with actions. The assumption is that 'motor activity strengthens recall' (Roberts, 1998), meaning that the link learners make between the language and the physical action enhances memorization.

In practice, teachers tend to spend about 120 hours asking learners to listen to sentences and to carry out actions indicating their comprehension before they encourage speaking. Pupils only speak once they feel ready. They are eventually able to give instructions or to tell stories with the help of gestures.

Shortcomings

This approach is helpful in the very early stages of language learning but needs to be complemented by other approaches. Issues related to the method are its teacher-centred nature (the teacher is in control of the grammar-based curriculum) and the paucity of language structures that are eventually useful in real situations of communication.

Main ideas

Table 4.4 Summarizing table of Total Physical Response

Total Physical Response	
Time span	1970s and 1980s
Big idea	Motor activity (physical actions) enhances memorization and therefore furthers learning
Engagement of the mind	Behaviourist
Deductive/inductive	Inductive
Use of L1/FL	FL
Authenticity of language	Focus on imperatives (teachers give instructions for action). The language used in the classroom is seldom used in real-life situations.
Language skills	Listening, speaking and some reading.
Main activities	Teachers give instructions in the form of imperatives or tell stories which the learners enact. Eventually, learners use the language orally.
Technology/resources	Minimal use of technology
Theoretical underpinning	Structural linguistics (grammar-based curriculum); humanistic approaches to language learning

4.2.5 Communicative Language Teaching

Around the 1960s more and more sociolinguists were discontented with the exclusive focus of linguistics on grammatical competence. Rather than finding out what learners could possibly say in the light of their knowledge of language, they wished to study a person's actual language use. Hymes (1972) was one of the first to propose a theory of language as communication. He posits that *communicative competence* implies:

- knowledge of the language
- ability to decide whether an utterance is formally possible
- ability to adapt an utterance to the context
- ability to use the language to have something done.

His concept of communicative competence thus comprises a linguistic, sociolinguistic and pragmatic component.

Canale and Swain (1980) and Canale (1983) proposed a pedagogical framework based on communicative competence. They distinguished four components:

- linguistic or grammatical competence: knowledge of phonology, morphology, syntax, semantics and lexis
- sociolinguistic competence: knowledge of the sociocultural rules of language and styles required to use language appropriately with regard to contextually defined choices such as formality and politeness
- discourse competence: knowledge of the rules governing the structure of texts (selection, sequencing and arrangements of words, structures and sentence patterns)
- strategic competence: knowledge of verbal and non-verbal strategies relevant to language learning, processing and production.

It follows that communicative competence and the ability to apply this knowledge go beyond the acquisition of mere grammar, favoured through Grammar-Translation, or of sociolinguistic skills, developed through Audiolingualism. Communicative competence should be the aim of language teaching and the means to achieve that end (Brumfit, 1994).

In the early 1970s, the European Council encouraged a more meaning-based approach centred on communicative competence. The objective of language learning was to facilitate European integration through enabling citizens to communicate in brief encounters with foreigners in predominantly tourist and professional settings. The Council of Europe called for a substitution of structural curricula with notional/functional syllabi. This type of curriculum is grounded on the analysis of communicative situations. The aim is to help learners develop the language needed to express a range of *notions* (concepts such as time, location or dimension) and *functions* (akin to speech acts such as greeting somebody, complaining, expressing opinions) in a variety of contexts. In a first step teachers identify the notions and functions, in a second, they define the relevant vocabulary and grammar needed to express these ideas.

With this new type of curriculum came a shift from a teacher-centred to a learner-centred approach. The role of teachers is to help learners reach their personal learning goals and to become more independent. This requires flexibility on the part of teachers since it is impossible for them to determine in advance the exact content of language lessons, and to control every aspect of teaching.

The publication of Krashen and Terrell's (1983) *Natural Approach* was another important drive towards meaning-based approaches. The authors claim that communication is the primary goal of language teaching, that (listening and reading) comprehension precedes production and that production simply emerges under the right conditions. For this to occur, learners need to have sufficient exposure to comprehensible input in a stress-free environment. The role of teachers consists of providing learners with enough linguistic input. The focus is on comprehension. Learners are not pushed into the use of the second language early on to avoid their *affective filter* (Krashen, 1982) going up. Teachers avoid formal instruction (e.g. teaching grammar, encouraging drills) and corrective feedback because they believe that they interfere with the natural developmental process (see Chapter 3; Krashen, 1981, 1982).

While the Natural Approach has dominated in the USA, CLT became the dominant approach in Europe in the 1980s (Widdowson, 1978; Littlewood, 1981; Brumfit, 1984). The emphasis lies on meaning and the focus is on spoken rather than written language. CLT came in a strong and a weak version. The aims of both are identical: to help learners express themselves fluently and appropriately in a range of situations. The means and the aims are similar: communication. The main teaching method was simulation: teachers created artificial simple interactions where learners imagined a particular situation and practised the language they would use if they were in that particular situation.

In the strong version, the role of the teacher is to:

- provide learners with linguistic input (e.g. in the form of stories or authentic materials)
- engage learners in conversation, promote negotiations and help learners express themselves in the target language early on
- suggest communicative activities and encourage language use in meaningful and purposeful ways.

Teachers neither correct errors nor teach grammar formally. It is up to the learners to analyse the language and to acquire the grammatical rules inductively.

In the more popular weak version teachers propose more structured activities enabling learners to practise sentence patterns inside and outside the classroom and to expand the acquired vocabulary to a range of settings. The focus lies on meaning and authentic purposeful language use.

Lessons typically follow the Presentation-Practice-Production model, also known as the PPP model:

- Presentation: the teacher presents linguistic material.
- Practice: learners practise structures and sentence patterns in a controlled way, often in group work. Typical activities are small- and whole-group discussions and role-plays.
- Production: ideally, learners progress to the stage of free production.

Both versions include a cultural component. Students learn typical greetings, gestures and non-verbal behaviour to act in culturally appropriate ways.

Shortcomings

Unfortunately, the breadth of the approach has resulted in misinterpretations of the main concepts. Some teachers have over-emphasized the role of the learner and left language learning entirely in the hands of the students. The lack of guidance has resulted in limited progress of the learners' competence. Other teachers continued to be teacher-centred and, therefore, did little to foster autonomous learning and to encourage creative language use. They stuck to the content of the books and failed to use authentic materials. Students learned set phrases and formulaic speech and 'imitated "real-life" language use' (Allwright, 2000: 3). For example, they learned to book train tickets for trips they would never undertake, but they never thought about or discussed various possible routes to the destination. Research studies showed that learners failed to acquire language that could be used in authentic situations of communication. Besides, CLT requires little focus on form, a principle which is not compatible with the concept of communicative competence as defined earlier. Teachers tended to correct errors if they interfered with communication. They taught little grammar since it was believed that grammar is acquired inductively.

In addition, some learners felt frustrated and under pressure to perform because teachers encouraged responses in the target language very early on.

Research studies into CLT have shown that learners who develop basic comprehension and communicative skills in the early stages of the learning process do not develop these abilities to advanced levels. Most fail to achieve a basic level of grammar (Harley and Swain, 1984; Swain, 1991; Lightbown and Spada, 2003). The OFSTED reviews in secondary schools in England indicate that learners generally speak with acceptable accuracy in routine situations, but their accuracy and fluency deteriorate when they speak at greater length or in new situations. Learners' pronunciation and intonation can be poor (Harris *et al.*, 2001).

Main ideas

Table 4.5 Summarizing table of Communicative Language Teaching

Communicative Language Teaching	
Time span	1980s
Big idea	Learners are encouraged to express different functions of language. Teachers provide them with the necessary linguistic input. Error correction is minimal. The focus is on meaning rather than form.
Engagement of the mind	Mentalist
Deductive/inductive	Inductive
Use of L1/FL	FL
Authenticity of language	In theory, learners are to communicate with a range of speakers inside and outside the classroom, hence, encounter and produce language in authentic situations of communication. In practice, they often learn set phrases and formulaic language.
Language skills	Listening and speaking, some reading and writing. There is little emphasis on grammar.
Main activities	Role-plays, games, drama, pair or small-group activities
Technology/resources	Overhead projector, audio and video recordings, computers
Theoretical underpinning	Chomskyan linguistics, notional/functional syllabus

If the objective of CLT was to develop communication skills and intercultural competence, the aim of recent approaches is to develop social actors. This has to be seen in the light

of the progressive integration of citizens in Europe. As Puren (2002, 2006) explained, the French (and for that matter all European citizens) are likely to study or work for a period abroad or even to use a foreign language when working in France. While learning how to start basic conversations with 'foreigners' in brief encounters, coming to know and understand others, and accepting differences between oneself and the target culture, were valid objectives in the 1970s, they are too narrow at the beginning of the twenty-first century. The European Commission wants citizens to be able to *act* together and to create similarities in their differences. This 'perspective co-actionelle co-culturelle' as Puren (2002) labelled it, underpins the Common European Framework of reference for Languages (Council of Europe and Council of Cultural Co-operation, 1996). Before I describe the popular *Task-based Instruction* encouraged by the Council of Europe I outline *Form-focused Instruction*. Both methods are post-communicative approaches or *neo-communicative didactics* (Stein, 2000a).

4.2.6 Form-focused Instruction

The issues related to CLT have prompted a move towards a greater focus on form within a communicative approach. The label *Form-focused Instruction* (FFI) is often used to describe the new approach. Long (1997) distinguishes between what he calls 'focus-on-form' and 'focus-on-formS'. The latter refers to traditional methods such as Grammar-Translation and Audiolingualism characterized by a structured and sequenced curriculum. By contrast the *focus-on-form* approach is embedded in meaning-based instruction like the weak version of CLT. Learners are exposed to meaning-based activities and their attention only shifts to formal aspects of the language when the teacher or students encounter a problem and 'notice a gap' (Swain, 1985) between the interlanguage and the speech that should be produced. The focus on form is thus incidental, contrary to the traditional approaches where it is the main concern of language teaching.

Research studies have shown that form-focused instruction and corrective feedback within communicative programmes are more effective in fostering foreign language learning than approaches that are limited to an exclusive focus on either accuracy or fluency (Savignon, 1972, 2002; Spada, 1997; Montgomery and Eisenstein, 1985; Ellis, 1995; Stein, 2000a; Lightbown and Spada, 2003).

Shortcomings

Focusing on form in a meaningful context is easier said than done. Teachers could easily slip into Grammar-Translation or Audiolingualism.

Main ideas

Table 4.6 Summarizing table of Form-focused Instruction

Form-focused Instruction	
Time span	From 1980s
Big idea	In order for learners to develop fluency and accuracy, the focus needs to be on form within an overall meaning-based context
Engagement of the mind	Mentalist
Deductive/inductive	Deductive
Use of L1/FL	Mainly FL
Authenticity of language	Learners often begin with set phrases and formulaic language and progress to more relevant and 'real' language in more authentic situations of communication
Language skills	All four language skills
Main activities	Role-plays, stories, drama, games, pair or small-group activities
Technology/resources	Computer, authentic materials
Theoretical underpinning	Research into the effectiveness of methods of second language teaching

4.2.7 Task-based Instruction

Task-based Instruction (TBI) (Carless, 2003; Ellis, 2003; Nunan, 2004) is based on socio-cultural theory. The focus lies on completing a task with a problem-solving element. A task is a meaning-based activity which takes account of the learner's linguistic proficiency, needs and interests and represents real-life situations (Skehan, 1989; Klapper, 2006). Examples are role-plays, communication games, discussions and debates which bring the real world into the classroom.

In order to complete the task the learners interact with a range of partners and use various (authentic) resources. They negotiate meanings in the first or the foreign language depending on their experience and skills. Solving tasks often requires them to use all four language skills in a culturally appropriate way. The authentic materials and the communication with native speakers provide them with insights into the ways of life of the target culture and with opportunities for common activities. The use of ICT is an inherent part of the method. Researching information on the internet or writing emails are regular classroom activities.

Many task-based lessons are built on the structure proposed by Willis and Willis (1996):

- *pre-task*: the teacher introduces the learners to the task and may at this point highlight useful vocabulary and structures
- *task:* learners complete the task alone, in pairs or small groups
- *planning*: learners plan a short oral and written report to tell their classmates how they progressed
- *report*: learners report to the class

- *analysis*: the teacher analyses the linguistic productions and highlights those aspects that need to be practised
- *practice*: learners practise aspects of the language where the teacher has noticed gaps
- *feedback:* the teacher gives feedback on the content, language and procedures used to complete the task.

Compared to traditional drills used in Audiolingualism, tasks are non-repetitive, meaningful and based on the learners' needs. They require learners to practise language 'directly' rather than using structures in isolation and to practise many skills at the same time. In traditional drills, learners focus on one or a few aspects at a time. While they might produce a particular structure correctly under these conditions, they could encounter problems with the same structure once they speak freely and focus on a range of aspects at the same time. Peterson (1975: 94) states that learners perform better if they learn to use all language skills as a whole as soon as possible.

Another advantage of the approach is its motivating effect. The wish to use language has repercussions on a range of levels (Johnson, 2001: 259–60):

- Learners are likely to remember the language used. Stevick (1976: 188) explains that meaning ('what happens inside and between people') is related to memory.
- They develop both accuracy and fluency. The interactions provide learners with many opportunities to get linguistic input, to negotiate meaning, to hypothesize about language, to test their hypotheses and to use language. It is inevitable that they will make errors and 'notice the gaps' between what they are able to say and want to say. The incidental focus on formal aspects, the feedback and practice enable them to acquire those new linguistic structures they are 'developmentally ready for'.
- Learners develop some knowledge about the language as a system.

Ellis (2003) summarizes the benefits. He holds that task-based teaching offers the opportunity for 'natural' learning inside the classroom, is intrinsically motivating, focuses on meaning and form, emphasizes the product and the process and is compatible with a learner-centred approach. The approach not only increases learners' motivation and confidence (Frost, 2005), it is also an efficient tool for learning languages (Long, 1997; Ellis, 2003) and for developing strategic competence. The wish to produce language, the fact of having control over their learning and the expectation of having to explain the procedures used to solve the task, require learners to take risks, to develop efficient strategies and to negotiate procedures (Allwright, 2000; Swain, 2000; Coyle, 2000). It has been shown that sessions where learners reflect on their strategy use have the potential to foster their strategy development (Donato and McCormick, 1994; Quicke and Winter, 1994; Coyle,2000; Stein, 2000a).

The Storyline Approach is an example of Task-based Instruction. The method was developed in the 1970s in Scotland to ensure a more integrative approach to teaching. Educationalists recently used the method to teach foreign languages as it provides a purposeful and communicative context and makes links to the real world. The holistic approach is learner-centred: it is based on the pupils' prior experiences and harnesses their creativity and desire to learn. While teachers develop the outline of the storyline and ensure that it is logical, learners fill in the detail and content. This provides them with a feeling of security and, more importantly, ownership. The identification with the characters and the stories and the sense of achievement propel the learning process.

Shortcomings

As with every approach, TBI has its shortcomings. Negotiation around the tasks is an important part of the learning process but beginner learners are likely to find it difficult or even impossible to use the target language for this purpose. Relying on the first language at these moments reduces the amount of language learning and might have a demotivating effect. In addition, the syllabus puts a lot of pressure on the teacher. Contrary to a linguistically structured or notional/functional curriculum (content-based), a procedural or task-based curriculum (Prabhu, 1987) does not prescribe the linguistic items that will come up in the lessons. Rather, it outlines a range of activities. Learners will use whatever language is necessary to solve a task and teachers will need to take instant decisions on ways to promote negotiation, on the types of error to correct and the linguistic forms to focus on. Further, the learner-centred nature of the approach means that learners are likely to do and learn different things in the same lesson. This calls for good monitoring and assessment skills and a lot of flexibility on the part of teachers. Finally, there could be a danger that teachers or learners believe that participation in tasks is a sufficient element for learning a language. While it is the essence of the method, 'doing' is not enough. Finally, the method has been criticized for not taking account of the insights derived from the cognitive, in particular the information-processing view of language learning (Klapper, 2003). Cognitivists agree that learners acquire language through exposure and meaningful interaction, but endorse the use of effective memorization and practice because the latter leads to the automatization of language skills and improved accuracy of the linguistic productions.

Main ideas

Table 4.7 Summarizing table of Task-based Instruction

Task-based Instruction	
Time span	Around 2000
Big idea	Combining a focus on meaning and form and process and product. Learners solve tasks in meaningful and authentic interactions.
Engagement of the mind	Mentalist
Deductive/inductive	Both
Use of L1/FL	The amount of FL increases with the learners' proficiency
Authenticity of language	The tasks are related to 'real-life' aspects and learners use language in real situations of communication
Language skills	All four language skills
Main activities	Role-plays, stories, drama, games, pair or small-group activities
Technology/resources	Computer, data projector, interactive CD-ROM, interactive whiteboards, use of internet (authentic materials, video conferencing)
Theoretical underpinning	Research into SLA and effective second language teaching, Prabhu's (1987) procedural (task-based) syllabus

4.3 Main points to remember

The review of teaching methods has shown that over time language teaching has changed in many respects:

- *change of focus*: from form (Grammar-Translation, Audiolingualism) to meaning (Communicative Language Teaching) to approaches emphasizing both meaning and form (Form-focused Instruction, Task-based Instruction)
- *change of aims*: development of analytical and logical skills, communicative competence, intercultural competence
- *change of syllabus*: grammatically sequenced (as in Grammar-Translation), notional/functional syllabus, task-based syllabus
- *change of pedagogy*: teacher-centred and learner-centred models.

If the aim has been to find a universal method for the optimum teaching of modern languages, one has to recognize that no one single best method exists (Whitehead, 1996). This is not astonishing since the 'success' of methods depends largely on the learners, the teachers, the situation and the overall context and the particular feature of language that needs to be learned. Today, all approaches are still in use in some form or other. Teachers tend (and need) to be eclectic and flexible, but it is fair to say that most teachers use a variation of CLT.

Even though there is no agreement on a 'best' method apart from the principle to draw both on meaning-based and form-focused components, practitioners defined principles of effective teaching:

- Start where the learners are. Activate and build on learners' experiences and knowledge.
- Encourage learners to create their own conceptual model first (to hypothesize and test their hypotheses).
- Promote meaningful interaction with the target language.
- Make learning enjoyable and create a supportive atmosphere where learners feel safe and free to take risks.
- Develop an appropriate and coherent curriculum that is based on learners' needs and allows for rich, authentic, varied and challenging input.
- Vary teaching methods: further learners' active participation and full engagement, cater for different learning styles and use multi-sensory methods.
- Use cooperative strategies and vary social groupings.
- Provide a range of authentic resources and extensive support to further learners' understanding.
- Treat and display learners' work with respect.
- Give learners constructive feedback on their work and their learning progress.
- Correct errors sensitively.
- Give learners some control over their learning, foster autonomy and develop learning strategies.
- Involve parents and inform them about their children's learning.

By applying these principles, it is likely that learners will develop into competent, motivated and confident language users. (Note that learning never happens automatically.)

What Children Say about Learning Foreign Languages

5.1 Introduction

After two theoretical chapters I continue with a case study of six monolingual English children's experiences of learning foreign languages. The six nine-year-old, working-class children lived in Dartford, a small town less than 30 miles east of London and easily accessible from Europe. I describe how Anne, Jane, Sandy, Paul, Mike and Larry (pseudonyms) learned French, German and Japanese formally and informally at home, on holiday and at school. Some had further opportunities to use languages in Cubs and the local football club. Note that these children's definition of 'using a language' and 'being able to speak' means using *some words* in that language.

In this chapter I illustrate the many different ways in which children learn and adults teach languages, make links to previous chapters and put some flesh on theory.

Food for thought

- Think about your own experience of learning foreign languages. When, where and how did you learn them?
- In what situations did you learn best?

All too often, the topic of foreign language learning is confined to teachers and schools. Many guidelines written for parents appear to be underpinned by the beliefs that, first, children are not exposed to foreign languages at home and, therefore, have few opportunities to acquire language in a natural way and, second, that parents are not knowledgeable about ways of fostering their children's learning process. I argue that the parents of these six children were interested in developing their children's foreign languages and were knowledgeable about ways of doing so. They, both intentionally and unintentionally, created practices that enabled their children to familiarize themselves with a range of languages and cultures and to improve their linguistic competence.

The children's experiences of foreign language learning differed at home and school. I describe the range of existing teaching practices and compare them both with children's perceptions and with the productive learning setting at home. The comparison illustrates children's awareness of their learning environment and the active role children played when learning languages. I close the chapter with the six children's vision of how languages should be learned.

5.2 Description of the study

The data of this chapter stem from a longitudinal study carried out in 2002 in the six children's homes and their school, West Hill Primary School in Dartford (Kirsch, 2006a). The following table gives an overview of the languages these six children learned in the calendar year 2002:

Table 5.1 Overview of language teaching in the calendar year 2006

Class/Children in	Period of time	Time allocation	Language	Teacher
Year 4	January–July	5 min per day	French	Mr Brown, class teacher
	January–July	30 min per week	Japanese	Miss Smith (secondary teacher) and two A-level students from the nearby Specialist Language College (SLC)
Year 5	Six lessons between September–December	45 min per week	German	Miss Lee (secondary teacher) from the nearby SLC
	Six lessons between September–December	10 min per week (revision of the German lessons)	German	Mrs Moore and Mrs Freeman, class teachers
	September–December	5 min per day	French	Mrs Moore and Mrs Freeman, class teachers

Note that although the six pupils attended two different Year 5 classes they learned the same languages for the same amount of time.

The parents of all six children had studied at least one foreign language at secondary school (e.g. French, German or Spanish) for a couple of years, and either one or both the parents of Anne, Jane and Larry had O-level qualifications in one language. Apart from Larry's mother, all revealed that they had had a bad experience. However, or maybe therefore, they were all very positive about the study of foreign languages at primary school. No parent used foreign languages regularly. Apart from two mothers, all parents were employed in local shops, smaller companies or bigger industries.

All children apart from Sandy had family members studying languages formally or informally at the time of the study. Anne's, Jane's and Mike's older brothers studied languages at secondary school, while Paul's and Larry's younger siblings had their first contact with foreign languages (FL) at primary school. Jane's grandmother and Mike's father attended language courses and Sandy's grandfather had attended one several years ago.

Data were collected using an ethnographic approach. I relied on interviews, observations, questionnaires and elicitation procedures such as role-plays. I also took field notes, tape-recorded interviews and lessons, took pictures, collected documents and kept a research diary. The children documented their experiences of using and learning languages in a diary, with a digital camera and a tape recorder. The variety of methods used enabled me to convey a rich contextualized portrait of the locally specific actions and events happening at home and at school.

5.3 A first look at children's experience of learning languages

Asked 'What have you done to learn languages?' children listed a range of activities in which they engaged on their own and with family members, teachers or acquaintances. The excerpts below give a flavour of the interviews. In brackets are the codes I used in the graphs and tables.

CK (C. Kirsch):	How did you learn French?
L (Larry):	I know quite a bit of French because we went there twice. And the first time, I had to learn some words to go to the baker, so I said what I wanted. I also spoke to the other children. (*Memorizing, finding native speakers, speaking*)
CK:	What else?
L:	I try to read. I don't know why I do that but each time when I go to the supermarket with my mother I look at the receipt and try to figure it out. Yes. And then I often tried to read things on signs, on the road, and tried to figure out what it meant. (*Reading, inferring meaning*)
CK:	How did you learn French?
A (Anne):	We do some French at school. We do games. Yesterday, we did one where we had to go out of the classroom and then we had a, like a ball, in someone's desk and we had to go and ask in French have you got the ball and the child who had it had to say 'Je m'appelle Georges'. (*Playing games*)

CK:	How do you learn Japanese?
P (Paul):	Teachers and students talk to us and we try to remember. (*Listening, memorizing*)
CK:	And that's all?
P:	Uh, we sometimes write things down. We speak to our neighbour. In the lesson today we could speak more, that is better, because it is like individual lessons. (*Writing, speaking*)
CK:	How did you learn German?
J (Jane):	I was asking my stepdad to learn some German. We took the dictionary and we read the words. He said them and I taped them. (*Getting help, using reference books, reading, speaking, listening*)
CK:	So he said them and you were saying them back to him?
J:	Yes. I couldn't remember some words. So I wrote down words like 'mein'. I wrote it down just the way you say it. And then I practised the words from time to time. (*Memorizing, repeating, writing, practising*)

The interviews illustrate how outspoken the children were about learning languages. They had some experiences of using and learning languages at home, on holiday and at school which they were eager to share with me. Figure 5.1 (home) and Figure 5.2 (school) represent the activities listed according to the languages and settings. Apart from the activities which came up in the excerpts above, children listed watching TV, singing songs, using computers, speaking about languages, reflecting about language learning and studying typical artefacts of a country.

5.4 Learning languages at home and on holiday

Below I outline the language learning practices described from the point of view of the children and their parents.

5.4.1 Children's perceptions

All children mentioned activities in the course of which they encountered and learned languages with their parents and relatives at home and on holiday. Figure 5.1 represents all actions. It indicates that the most frequent activities were listening, speaking, reading and writing and that most occurred in French.

Children encountered foreign languages when they, sometimes together with their parents and siblings, listened to music or watched television, listened to their older siblings doing homework or listened to native speakers on holiday. All parents had taken their

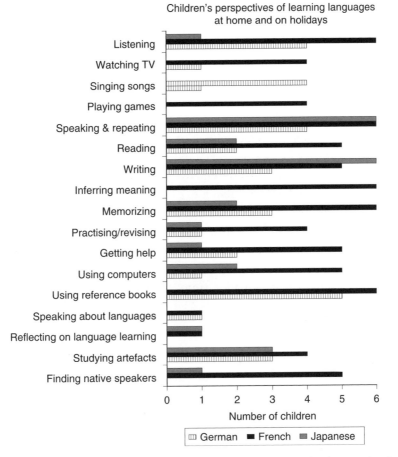

Figure 5.1 Language learning activities in which children reported that they engaged at home and on holiday.

children to France either on holiday or on day trips to do shopping. This was possible because of the proximity of Dartford to the Channel Tunnel.

Children repeated words after family members or used words in foreign languages when they told their parents about their learning experiences at school. In addition, some used some utterances abroad, for instance when they ordered a drink or bought some food at the local supermarket. They tried to make sense of signposts, labels on food and captions in magazines. Some even tried to read story books in French. These guessing and reading activities were initiated either by the parents or by the children, who were driven by their curiosity to make sense of the world around them (Bruner, 1990; Kress, 1997). These activities show that children are careful listeners and observers of their linguistic environment (Kenner, 2000).

Writing, namely copying words, enabled children to memorize and practise. For example, Mike practised his name in Japanese Kanji. Formal practice was also mentioned. Jane practised some German words with her stepfather and Larry worked through three French primers with his grandfather.

All children had access to a computer at home and most children made use of it, for example, by looking up information about other countries on the internet together with an older family member. One boy had a computer game that he played in languages other than English, and the parents of two children had CD-ROMs in French which their children used occasionally.

All families had dictionaries and children, again either on their own or with siblings or an adult, used them to look up words. Mike's mother asked her two sons to find a new word every day. Mike revised all words at the end of the week. Anne's mother had bought a phrase book which she expected her two children to use on holiday.

Many parents reported that they spoke about language learning with their children. These conversations seem to have been important to Anne who was the only child who mentioned them in the interviews.

The list of activities is certainly impressive. In order to check the trustworthiness of my data, I had to compare the information from children with the activities in which parents reported engaging their children.

5.4.2 Practices offered by parents

Research findings in the field of second language socialization have revealed the rich practices in which all parents (or family members) involve their children in order to help them learn a second language. Among these practices are doing games; pointing at pictures of relatives and naming them; reciting rhymes; playing school; telling stories; looking at labels; and reading books (Gregory and Williams, 1998, Gregory *et al.*, 2000; Nieto, 1999; Brooker, 2002; Bayley and Schecter, 2003; Lamarre with Paredes, 2003). It was suggested that practices which further language learning 'happened most of the time within the framework of everyday life and entertainment' (De la Piedra and Romo, 2003: 51) rather than being specifically organized to teach languages (Heath, 1983; Schieffelin and Ochs, 1986; Wells, 1987; Taylor, 1994). Brumfit (1995) has claimed that children learn languages in a 'conscious/organized and unconscious/accidental way' (p. 9).

The activities in which parents engaged with children in my study resemble those I found in the above literature. In addition, they mirror the ones outlined in the practical guides for parents written by Farren and Smith (2003) and Arndt and Effgen (2005). None of these parents had ever read a book on how to help their children learn foreign languages. Nevertheless they intentionally and unintentionally presented children with an average of 13 different opportunities to encounter and learn foreign languages. Table 5.2 lists all practices in which parents, siblings and grandparents engaged with the children or in the presence of them.

In some of these language events, children were at the 'periphery' (Lave and Wenger, 1991), in others, they were more directly involved in the interactions with more competent speakers

Table 5.2 Language learning practices offered by the relatives (parents, siblings and grandparents) to the six children at home and on holiday
The capitals stand for the children's names

Language encounters/children's relatives	A	J	S	P	M	L
Meeting acquaintances speaking foreign languages	√	√	√	√		√
Listening to music, watching TV	√		√ rare			√
Studying languages	√	√		√	√	√
Using the odd word	√	√	√	√	√	√
Participating in social events	√		√	√		√
Going abroad	√	√	√	√	√	√
Using target language on holiday	√		√ rare	√	√	√
Guessing labels	√					√
Talking about language learning	√	√	√	√	√	√
Speaking about languages	√	√	√ rare			√
Playing games	√		√		√	√
Singing songs	√					√
Using computers	√	√	√	√	√	√
Teaching vocabulary	√	√	√	√	√	√
Using reference books	√	√	√	√	√	√
Encouraging language use	√				√	√
Encouraging formal practice					√	√
Developing language learning strategies	√				√	√

and, hence, could participate more fully in the life of the community (e.g. going abroad). Some events enabled children to raise their awareness of different languages and cultures (e.g. meeting acquaintances), others to develop competence (e.g. teaching vocabulary). Some *just happened*, others were deliberately organized by family members for the purpose of practising languages (e.g. revising vocabulary items, working through primers). On many occasions, however, parents did not plan language learning activities consciously. It just happened that they used languages when doing homework with an older sibling, when ordering food on holiday or when listening to music in a language other than English.

The interviews show that the children recognized the potential that these situations hold for language learning. This indicates that they analysed events in which they were not directly involved and began to pay particular attention when they spotted an opportunity for learning. They listened to and observed people using languages; asked questions; deciphered labels; copied words and practised utterances. All children initiated activities with family members even when the latter did not have teaching in mind. The fact that children picked up some languages and learned about languages and cultures in situations that were not conceived of as learning arrangements is in line with findings from Ward (1971), Heath (1983), Rogoff (1990, 2003), Schieffelin (1991), Taylor (1994) or De la Piedra and Romo (2003). The authors show that children learn skills through overhearing and observation in situations that have not been specifically set up with a learning intention. Driven by either a wish to make sense of situations where foreign languages were used, or their goal to improve their knowledge, children actively create an opportunity for learning.

The comparison of the parental practices outlined in Table 5.2 with the children's perceptions of their language learning opportunities represented in Figure 5.1 reveals a good correspondence. This does not only illustrate the trustworthiness of my data but it is also a sign of children's positive attitudes, their interest in languages and their endeavour to learn.

5.5 Learning languages at school

Next, I present the learning activities in which children reported engaging at school and the practices I observed in Years 4 and 5.

5.5.1 Children's perceptions

The six children whom I studied had learned some French with their class teachers in Years 3 and 4 and some Japanese with a secondary specialist in Year 3. In the calendar year 2002 they learned French with Mr Brown (the class teacher) and, from January to July, they enjoyed half an hour weekly of Japanese both with Miss Smith, a secondary specialist, and two A-level students. From September, Anne and Larry attended Mrs Moore's Year 5 class whereas Jane, Sandy, Paul and Mike attended Mrs Freeman's mixed Year 5 and 6 class. Miss Lee, a secondary specialist, taught German in these two classes. In the first term, she taught six weekly lessons of 45 minutes to each class. (She taught each class for six weeks in each subsequent term.) The Year 5 teachers revisited the content of the German lesson and continued with the provision of French. I observed language lessons and some core subjects and interviewed teachers about their practices.

When I asked children about 'the things the teachers did with them in their language classes', they listed 16 activities presented in Figure 5.2. The figure shows that only a few children mentioned carrying out activities in German. In fact, at the time I carried out my last interviews in November 2002, Anne and Larry had only had six weeks of German with the secondary teacher while the other four children had only just started their tuition.

A quick comparison of children's reported activities in the home with the school setting (Figures 5.1 and 5.2) indicates that there are more similarities between the two settings than differences. Children engaged in activities requiring the *four language skills* and *memorizing* in both settings independently of the language. However, those who went on holiday had more language learning opportunities since they could hear and produce the foreign language. *Practising/revising, studying artefacts; getting help* (and feedback) and *playing games* are similarly mentioned in both settings. The same is true for *speaking about languages* and *reflecting on language learning*, though these actions are rare and language specific. *Using dictionaries* and *computers* happened exclusively at home, though such tools certainly have their place at school.

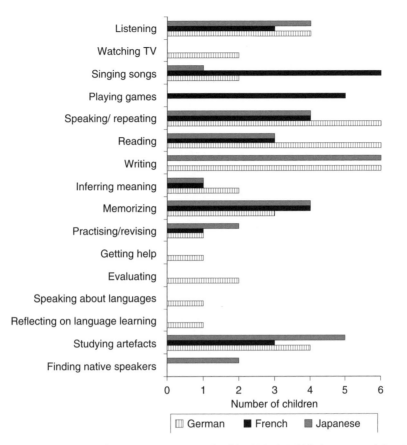

Figure 5.2 Children's perspectives on learning languages at school (activities in which they reported that they engaged at school).

A more detailed look reveals that the two contexts differ most when it comes to learning Japanese and German. Most teachers adopted a formal approach whereas children lacked a structured learning environment at home. Children could only engage in the same activities if they *brought* the language home. This was the case, for example, with Jane and Larry who were very eager to learn German. They initiated reading and writing activities with family members, carefully listened to them, repeated words after them, inferred meanings, memorized words and increased their knowledge of Germany by looking up information in books. They created continuity between their experiences at home and at school by producing a learning context at home which partly resembled school. According to Dewey (1916), students need strong goals in order to build continuities and to ensure future learning. Without motives and interests, they will neither identify with a subject nor throw themselves fully into their work. The continuity between settings is not just *there*: it needs to be *created*.

Differences in the type of language learning activities seemed to be least pronounced in French. Many children engaged in similar language learning activities at home and at school. This does not mean, however, that the two settings were similar. The meaningful language use that the parents of Anne, Mike and Larry encouraged at home and on holiday was in stark contrast to the not very challenging *fun activities* dominating at school. Oral language use was reduced to a minimum. Being interested in improving their competence, Anne, Jane and Larry interpreted the school setting as a *learning environment* and behaved accordingly. They reported listening, speaking, reading and memorizing although Mr Brown did not put any emphasis on these activities (see Table 5.3).

Children were aware of how language learning processes differed at school and at home and were able to critically compare outcomes. For example, all children agreed that they learned little French in Year 4 and that they did not increase their proficiency as much as they had hoped. They criticized the lessons on the grounds of their non-challenging content, the slow pace and the unsuitable, childish activities. They believed that singing, playing and studying artefacts were not effective ways of *learning* the language.

Larry:	I would learn most of [French] when I went on holiday this year and the year before and the year before that. So that is when I learned the most because it didn't, no, because we have not been through any French at school at all.
CK:	Well, I mean, you did the songs last year.
Larry:	Oh yeah, but that did not really teach us anything.
Sandy:	Because in the French ones we didn't do that many things on it because Mr Brown didn't really do anything with us about it.

They concluded that singing and playing, though enjoyable, did not help them to develop proficiency in the foreign language. On the other hand, they considered the speaking, reading and writing activities that they had experienced at home and in some German and Japanese lessons to be effective.

In order to understand children's explanations and to value the extent to which they were aware of their language learning environment, it is necessary to have some background information about the school. I describe the provision for foreign language learning in the following section.

5.5.2 Practices organized at school

West Hill Primary School, a popular, average-sized, mixed school in Dartford, was attended in 2002 by nearly 500 pupils aged five to eleven. Ten per cent of all pupils came from a minority ethnic background, the largest proportion being Asian. The number of children with special educational needs was 14 per cent in 2004, which was below the national average.

The head teacher's decision to offer foreign languages as a timetabled subject was influenced by a range of factors: the closeness to France, the national push for foreign languages,

Kent County Council's policies and work on early language learning and her own desire to offer a broad and balanced curriculum enabling children to get first-hand experience of a variety of subjects. In 2000, she put the deputy head in charge of introducing FL across the board and sent several teachers to in-service training sessions. These teachers were introduced to the *sensitization approach* (see Chapter 1) and the language programme *pilote* (Rumley and Sharpe, 1999) and learned how to use songs, games and rhymes to embed languages in routine activities throughout the day. It is, therefore, not surprising that the school implemented a sensitization approach, the model used in every fifth school in Kent (Driscoll *et al.*, 2004). The aims, the teaching time and the content of the language lessons were similar to those of other schools providing early language learning at the time (Powell *et al.*, 2000; Driscoll *et al.*, 2004).

In 2000, the teachers at West Hill Primary agreed to develop positive attitudes and to raise children's awareness of languages and cultures. One way of promoting the diversification of languages was through displays, posters and books that acknowledge the diversity of society; another through establishing links with primary schools in Japan and Sardinia. The schools regularly exchanged typical art and craft works which they then exhibited in the corridors of their respective schools .

Those teachers who were confident in French or Spanish used languages in daily routines sang songs and played simple games in foreign languages. This meant that pupils' exposure to languages depended largely on the interest and competence of their particular class teacher.

Table 5.3 Language learning practices used by seven tutors at school

Language learning practices	Primary teacher			Secondary teacher	
	Mr B (F)	Mrs M (G, F)	Mrs F (G, F)	Miss L (G)	Miss S (J)
Using languages for rituals (e.g. register)	√	√	√	√	√
Speaking about a country/culture	√	√		√	rare
Singing songs	√	√	√		√
Playing games	√			√	√
Listening exercises	√	√		√	
Teaching vocabulary	rare	√	√	√	√
Conversing		√	√	√	√
Reading sentences and short texts		√	√	√	
Writing in order to communicate		√		√	
Practising			√	√	√
Revising		√	√	√	
Developing knowledge about language		√	√	√	
Teaching learning strategies		√	√	√	rare

The language tutors' names are abbreviated (Mr Brown, Mrs Moore, Mrs Freeman, Miss Lee, Miss Smith) and the letters in bold below their names indicate the language(s) they taught (French, German, Japanese). A tick means that they used a particular practice.

The language coordinator (Mrs Moore) soon realized that the school needed the help of the local Specialist Language College (SLC) if FL was to develop. From 2001, secondary school teachers from the SLC taught Japanese and German to children in Years 2, 3, 4 and 5 in the presence of the primary generalists. This background information is necessary to understand the provision and practices I observed in 2002.

Table 5.3 outlines the practices the primary and secondary teachers used in their Japanese, German and French lessons. It shows that children engaged in activities which were sometimes contrasting, sometimes complementary. Their experience depended entirely on the language and the teacher. The teachers' language competence, confidence and understanding of language learning and learning theories influenced their aims which, in turn, shaped their choice of teaching practices. (This relationship between a person's beliefs and goals, their sociocultural context and the ways they engage in tasks has been well studied by many, among them Platt and Brooks (1994), Nardi (1996) and Holland and Reeves (1996).)

Below I give some details about the teachers and their practices. The specialist language teachers (Miss Lee and Miss Smith) and the Year 5 teachers (Mrs Moore and Mrs Freeman) had a degree in languages and had the linguistic competence and confidence to teach languages. They developed pupils' linguistic skills, knowledge about countries and knowledge about language (KAL). The two Year 5 teachers and Miss Lee (the German teacher) were interested both in the product and children's learning processes and chose methods that were largely underpinned by social constructivism. They put communication at the centre of the lessons, focused on the four language skills and helped children develop both fluency and accuracy in a meaningful communicative context (Savignon and Berns, 1984). Without being aware of it, they used *neo-communicative methods* (Reinfried, 1999; Wolff, 1999). They taught vocabulary, encouraged meaningful language use and practised aural, oral and literacy skills. They expected pupils to speak accurately and drew their attention to particular features of the language such as spelling and plurals. Mrs Moore and Mrs Freeman had initially believed that grammar and literacy had no place in language lessons at primary school. They changed their view when they witnessed the pupils' interest in German literacy and realized that Miss Lee increased their knowledge of English and German.

Miss Smith, the Japanese teacher, created a safe learning environment where children had ample opportunities to listen and practise. She switched between behaviourist and social constructivist learning theories which was reflected in her endeavour to combine the drilling of words and sentence structures in an audiolingual tradition with a more communicative approach. Her aim was to develop children's linguistic proficiency but she also raised their awareness of Japanese culture, for example by teaching some Kanji.

Mr Brown, the Year 4 teacher, adopted a *sensitization approach* when he taught French. His aim was the development of positive attitudes towards languages and cultures through the use of songs, games and cultural artefacts. His teaching was largely based on behaviourism. Mr Brown had GCSE French and felt less confident in developing children's linguistic competence. Besides, he explained that it was inappropriate to aim at competence at primary school.

A comparison of Table 5.3 with Figure 5.2 reveals many similarities. It highlights children's awareness of their learning environment. As a group, they recalled all the activities done in their lessons although there were differences between the children. However, there are also interesting differences which point to a discrepancy between a teacher's intentions and the children's understanding of the purpose of the foreign language lessons. For example, some pupils remembered reading and memorizing vocabulary in their French lessons even though Mr Brown did not focus on these aspects. In fact, these two activities only happened when he introduced the class to a French memory game. The fact that these children recalled these activities indicates that they considered them to be important. As pointed out before, they wished to improve their competence in French. Children could well have engaged in the French activities on a deeper level than one might have expected by simply observing lessons.

In the next section, I illustrate the children's considerable knowledge of effective teaching methods. They were able to design an effective learning programme by building on their own learning activities and experiences.

5.6 Children's vision of language teaching

In order to examine what practices children found useful and effective, I organized a role-play: they were MPs who had to decide on the language provision in an LA, in particular on the choice of a language, teaching time and teaching methods. They had a quarter of an hour to discuss the issues before they called me, the journalist, into their office.

Both groups, one of girls, one of boys, decided to make French a compulsory language because of the location of the country. The boys explained in addition that French is easy to learn while the girls pointed out that it has the same alphabet as English and is widely spoken in Europe and Africa. The girls insisted that each English school should have a project with an African school so that schools could exchange resources and teachers. As for timing, both groups suggested that French should be taught from Year 2 to Year 6 for two hours a week. They also listed similar aims for FL teaching: the development of oral and written communication skills and of some knowledge and understanding of the countries where French is spoken.

The children listed a range of learning activities: singing; watching TV and videos; listening to tapes and the radio; talking to teachers, classmates and French-speaking people; reading posters and books; writing; looking up words in dictionaries; working on the internet; taking photos; taping French native speakers and studying maps. Both groups made school trips to France a compulsory part of the learning programme. They wanted learners to engage in regular activities with French native speakers, for example by skiing in the Alps.

It is important to note that the suggested methods were not empty words but had been thought through carefully. Because children found watching TV in a language other than English difficult, they proposed films with subtitles. Being concerned about cultural awareness, they added that the videos should present particular features of France. Since they themselves struggled with reading, they stressed the need for regular practice with teachers at school and with parents at home. To increase exposure and practice, the girls suggested the display of posters with useful words and phrases in public places (e.g. roads, gardens, squares).

The exhaustive list of interactive methods mentioned above allows both for language acquisition and formal language learning. The activities are characteristic of a *whole language approach* where learners use all four skills in authentic situations of communication both outside school and in formal settings. Apart from developing language competence, these methods foster the development of knowledge of culture and of geography of French-speaking countries. Such a rich and productive learning setting as described by these children rarely exists in schools but made perfect sense to them in the light of their own experiences. The role-plays have therefore illustrated two things: first, these children understand that language learning is a social process involving a variety of people and, second, they know that there are many different ways of creating productive language learning environments.

5.7 Conclusion

This chapter has illustrated that the six children familiarized themselves with languages and developed their language competence by drawing on a range of facilitators such as family members, holiday acquaintances and teachers. In addition, they encountered languages with coaches or instructors in clubs. The range of settings and people involved in children's language learning confirms the extent to which young children's learning interactions occur within 'organized, flexible webs of relationships that focus on shared, cultural activities' (Rogoff, 1990: 97). This confirms that foreign language learning is taken seriously by British people and that much work has been undertaken to sensitize young children to languages and cultures early on.

The positive attitudes of the parents of these six ordinary and working-class children towards early language learning were reflected both in the creation of rich and varied language learning opportunities and in their children's developing attitudes and skills. Like most parents, they cared about their children's interests and developments. The arrangements they created, whether intentionally or unintentionally, for the purpose of entertainment or education enabled their children to foster an interest in a range of countries and cultures and to develop positive attitudes to languages and language learning. They used languages with a range of interlocutors, drew on a variety of material resources and increased their vocabulary and linguistic competence. In addition, they developed some knowledge of language learning.

Naysmith (1999) showed that children who have been exposed to foreign languages and had some experience of using and learning these tend to be confident and well prepared for formal language teaching because they are *receptive* and able to build on prior skills and knowledge. These six parents are likely to have given their children a headstart in learning additional languages. It is therefore important to understand, recognize and acknowledge parents' expectations and skills when it comes to helping children learn languages. Unfortunately, educationalists often seem to be unaware of the range of productive arrangements made by family members at home (Vincent, 1996; Huss-Kessler, 1997).

The comparison of home with school contexts in my study shows more similarities between settings than one might have expected. Children engaged in many activities both at home and at school, particularly when it came to oral and written language use and to memorization. Children did not engage in either numerically more or in qualitatively more complex activities (e.g. evaluating their own learning process) at school – where one might imagine they had a better opportunity to do so – than at home. They had less access to resources than at home and fewer possibilities to use languages in authentic situations of communication. The home context seemed to offer the following advantages: children had role-models in relatives who learned and used languages; they could count on the assistance of a range of competent speakers and they had access to a range of interactive resources.

Teachers should have productive dialogues with parents in order to find out more about children's experience of using languages outside school and to create continuities between the two settings. Collaboration with parents (as well as with primary and secondary teachers) and continuity between home and school should be among the priority topics at initial teacher training and in-service training. Research findings have indicated that high levels of continuity between the home and school settings are closely related to children's subsequent achievement, their social and cognitive development and their sense of self (Scollon and Scollon, 1981; Michaels, 1986; Heath, 1983; Cochran-Smith, 1984; Pollard with Filer, 1996; Anning and Ring, 1999). Failure to take account of and build on children's language learning experiences outside school could in addition result in children perceiving FL as a useless experience (Dewey, 1933). This could be the case if children with high expectations who want to *learn* a language are continuously exposed to mere fun activities with the aim of familiarizing them with languages.

Finally, this chapter has highlighted children's awareness of their language learning settings, their interest in learning languages, their reflective and analytical skills, their understanding of ways of learning languages and their active engagement. Driven by either a wish to make sense of situations where foreign languages are used, or their goal to improve their knowledge, they actively created learning opportunities (Nardi, 1996). They observed, overheard and engaged with more competent speakers whether these people intended to teach them foreign languages or not. These findings are encouraging at a time when many parents and teachers put considerable effort into early language learning.

6 Introducing Children to Foreign Languages

6.1 Introduction

As shown in Chapter 1, teachers throughout the world use similar strategies to introduce learners to foreign languages: they draw on games, songs and rhymes, tell stories and use languages throughout the day, for example in daily routines. Chapters 2 and 5 have illustrated that the teachers at Portway, Cardwell and Westhill Primary Schools used these strategies effectively to familiarize pupils with foreign languages, teach basic skills and develop positive attitudes to learning.

Food for thought

- Regular exposure to a foreign language is a prerequisite for language learning (see Chapter 3). Think about your own experience of learning languages. How have your teachers ensured that you heard or saw a foreign language as often as possible, perhaps even on a daily basis?
- In what ways have your teachers used rhymes, games, songs and stories? How do you think they can enhance language learning?
- Practice and revision of key vocabulary and grammar points are a necessary part of the learning progress. How have you learned vocabulary and grammar?

In this chapter I look at ways in which teachers can create an inviting physical environment and social climate that encourages the daily use of foreign languages. Embedding languages in the life of the classroom and integrating them into the curriculum are excellent strategies for doing this. Highly enjoyable *five-minute activities* such as games, rhymes or songs are invaluable in getting pupils to use the target language and practise one of the four language skills. The use of stories is an ideal way of introducing pupils to longer sequences of language and to work in a holistic way. I give practical examples and offer some guidance on how to use these activities successfully.

Although the emphasis of this chapter is on fun and enjoyment, I would like to stress that language learning is more than amusing children with playful activities for five minutes a day. For pupils to acquire a language, lessons need to build upon each other and offer a range of communication situations. This enables learners to *do* something in the new language and to make progress. Satchwell (1997) reminds us that this requires rigorous planning by the teacher:

> Simply stringing together a series of unconnected games and activities which will entertain and amuse the pupils is not sufficient, even with the four- and five-year-olds.
>
> (p. 26)

6.2 The physical environment

When entering schools visitors are often greeted with welcome posters in a range of languages (see Figures 2.1 and 10.1). Where foreign languages feature high on the agenda they are likely to see multilingual labels, displays of work, friezes, posters or resources (see Figures 6.1 and 6.2 as well as 10.1 to 10.4). Figure 6.1 shows an excerpt of a display of writings, cards, drawings and artwork from Japanese pupils. The poster exemplifies the project work undertaken between West Hill Primary School and a class in Japan. Such symbols can have a stimulating and motivating effect, and encourage learners to engage with foreign languages.

On entering a classroom, a visitor can get a fairly good impression of the use of foreign languages. Figure 6.2 shows resources used by a teacher at Westhill Primary School to write the date and time in French. The questions and answers in German and the Swiss German greeting 'Sali . . . Grüezi Frau Klee' indicated that the teacher also practised some German. Some walls were decorated with posters with instructions in French and some pieces of furniture had multilingual labels attached. The labels, greetings, instructions and key questions were a useful resource in the language lessons and served as a memory aid (Martin and Cheater, 1998).

The following section explores some reasons for using the target language in the classroom and offers some practical suggestions.

Figure 6.1 Japanese artwork.

6.3 Using the target language

Immersion is the ideal situation for language learning at school (see Chapter 1, section 1.6). It can be achieved if teachers use the target language both as a medium of communication in language lessons, and as a means of instruction in subjects other than modern languages. This method is known as Content and Language Integrated Learning (CLIL). Learning new concepts or revisiting old ones in a different language has several advantages:

- Pupils improve their language skills.
- Pupils are likely to learn subject matter at a *deeper level*. The opportunity to think about concepts in two languages and from different perspectives facilitates understanding and reinforces learning.
- The opportunity to apply knowledge and to practise language skills across subjects engages pupils in higher order thinking skills and enhances their ability to transfer skills.

CLIL is used throughout Europe (Eurydice, 2006) but the status and provision is complex and depends on the country. Using CLIL effectively requires good language skills on the part of both the teacher and the learners. Its use is often limited to secondary schools or to primary schools where much time is spent on learning foreign languages (e.g. Luxembourg, Finland, Netherlands).

Figure 6.2 Resources for writing the date and learning the time in French.

In most countries, primary school teachers enhance the exposure to the foreign language by using it as a medium of instruction in the language lessons and by using it throughout the day, for example in routine activities such as taking the register. Listening to a foreign language in context (e.g. classroom instructions) and on a regular basis contributes to learning in the following way:

- It exposes pupils to the words, sound patterns, rhythm and intonation of the new language.
- It offers comprehensible input.
- It encourages pupils to make sense of the overall meaning of an utterance rather than translate single words.
- It helps pupils memorize pieces of language which they can analyse and break down at a later stage in their learning process.
- It strengthens pupils' confidence in their language skills.
- It fosters the development of pupils' attention span and listening skills.
- It furthers the development of communication strategies. Pupils have the opportunity to observe the teacher using mime, gesture and visuals, and to use these techniques themselves to convey meanings.

In order to develop classroom language, pupils need to learn specific vocabulary and sentence structures. Teachers will need to ensure, for example, that pupils know the names of the most common classroom objects and some ways of asking for equipment. Learners will need to be able to perform simple speech acts such as asking for clarification or permission, making apologies and giving basic explanations.

Teachers can introduce classroom language as separate vocabulary items, practise them in games such as 'Simon says' (see section 6.4.3) and encourage the design of visuals as a memory aid. To help learners memorize the new language, they need to use the new phrases consistently and to make learners use them as well. As pupils become more confident and competent, they can use longer, more complicated utterances and integrate new vocabulary into old structures. The context will help them understand the meaning. If the classroom climate makes learners feel safe and secure and if it encourages them to take risks, they will begin to use the foreign language themselves with increasing competence.

The use of puppets

Research findings have shown that puppets are an excellent way of promoting positive attitudes towards the use of the target language. Pupils often lose their inhibitions about speaking either to or *through* the puppet when holding it themselves. It seems suddenly less threatening to use the language and run the risk of making a mistake. Teachers can use them to present new language, to promote spontaneous dialogue and to act as a role-model. Their puppets may or may not be native speakers and may or may not correct mistakes (Satchwell, 1997).

Teachers are good role-models and should use the foreign language as frequently as possible. Whatever their level, they should master the vocabulary, pronunciation, intonation and structures they use, and be confident in what they say. Teachers who are unsure of the target langue are better off using less language well and correctly than trying to use more language incorrectly. It is important that they start slowly and build up their repertoire over time.

When using the target language, teachers need to take account of the linguistic needs of all their pupils. If they feel a need to re-explain or to clarify a misunderstanding they can revert to the main language (e.g. English in the UK). They could, for example, ask a competent linguist in the class to rephrase what has been said. Ideally, the teacher should have discussed with the pupils when and under what circumstances English can be used in foreign language lessons. It is crucial that they avoid alternating between languages on a regular basis; this would only be confusing and result in developing *lazy learners*. Rather than listening carefully to the explanations in the foreign language and trying to make sense of them, pupils are likely to learn that they only have to wait for the English translation. They would, therefore, probably not make as much effort as is needed to participate in the language lesson.

6.4 Using rhymes, songs and games

In this section, I present some benefits of working with poems, rhymes, tongue-twisters and songs, give some concrete examples of how these literary forms can be used and point out some pitfalls. Some methodological considerations on how to develop listening, pronunciation and speaking skills are provided in Chapter 7.

6.4.1 Benefits of using rhymes, poems and songs

Many language teachers have described the benefits of using rhymes, songs and games in foreign language classes as follows:

- Rhymes, poems and songs are very popular with young language learners who tend to be familiar with this type of literacy from school or home. Children do not shy away from poems and songs in foreign languages.
- Teachers are equally familiar with them and thus may find them a good way into the teaching of foreign languages.
- They promote positive feelings.
- The rhythmical patterns facilitate and accelerate learning.
- They are a good means of developing listening, pronunciation and speaking skills. Pupils do not tire of listening to and repeating them over and over again. They join in with the parts they know and acquire more sounds, words and sentences with each successive performance until they gradually master the text.
- These forms of literacy help pupils get into the rhythm of a language and learn to pronounce sounds and words confidently, accurately and with expression.
- Pupils are more likely to remember the new words and structures because they are repetitive, meaningful and presented in predictable patterns and larger chunks. The internalization of sounds, words and sentence patterns brings learners a step closer to using these in other contexts.
- Rhymes, poems and songs can initiate a range of activities:
  o listening (e.g. listening out for particular sounds and patterns)
  o reading (e.g. putting strips of paper with lines of the lyrics of a song into the right order)
  o drawing (e.g. illustrating a poem)
  o performing actions (e.g. finger rhymes)
  o playing and enacting
  o performing in front of an audience
  o creating new texts by drawing on the key vocabulary learned or substituting words
  o practising intonation, pronunciation and structures.
- Poems or songs about typical traditions or cultural artefacts (e.g. Christmas songs) are helpful in developing pupils' cultural awareness and understanding.
- Working on rhyming words and discussing the layout of the texts helps pupils to develop their knowledge about language.
- Pupils come to realize that they can enjoy, sing and comprehend traditional songs without having to understand every single word (Martin and Cheater, 1998). This understanding is important when they tackle longer pieces of language.

Many teachers take advantage of the popularity and repetitive structure of songs to practise key vocabulary in an *enjoyable* way. They make up their own songs based on well-known tunes. Since pupils already know the melody, rhythm and beat they can concentrate on the new language. When teachers replace words in the original songs by words in the same or another language, they have to pay attention to both the number of syllables and the intonation pattern. If one of the aims is to teach pupils the correct pronunciation of words, then teachers have to make sure that the intonation of all the substituted words is correct. Below is a list of English songs that teachers in England often use as a starting point to create new versions of songs in other languages:

- Clementine
- Green Bottles
- Humpty Dumpty
- Jingle Bells
- Lavender's Blue
- London's Burning
- Nuts in May
- One Finger, One Thumb
- She'll be Coming round the Mountain
- Ten Little Indians
- The Farmer's in his Den
- Three Blind Mice
- Twinkle, Twinkle Little Star
- Old MacDonald

Many ways of exploring a poem

I exemplify here the many possible ways in which a poem can be explored by looking at a French poem for Easter (Example 6.1).

Example 6.1 Excerpt from a French poem for Easter

J'ai trouvé un bel œuf bleu.	*I found a blue egg*
Bleu comme la rivière,	*Blue like the river*
Bleu comme le ciel.	*Blue like the sky*
Le lapin l'avait caché	*The rabbit had hidden it*
Dans l'herbe du pré.	*In the grass in the meadow.*
J'ai trouvé un bel œuf jaune.	*I found a yellow egg*
Jaune comme de l'or,	*Yellow like gold*
Jaune comme un canari.	*Yellow like a canary*
Le lapin l'avait caché	*The rabbit had hidden it*
Derrière un pommier.	*Behind an apple tree.*

Martin (2002: 43–4)

When working on the development of oral skills, teachers could, for example:

- work on particular sounds (phonemes) and rhyming words (e.g. [ø] in *bleu*)
- work on the sound-letter correspondence (e.g. [e] in *milliers, soulier*)
- practise the pronunciation of words
- teach vocabulary (e.g. *œuf, bleu, rivière, lapin, pommier*).

Teachers can foster the development of literacy skills by asking pupils to:

- read the poem
- copy-write

- write an additional verse
- discuss the structure of the poem.

  Teachers can develop knowledge about language through:

- work on the sound–letter correspondence
- comparison of words and work on the etymology (e.g. *rivière*/river, *bleu*/blue, *canari*/canary)
- reflections on the place of the adjective in relation to the noun (e.g. *œuf bleu*/blue egg).

  Finally, the poem helps to develop cultural awareness by providing some insights into the ways in which Easter is celebrated in France. The Easter bunny traditionally hides eggs in the garden (or the woods) and pupils go egg-hunting on Easter Sunday. Pupils can compare this tradition with traditions in other countries where children make an Easter nest with twigs and put it in the garden or the house. Parents fill it with real coloured eggs or chocolate ones. Note that I do not suggest that teachers use a poem in *all* these different ways. This could eventually spoil the sheer enjoyment of reading a poem.

6.4.2 Working with rhymes, poems and songs

In this section I have grouped rhymes, poems and songs according to three themes that teachers can explore in daily routines or language lessons at an early stage. The *greetings*, *introductions* and *body parts* exemplify how rhymes, poems and songs can be embedded in the curriculum.

Greetings

The first example in French and Italian is taken from Martin and Cheater (1998). It combines simple greetings such as *bonjour/au revoir* with members of the family. When introducing the rhyme, teachers can build on *bonjour* and *buongiorno* which pupils might already have heard at home, on holiday or through taking the register. They can encourage the learners to substitute these greetings with other forms such as *bonsoir/buonasera*, *salut/ciao* or *saluti* or *salut/arrivederci* (goodbye, cheerio). The same vocabulary can be revisited during registration and in circle time and be 'recycled' in made-up songs and other rhymes.

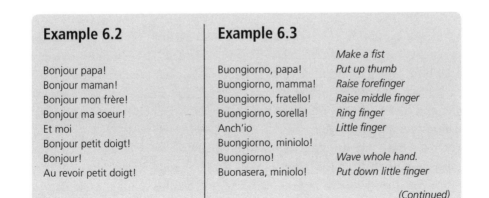

Example 6.2

Bonjour papa!
Bonjour maman!
Bonjour mon frère!
Bonjour ma soeur!
Et moi
Bonjour petit doigt!
Bonjour!
Au revoir petit doigt!

Example 6.3

	Make a fist
Buongiorno, papa!	*Put up thumb*
Buongiorno, mamma!	*Raise forefinger*
Buongiorno, fratello!	*Raise middle finger*
Buongiorno, sorella!	*Ring finger*
Anch'io	*Little finger*
Buongiorno, miniolo!	
Buongiorno!	*Wave whole hand.*
Buonasera, miniolo!	*Put down little finger*

(Continued)

Example 6.2 – cont'd	Example 6.3 – cont'd	
Au revoir ma soeur!	Buonasera, sorella!	Put down fourth finger
Au revoir mon frère!	Buonasera, fratello!	Put down middle finger
Au revoir maman!	Buonasera, mamma!	Put down forefinger
Au revoir papa!	Buonasera, papa!	Put down thumb
Au revoir!	Buonasera!	Finish with fingers in a fist
		Wave whole hand.

Below is an example of a *home-made* song that teachers can use to teach, practise and revise greetings.

> ### Example 6.4
>
> **Guten Morgen Lied** (*Melody: She'll be coming round the mountain*)
> Guten Morgen, guten Tag, Auf Wiedersehen. (2x)
> Guten Abend, gute Nacht
> Abend, gute Nacht
> Guten Morgen, guten Tag, Auf Wiedersehen.

Introducing myself

Being able to introduce oneself in a foreign language is very important to pupils. A nice way to recycle the vocabulary on greetings and to move on is to teach a home-made song such as the following:

> ### Example 6.5
>
> **Ich stelle mich vor (introducing oneself)** *Melody: Sur le pont d'Avignon*
> Guten Tag, guten Tag.
> Ich bin Paula, ich bin Paula.
> Guten, Tag, guten Tag.
> Ich bin Paula, wer bist du?

The finger rhymes below (Martin, 2002) are a good example of ways in which the same basic vocabulary can be introduced, rehearsed and expanded. The first one is based on 'Two little dickie birds' which many pupils know (Example 6.5). They can therefore concentrate on the new language rather than the meaning of the text. They are likely to know the greetings *Guten Tag* and *Auf Wiedersehen*, and can therefore concentrate on the new phrase *Ich heiße* used to introduce oneself.

Teachers can introduce this little rhyme with visuals, for example a picture of two birds sitting on a stone, or they can use finger puppets. Pupils can join in with the parts they know and gradually say the whole rhyme. Eventually, they can use the rhyme as a template to create a short role-play. All they need to do is substitute the names and greetings. The realization that they are able to use a foreign language to express something personal will give them a feeling of success and progress.

Example 6.6

Zwei kleine Vögel	*Wiggle finger puppets on finger.*
Auf einem Stein.	
Ich heiβe Hans.	*Raise one puppet in the air.*
Ich heiβe Hein.	*Bring 1st one down and the 2nd one up.*
Guten Tag, Hans.	
Guten Tag, Hein.	*Bring 2nd one down and the 1st one up.*
Auf Wiedersehen, Hans.	*Bring 2nd one up and hide behind the back.*
Auf Wiedersehen, Hein.	*Bring 1st one down and hide behind the back.*

Examples 6.7 and 6.8 provide many opportunities to develop language that figures in many conversations. Once children know some basic greetings, they can be introduced to the question 'How are you?' and some possible follow-ups. In this way they familiarize themselves with cultural differences. While English people tend to repeat the question, other nationalities, such as the Spanish, answer it. While Spanish, Belgian or French people welcome each other each with a particular number of kisses, other nationalities use hugs or are more formal.

Example 6.7

Deux petits escargots dans le jardin.	*Two fists with two thumbs pointing to each other.*
Bonjour!	*Raise thumb of one hand.*
Bonjour!	*Raise thumb of the other hand.*
Deux petits escargots dans le jardin.	*Two fists with two thumbs pointing to each other.*
Bonjour!	*Raise thumb of one hand.*
Bonjour!	*Raise thumb of the other hand.*
ça va ?	*Raise thumb of first hand.*
Oui, merci. Et toi?	*Raise thumb of second hand.*
ça ne va pas.	*Raise thumb of first hand.*
Il pleut.	*Wiggle fingers of second hand to show rain falling.*
Je rentre. Au revoir!	*Thumb of first hand 'enters' the fist.*

Example 6.8

	Children can do this finger rhyme in pairs.
	They put their hands together.
Toc toc.	*Thumbs*
¿Quién es?	*Little fingers*
(Name of a child)	*Index fingers*
¡Hola . . .(the name of the child)!	*Ring fingers*
¡Hola! ¿Cómo estás?, Muac Muac!	Middle fingers (go side by side pretending two hugs and then two kisses – touching twice)
	This finger rhyme needs a lot of coordination and practice.

Body parts

Some songs are ideal for building up vocabulary of a particular semantic field. Examples are the traditional French songs 'Alouette, gentille Alouette' (body parts), 'Loup y es-tu?' (clothes) and 'Sur le pont d'Avignon' (professions). The popular song 'Head and shoulders, knees and toes', translated into many languages is ideal to practise body parts (Example 6.9). The words for the different parts of the body are eliminated and replaced by gestures after each successive singing. Because of its repetitive nature and the actions children find it easy to learn versions in various languages. Apart from learning new words they begin to comprehend that gestures are an important way of conveying meaning.

Example 6.9 'Head and shoulders, knees and toes'

Head and shoulders, knees and toes	Kopf und Schultern, Knie und Zehen
Knees and toes.	Knie und Zehen.
Head and shoulders, knees and toes	Kopf und Schultern, Knie und Zehen
Knees and toes.	Knie und Zehen.
Eyes and ears and mouth and nose.	Augen, Ohren, Mund und Nas'.
Head and shoulders, knees and toes	Kopf und Schultern, Knie und Zehen
Knees and toes.	Knie und Zehen.
Tête, épaules, genoux, pieds	Cabeza, hombro, pierna y pie
Genoux, pieds.	Pierna y pie
Tête, épaules, genoux, pieds	Cabeza, hombro, pierna y pie
Genoux, pieds.	Pierna y pie
Yeux, oreilles et bouche et nez.	Ojos, oidos, boca y nariz
Tête, épaules, genoux, pieds	Cabeza, hombro, pierna y pie
Genoux, pieds.	Pierna y pie.

One can think of a range of follow-up activities for this song:

- comparing words for the same body parts across languages. The comparison of the English word 'knee' and the German word *Knie* triggers conversations about etymology and the origins of the two languages
- finding rhyming words across languages (toes/nose; *nez/pied*)
- introducing pupils to the written word once their pronunciation is secure
- considering sound-letter correspondences to develop pupils' knowledge of pronunciation (e.g. the letter 'k' in 'knee' is not pronounced)
- speaking about the use of capital letters (e.g. 'knee' and *Knie*)
- comparing the number of conjunctions in the German and the French song. This exercise asks pupils to explore the number of syllables in words and to consider the rhythm of the song.

For a collection of rhymes and poems that can be used to work on greetings, classroom instructions, the weather, days of the week or counting, I refer to Satchwell and De Silva (1995), Martin and Cheater (1998), Skarbek (1998) and Martin (2002).

6.4.3 Games

Martin (1995), Satchwell and De Silva (1995), Tierney and Dobson (1995), Driscoll (1999a), Rumley (1999) and Stein (2000b) give many reasons why games can be an efficient means of teaching foreign languages:

- They are enjoyable and appeal to pupils' sense of fun.
- They have a motivating nature and as a result pupils want to play them several times.
- They engage the *whole learner* by calling on their likes, fears and cognitive powers.
- They are meaningful scenes of interaction (e.g. participating in a guessing game, asking for a card in a card game). Players develop real plans and use strategies to win.
- Games promote participation, foster pupils' social skills and develop their ability to work together.
- Many games have a repetitive character and require pupils to use the same limited amount of vocabulary and sentence structures over and over again. Pupils practise in a focused and rigorous way without even noticing.
- Familiar games such as bingo, dominoes, noughts and crosses, Pelmanism or Kim's game have the advantage that they can easily be adapted to language learning. This means that pupils know the game and that no time is lost with unnecessary explanations.
- Games encourage independent work.

In what follows I present some games that can be used in foreign language lessons. For further ideas I refer to Martin (1995), Satchwell and De Silva (1995) and Tierney and Dobson (1995).

Games with numbers and words
Bingo

Bingo is an ideal game for practising receptive skills. Each pupil gets a squared piece of paper with numbers or words in each square. Pupils have different sheets. The teacher (or a child) calls out the symbols and pupils cross them out on their card. The first player who has crossed out everything is the winner. In order to check whether the winners have played correctly the teacher can ask them to read out all words on their card.

In the French game Loto, the player who has crossed out three symbols either vertically, horizontally or diagonally calls out '*Quin*' and is a first winner. The pupil who has crossed out everything says '*Carton plein*'.

Noughts and crosses

In this game, pupils play in teams. The teacher fills a 3 × 3 matrix with characters. When a pupil reads a character correctly, the teacher marks that specific field with a nought or a cross, depending on which team the pupil is in. The winner is the team that has three noughts or crosses either vertically, horizontally or diagonally. Apart from identifying symbols correctly, pupils have to play strategically.

Card games
Domino

The domino cards below can be used to create a simple question-and-answer reading exercise in Italian. The aim is to find a domino card that holds the answer to a question asked on another domino card.

Example 6.10 Domino game

Example: Domino card 1: *Question* Come ti chiami? Domino card 2: *Answer* Mi chiamo Paolo.

Inizio	Come ti chiami?	Mi chiamo Paolo	Quanti anni hai?	Ho cinque anni.	Hai fratelli?	Houna sorella.	Hai animali domestici a casa?

Domino card 1   Domino card 2

Pelmanism

Two sets of cards are arranged face down in front of pupils. One set could have pictures, the other the words labelling these pictures. A child turns over one card from each pile and names the cards. If the cards match and the label is correct, the child can keep both cards. The winner is the player with the most cards.

Happy families

This card game comprises distinguishable families (e.g. animals, clothes, food). Generally, each card displays a big picture in the centre and three small ones of the other family members on the bottom. The cards therefore tell a player both which members they have already and which ones remain to be collected. The aim of the game is to collect all the cards of the same family.

Pupils ask other players for a particular card. If the person asked has the card, he/she has to pass it on and the first player can continue. If the person does not have the card, the next player continues.

Memory games
Kim's game

Teachers show pupils concrete objects or visual representations and ask them to memorize the items. Pupils then close their eyes and the teacher takes one object away. The players guess what object is missing. Alternatively, the teacher covers all the objects and pupils try to remember as many as possible.

'I went to the market and I bought . . .'

This or a similar sentence can be the incentive for pupils to compose a very long sentence full of nouns. Each pupil repeats what the others have said and adds an additional item.

Guessing games
Treasure box
The teacher has a box with items of the same sort (e.g. clothes, food items). The teacher describes an item and pupils guess which one it is. This game offers a lot of comprehensible input.

A similar game consists of pupils guessing what the teacher sees or is thinking of without the adult giving any hints. The open-ended nature of the game encourages all pupils to participate.

Create peek-a-boo stories
The teacher uses books with flaps (commercial or home-made), describes the pictures hidden below the flap and asks pupils to guess what they are.

Hangman
This is a very popular game for guessing words. The teacher writes a blank on the board for each missing letter. Pupils guess letters thereby drawing on their knowledge of both the alphabet and possible grapheme (letter) combinations until they are able to guess the whole word. If a pupil says a correct letter, the teacher writes it on the board in the correct space. For each incorrect letter he/she adds a line to the 'hanging man'. The game is over when pupils have either guessed the word ('pineapple' in Example 6.11) or used up all their chances (four more in this example).

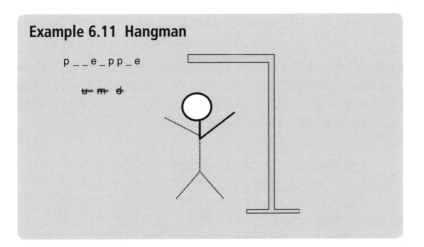

Example 6.11 Hangman

p _ _ e _ p p _ e

u̶ m̶ d̶

Hangman helps pupils work on their alphabetical skills and facilitates memorization of the oral and written word.

Physical games
Games that allow pupils to be physically active are particularly well suited to younger children and their natural desire for movement.

Fruit salad

The teacher names every child according to a fruit (or something else) and ensures that three or four pupils have the same name. When the teacher calls a fruit, every player with that particular name has to change seats. When the teacher calls 'Fruit salad', all the pupils change seats. The game can be made more interesting if the teacher takes away a chair after they have called the name of a fruit. The player who does not get a seat is 'out' but is allowed to call out the next fruit.

Simon says

This game is based on Total Physical Response. The teacher gives instructions to do something, most of which are prefaced with the phrase 'Simon says'. Pupils must act out only those commands beginning with 'Simon says'. Players who act on the wrong commands have traditionally been eliminated. The teachers should carefully think about this rule: he/she might like to come up with an alternative so that (young) pupils do not get upset and can continue to participate. In France and Germany, this highly popular game is called 'Jacques a dit' or 'Pumpernickel sagt'. The game is ideal for practising motion verbs.

What time is it, Mister Wolf?

In order to play this popular game pupils need to know the numbers in the target language and some key phrases such as 'What time is it, Mister Wolf?' ('*Quelle heure est-il, Monsieur Loup?*'). The wolf gives pupils a time (e.g. '*Il est deux heures.*'), and the children walk towards it making as many steps as mentioned in the sentence. When the wolf answers 'Time for lunch', all the pupils run away. The child who is caught by the wolf is the wolf in the next game.

Skipping songs

This German game can easily be played in PE. Two pupils turn the rope and give instructions to a third who skips and acts on the instructions (e.g. 'Show your leg'). At the end of the game, the two pupils ask 'How old are you?' and count the number of times the child in the middle manages to jump without touching the rope.

Example 6.12 Jumping game

	Instructions
Teddybär, Teddybär, dreh dich um.	*Turn around.*
Teddybär, Teddybär, mach dich krumm.	*Bend over.*
Teddybär, Teddybär, zeig deinen Fuß.	*Show your leg.*
Teddybär, Teddybär, mach einen Gruß.	*Choose a greeting*
Teddybär, Teddybär, wie alt bist du?	
1, 2, 3, 4, 5	

6.4.4 Some considerations when planning

According to Rixon (1992), Stein (2000b) and Jones and Coffey (2006) games, songs and rhymes are excellent motivators and have an enormous potential for the development of language learning and metacognitve, cognitive and social skills. However, for them to be effective, teachers must follow a number of rules:

- Plan the activities carefully.
- Have a good understanding of linguistic progression.
- Know how to adapt activities to the needs of the class.
- Have good management skills, especially when doing games.

However, when games, songs and rhymes are used ineffectively (without targets and out of context), they can easily become mere entertainment and pleasurable interruptions in the school day which, in the long term, results in pupils in the long term being bored and losing interest. Effective planning is therefore necessary. Example 6.13 is a template for a lesson plan. Here are some points to consider when planning:

Example 6.13 Template for a lesson plan

Date		Subject	Lesson in sequence
Prior learning/Key point(s) for reinforcement from last lesson			**Learning objectives (LO)**
Time	**Link with the LO** **Starter** **Main body of lesson** **Plenary**	**Role of the teacher** (including activities, key questions, resources, TA, assessment points)	**Role of pupils** (including activities, anticipated areas of difficulty/ problems)
Homework			
Lesson evaluation			
<ul><li>To what extent have the learning objectives been achieved? *Were the methods, teaching strategies and resources effective? What could I have been done differently? What will I do next?*</li><li>Who has learned what?</li></ul>			

- Start with the learning objective and pupils' prior learning. The fun activity in the form of a game, song and rhyme is not the starting point.
- Carry out the activity yourself. This is an invaluable means of using the required target language, judging the difficulty of the task and thinking about the resources needed.
- Assess pupils' prior knowledge and consider different ways in which you can build on their knowledge to reach the learning objectives.
- Decide which, if any, language features need to be taught before the activities.
- Think of appropriate ways to teach the required language structures (e.g. use of gesture, mime and resources).
- Think of prompts and clarifications that might be needed during the activity.

- Plan short, clear and precise instructions.
- Plan for social organization, time and space. Ensure that all pupils can participate and think of the ideal place to undertake the activity.
- Think about an appropriate closing. Some games can get the children very excited and it might therefore be essential to finish off with an activity that calms them down.
- Plan for opportunities to assess what pupils have learned. Watching pupils is a good opportunity to monitor and record their performance. This also enables you to evaluate the effectiveness of your own teaching and to decide whether you need to revisit a particular language item.

While games, songs and rhymes are generally brief activities, stories include more language and require a longer lesson period.

6.5 Working with stories

Schools often assign a minor role to songs, drama or fiction in spite of the importance of these narratives in the development of pupils' language skills and sense of identity. Bruner (1996), for example, holds that one makes sense of the world through narratives which help one 'construct an identity and find a place in one's culture' (p. 42). Telling stories is one way people collectively build up a significant and orderly world. Indeed, pupils' stories reveal their ability to construct a meaningful world that they can control. They express their hopes, fears and wishes and even suggest solutions to problems.

Many educators have highlighted the benefits of using stories in the foreign language classroom:

- Pupils generally like listening to stories.
- Stories are an *easy* and *enjoyable* way into language learning.
- Working with stories harnesses learners' fantasy and imagination. Pupils generally like to find alternative endings, develop characters further, act out the story or create a new one.
- Stories develop and foster learners' concentration span, their listening skills and learning strategies. Children tend to listen with great care as they are keen to understand the content and eager to participate (Jones and Coffey, 2006). They learn to use textual and visual clues and to anticipate what comes next (Tierney and Dobson, 1995; Hurrell, 1999). They discover that it is not necessary to understand every single word in order to make sense of a story.
- Working with stories develops learners' ability to narrate events in a coherent way (Wells, 1987).
- Stories help develop learners' linguistic proficiency. They present pupils with authentic language, longer pieces of text and repetitive structures. Listening to longer pieces of work familiarizes pupils with the rhythm of a language and helps them develop a feeling for it (Jones and Coffey, 2006). The meaningful context and the repetitiveness of the language facilitate understanding, acquisition and memorization of new vocabulary and structures. At a later stage pupils break down the pieces of text, analyse the constituents and combine them with other words to construct new utterances.
- Stories are a good starting point to work on all four language skills and to take a holistic approach (see chapters 7 and 8).

- Big books are an ideal way to familiarize pupils with reading. Teachers can show the reading direction (to nursery children), point out particular letters and words and encourage pupils to join in.

Depending on their aims, teachers are likely to choose different types of stories. Familiar tales (e.g. 'Hänsel and Gretel', 'Three Little Pigs') encourage children to concentrate on the language (the sound, the vocabulary, the structures) rather than the content. Traditional stories offer interesting insights into cultural values, beliefs and ways of doing things. Books with particular themes are ideal to revise and develop vocabulary. Eric Carle's *The Very Hungry Caterpillar*, for example, is built around topics such as food and days of the week.

Some teachers prefer to write their own stories or work with stories written by pupils. This has the advantage that both content and language draw on children's prior experiences, background and prior knowledge. In order to adapt commercial books to the linguistic needs of the class, some teachers simplify the language or even write a completely new version of the story. They can still use the original book with the pictures if they cover the old text with Post-it notes.

Tierney and Dobson (1995) have identified the qualities of *good* stories:

- They have a good storyline which provokes curiosity and helps pupils anticipate what happens next.
- The language conveys the basic meaning and guides the reader through the text (e.g. suddenly, the first/second/third day). It is simple, repetitive, natural and reflects what children are likely to hear.
- The content is relevant, interesting, accessible and suited to pupils' needs.
- A restrictive range of repetitive structures facilitates memorization and encourages learner participation.
- Illustrations are clear, attractive and help to convey meaning.

6.6 Making cross-curricular links

Cross-curricular links between languages and other curriculum areas save time and give status to the foreign language. Cross-curricular links can be done at various levels.

First, teachers could liken the content of the language lessons to a topic already covered or to be covered in another subject. The list below, influenced by Satchwell and De Silva (1995), presents subjects and topics that have been linked to foreign languages:

- Mathematics (e.g. shapes, measurements, coordinates)
- English (e.g. 'knowledge about language', dictionary skills)
- Geography (e.g. location of countries and major cities on maps)
- Science (e.g. healthy food)
- Music (e.g. songs)
- PE (e.g. games)
- Arts (e.g. famous artists)
- Design and Technology (e.g. weather disk)
- ICT (e.g. word processing, text manipulation).

An example of a cross-curricular link between Foreign Languages and Geography can be found in Chapter 10, section 10.3.1.

It is crucial that the combination of two subjects does not come at the expense of the learner's progression in either of them. This could easily happen if the work is not at the cognitive level of the pupils. This is the case, for example, when Year 4 pupils do simple mental arithmetic in the foreign language using numbers up to 20. If the teacher wants to engage learners in this sort of activity he/she should make sure that the task is relevant, appropriate and at the pupils' cognitive level. The game Bip is a good example for practising the times tables. When practising the 1×7, for example, pupils are asked to replace every seventh number plus every number with the digit 7 with the word 'bip'. Counting to more than 70 in a foreign language at the same time as paying attention to the multiplications and the traps (e.g. 'bip' for 27 and 28) is a challenging exercise.

A second way to make cross-curricular links is through project work that is undertaken in a range of subjects. Tierney and Hope (1998) provide details about the activities in which pupils can engage in the course of a project on the European Union (pp. 17–20):

- Foreign Languages: pupils learn the names of some European countries and their capitals.
- Geography: pupils learn to describe their location with compass points and revisit some key geographical features in the foreign language. They use their knowledge of colours to describe European flags.
- Mathematics: pupils convert currencies.
- Music: pupils learn some traditional songs and dances, and talk about some famous European musicians.
- Design and Technology: pupils prepare some typical food.

The scheme, from the North Yorkshire County Council, used in the CiLT and NACELL (2006) *Training Manual for Teachers*, shows how foreign languages can be embedded in the curriculum of a Year 5 class. It provides a concrete example of the links between a language activity and a wide range of Core and Foundation subjects.

6.7 Main points to remember

In order to learn a new language, pupils need to be exposed to it, use it and practise it in a meaningful way. You can help pupils learn when:

- you are a good role-model and use the language as much as possible in language lessons.
- you use and ask pupils to use the foreign language throughout the day, for example in basic instructions.
- you integrate languages into the curriculum, for example by making cross-curricular links.
- you use games, songs, poems and stories in a meaningful way.

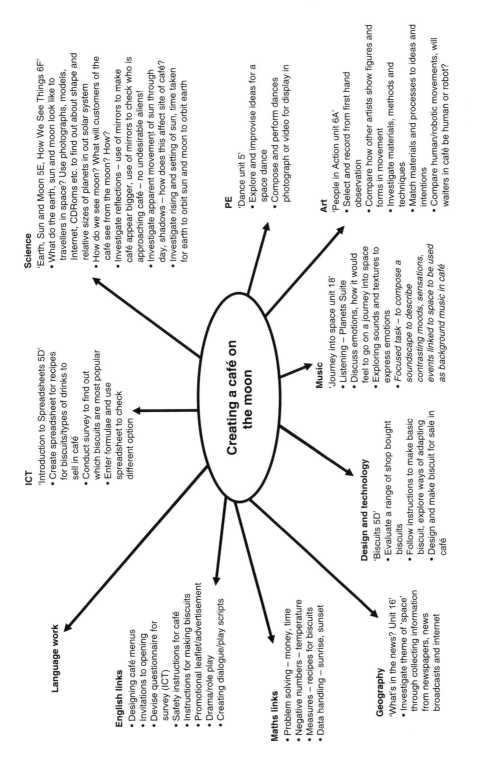

Science
'Earth, Sun and Moon 5E, How We See Things 6F'
- What do the earth, sun and moon look like to travellers in space? Use photographs, models, Internet, CDRoms etc. to find out about shape and relative sizes of planets in out solar system
- How do we see moon? What will customers of the café see from the moon? How?
- Investigate reflections – use of mirrors to make café appear bigger, use of mirrors to check who is approaching café – no undesirable aliens!
- Investigate apparent movement of sun through day, shadows – how does this affect site of café?
- Investigate rising and setting of sun, time taken for earth to orbit sun and moon to orbit earth

PE
'Dance unit 5'
- Explore and improvise ideas for a space dance
- Compose and perform dances photograph or video for display in

Art
'People in Action unit 6A'
- Select and record from first hand observation
- Compare how other artists show figures and forms in movement
- Investigate materials, methods and techniques
- Match materials and processes to ideas and intentions
- Compare human/robotic movements, will waiters in café be human or robot?

ICT
'Introduction to Spreadsheets 5D'
- Create spreadsheet for recipes for biscuits/types of drinks to sell in café
- Conduct survey to find out which biscuits are most popular
- Enter formulae and use spreadsheet to check different option

Creating a café on the moon

Music
'Journey into space unit 18'
- Listening – Planets Suite
- Discuss emotions, how it would feel to go on a journey into space
- Exploring sounds and textures to express emotions
- *Focused task – to compose a soundscape to describe contrasting moods, sensations, events linked to space to be used as background music in café*

Design and technology
'Biscuits 5D'
- Evaluate a range of shop bought biscuits
- Follow instructions to make basic biscuit, explore ways of adapting
- Design and make biscuit for sale in café

Language work

English links
- Designing café menus
- Invitations to opening
- Devise questionnaire for survey (ICT)
- Safety instructions for café
- Instructions for making biscuits
- Promotional leaflet/advertisement
- Drama/role play
- Creating dialogue/play scripts

Maths links
- Problem solving – money, time
- Negative numbers – temperature
- Measures – recipes for biscuits
- Data handling – sunrise, sunset

Geography
'What's in the news? Unit 16'
- Investigate theme of 'space' through collecting information from newspapers, news broadcasts and internet

Pupils are more likely to learn if they see evidence of progress in the following areas:

- an ability to use a language in a wider range of contexts and topics
- a deeper insight into how language works
- a better understanding of their own and others' cultures
- enhanced language learning skills.

Stories, games and songs can be an effective means of developing children's language when they are well integrated into a scheme of work.

Planning for continuity and progression is essential if pupils are to progress and become confident language learners and users. This requires the teacher to build on pupils' prior knowledge and to organize sequences of lessons enabling them to increase the amount, complexity, fluency and accuracy of their language use. Simply stringing together isolated 'fun activities' and carrying them out without a sense of learning outcome and context does not guarantee learning or progression. In fact, it does not even guarantee that the learners' motivation is sustained (see Chapter 5).

Developing Children's Listening and Speaking Skills | 7

7.1 Introduction

In the following two chapters I show how stories, poems, songs and structured exercises can be used to develop the four language skills. Listening, speaking, reading and writing reinforce each other and are rarely used independently. Students attending lectures, for example, are likely to use all four skills: they listen to a lecturer, discuss issues, read from presentation slides and take notes. Given that the four skills are often used simultaneously in real-life situations, it is important to foster the development of both receptive (listening and reading) and productive (speaking and writing) skills at school. Note that receptive skills are not *passive* skills: listeners and readers need to actively construct the meaning of the languages produced.

In this chapter I first examine the processes involved in listening and speaking. This understanding provides teachers with a useful starting point for the development of oral skills. I continue with suggestions for practical activities thereby referring to two different approaches,

---

Food for thought

- Did you find it easy to acquire listening and speaking skills? Why/Why not?
- What special talents do you have that you can use in the classroom to facilitate listening comprehension? Think of drawing, pantomime, use of ICT, etc.
- What authentic resources (e.g. native speakers, books, internet access) are available in your community? How can you initiate opportunities for communication?
- According to the Input Hypothesis (Chapter 3), children need comprehensible input to acquire a language. How can you make sure that your learners get enough input and that they understand it?
- According to interactionist and conversationalist theories (Chapter 3) learners need opportunities to use language and negotiate meaning in meaningful situations. How can you create such situations in your classroom?
- Did teachers or native speakers correct errors you made in a foreign language? How did they correct you and what was the effect?

---

a structural and a transactional approach to teaching foreign languages. I finish with some suggestions on how to correct errors.

7.2 Processes involved in understanding and producing language

The ability to understand an utterance in a foreign language and to respond appropriately involves more than proficiency in the foreign language. In order to make sense of the information and to continue a conversation, learners need to have some prior knowledge of the topic, the speaker and the situation at hand (known as background knowledge). They also need to have some understanding of the way speech is organized. This knowledge enables them to recognize, for example, that their interlocutor has asked a question and expects an answer. In order to reply, they will need some knowledge of how to communicate in a culturally appropriate and socially acceptable way. This helps them decide, for example, whether to use the formal *vous* or the informal *tu* in French.

The processes involved in producing and making sense of speech are of two types: *bottom-up* and *top-down* processes. Both occur simultaneously, both are interdependent and necessary for the understanding and production of speech.

Bottom-up (or data-driven) processing involves prior knowledge of the language system (phonology, grammar, vocabulary) (see also Chapter 9, section 9.2). The knowledge of the phonological system enables learners to break down the flow of speech into sounds or groups of sounds that can form words. The knowledge of vocabulary enables them to recognize words within phrases. A knowledge of grammar (e.g. inflection of verbs, the use of pronouns) is necessary in order to check the cohesion and coherence of a text (Celce-Murcia and Olshtain, 2000).

The bottom-up processes help learners predict words or structures and, therefore, accelerate and facilitate the meaning-making process. Beginners, however, often do not know what words can follow which and how sentences are put together. As a result they need more time to make sense of oral or written text. Language-learning strategies and metacognitive skills enable them to compensate for the slow processing. Metacognition is the ability to think about one's thinking, and, in this particular context, to think about ways of producing or understanding speech.

Top-down (concept-driven or knowledge-driven) processes involve activation of background information about the topic, an understanding of how discourse is organized with respect to different genres, purposes or topics and a knowledge of the particular context, situation and speaker.

In order to develop bottom-up processes, learners need to be exposed to the foreign language as much as possible. They need to listen to specific sounds and words while also developing their vocabulary, grammar and effective language learning strategies. In order to develop top-down processes, learners need to increase their understanding of how discourse is organized, to improve their world knowledge and to develop their ability to assess the particularities of the communication system at hand.

The next sections look in greater detail at ways of enhancing the development of listening and speaking skills, in particular the development of sounds, words and sentences. (Ways of developing grammar and language learning strategies are presented in chapters 9 and 11.) Since the choice of activities depends largely on the teacher's view of language learning and preferred teaching methods I briefly present the main characteristics of both a structural and a transactional approach.

7.3 A structural and a transactional approach to language learning

A structural orientation is characterized by its focus on form. The learning outcomes tend to be grammatical accuracy, vocabulary and general proficiency in the foreign language. Typical methods are Grammar-Translation and Audiolingualism but some also count the weaker version of CLT as a structured approach.

In this (traditional) approach the teacher generally introduces new sounds, words and sentence structures in isolation and then presents structured exercises to practise the language items. The idea is that presentation and practice will enable learners to produce language independently. This Presentation-Practice-Production (PPP) model is characteristic of a linear and teacher-centred view of learning.

The structured drills draw at times on behaviourist and at times on cognitive learning theories. Among the typical drills are substitution, gap-filling and spelling tests. Their aim is controlled composition and error avoidance (see Chapter 4). (The fact that teachers control the learning objectives and outcomes gives them the feeling of being in control. It is therefore possible that this model appeals to inexperienced teachers.)

The structured approach with its focus on form can be contrasted with a transactional approach with its focus on language use. The latter encourages learners to use language for a particular purpose, for example to negotiate meaning or to solve a problem. Task-based Instruction (TBI) is an example of a transactional approach. This communicative approach is underpinned by a sociocultural view of language learning and social constructivist theories. Activities involve collaboration and are built on real-life situations. The focus lies on meaning and form, product and process, the individual learner and the community.

Below I present activities in line with these two different approaches.

7.4 Developing listening skills

If pupils are to get into the rhythm of a language and develop a feeling for it, they need to have plenty of opportunities to listen to longer pieces of texts, to hear a range of speakers of different origins and with different accents, for example, native speakers, audio-recording, and to work with a variety of texts, registers and genres, for example, stories, letters, audio and video resources, advertisements (Cheater and Farren, 2001).

Children are often excited by the sounds of words in foreign languages. Harvey Taylor (1981) maintains that they develop their listening comprehension ability in different stages:

- *recognition of the target language*: they develop a feeling for the overall sound of a language (sounds, rhythm, cadences) and are able to identify it
- *recognition of isolated words*: they are able to recognize some isolated words such as cognates, familiar names or vocabulary studied previously
- *recognition of phrase boundaries*: they are able to recognize words, sentences and phrase boundaries, but much of the meaning still escapes them
- *listening for the gist*: they develop a feel for the global meaning and understand the topic or main point
- *true listening*: they can follow the meaning but many words are still unknown to them.

Although the appropriateness of Taylor's classification can be debated, the model offers a useful framework. In fact, it mirrors what happens in many classrooms: teachers choose poems, rhymes and songs to familiarize pupils with a new language; help them recognize salient sounds and work on comprehension at word, sentence and text level. This linear progression from small language items to whole texts is typical of a structured approach.

However, pupils do not necessarily learn language in this way. Detailed work on sounds, words and sentences only becomes relevant and useful if these items are fully integrated into meaningful language use. This explains why many teachers start with a story, hence, with authentic and meaningful language at text level. Once pupils have understood the meaning of the story, the practitioner proceeds to working with unfamiliar sounds, new vocabulary or particular grammar points. Since pupils wish to understand the story and are eager to use the language in a meaningful context, they are likely to engage with these language items at a deeper level and to remember them better.

In the following sections I describe different activities that teachers can carry out to help pupils identify and recognize sounds, words and sentence and to understand short texts. I refer to Chapter 6 for examples of how teachers can familiarize pupils with a new language.

7.4.1 Sound identification exercises

Learners need to be aware of individual sounds in order to develop accurate pronunciation and the ability to read alphabetic languages. *Phonemic awareness* is a person's ability to recognize that words consist of individual sounds, and to manipulate these sounds. Research findings have shown that children do not acquire phonemic awareness spontaneously. This ability can be taught, for instance through exercises that ask pupils *to identify* sounds. Teachers need to ensure that exercises that call for intensive listening and good concentration are enjoyable and help learners develop confidence.

Teachers are likely to focus on sounds (phonemes) in a foreign language that differ from the children's first language. In Britain, for example, teachers might be particularly interested in the French sound [y] as in *tu*, and the Spanish [ɲ] as in *español*. In order to help children recognize and identify salient sounds, they could choose texts with recurring phonemes. An example is the song 'Le petit ver' where the sound [y] appears five times.

Example 7.1 'Le petit ver'

Le petit ver	***The little worm***
Qui a vu tout menu	*Who has seen very small*
Le petit ver de terre?	*The little bare worm?*
C'est la grue qui a vu	*It's the crane which has spotted*
Le petit ver tout nu.	*The little bare worm.*

Source: www.ecole-plis.com/IMG/Chansons/chansons/lepetitver.htm

---

Popular exercises to develop phonemic awareness are identification, segmentation and sound/symbol identification exercises.

Identification

The aim of this type of exercise is to help pupils identify a particular sound. Some teachers choose familiar texts such as the song above; others prefer to work with unknown words because then the focus lies on the sounds rather than the meaning. The teacher reads the poem, isolates the sound and repeats it several times with a clear and accurate pronunciation to ensure that all pupils know which sound to listen out for. He/She could then invite pupils to respond with a particular response (e.g. raising a hand) each time they hear the sound.

Segmentation

Segmentation exercises encourage pupils to listen *into* the words, to isolate and put sounds together and to find words beginning and ending with the same sounds.

Below are possible exercises:

- enunciating the sounds in words to show one's ability to hear and say sounds correctly
- listening out for rhyming words (e.g. *vu, menu, nu, grue* in Example 7.1)
- finding words with the same sound (e.g. [y] as in *tu* or *lune*)
- discussing the meaning of particular sounds. For example, when pupils compare the German words *Hund* and *Hunde*, possibly helped by pictures of one dog and several dogs, they discover that the phoneme [ə] in *Hunde* forms the plural
- making pupils identify the number of syllables in a word
- clapping the rhythm of familiar words.

Sound/symbol identification

This type of exercise requires learners to match sounds with the appropriate letters and vice versa. Many examples of this type of exercise, such as work on the alphabet, are presented in Chapter 8 (sections 8.4.1 and 8.5.1).

7.4.2 Word identification

Below are some sample activities in word identification:

- provide short passages containing easily recognizable words (rhymes, songs, resources prepared for this occasion) and ask pupils to signal when they hear the particular word or phrase or to tick it off on a list
- play a version of 'Fruit salad' (see 6.4.3)
- ask pupils to place words in the order they hear them using pictures or other resources (e.g. Lego bricks)
- say two sentences that differ by one word and ask pupils to identify the difference.

7.4.3 Comprehension exercises at the word and text level

There is a range of ways to assess whether children have understood the meaning of words and simple phrases. The teacher can ask children to:

- match words/phrases with pictures (e.g. Bingo, Loto)
- mime words
- act out simple instructions (e.g. 'Simon says'; increase the complexity of the game by giving several instructions)
- draw according to instructions
- classify words (e.g. find the odd one out; group words into particular categories)
- agree or disagree with statements (e.g. show 'thumbs up/down')

- answer comprehension questions
- play 'Change the meaning' game (DfES, 2005a: 49). Pupils take turns to change the meaning of a sentence by changing one word. A first child says, for example, 'I buy a green apple' and a second 'I buy a green banana'. The others identify the word or even the word class (e.g. noun) that has been changed.

The last activities are more complex. They involve several skills (e.g. speaking, reading) and draw on children's knowledge of grammar.

If pupils have developed good listening and speaking skills, they can work in pairs and play the following two games.

Listen and draw

Two pupils sit back to back. One pupil has a card with a simple picture (e.g. a house) and the other has a blank piece of paper. The first pupil describes the picture, the second draws what he/she hears described. Then they compare their pictures.

Breakout

Two pupils sit back to back. Both have a picture of a maze. One pupil gives directions to get out of the maze, the other draws the escape path.

7.4.4 Text comprehension

Listening to longer texts is often beyond the learners' level of active performance. It is very important that teachers have a realistic expectation of what pupils can achieve and that they make their learning objectives clear. In each listening comprehension, pupils need to know if they are expected to listen for gist, meaning or a particular piece of information.

Before teachers present a longer piece of text, they might pre-teach key words, provide background information, show pictures or revise listening strategies. These activities activate pupils' vocabulary and background knowledge, promote curiosity and give them a real reason to listen to the text. (The support enables them to draw effectively on their bottom-up and top-down processes when listening.)

While teachers tell or read the story, they can aid children's understanding by showing prompts and using mime, gesture and intonation. To check comprehension, they can ask simple comprehension questions or ask pupils to guess what comes next. However, teachers must not ask too many questions or they will disrupt the flow of the activity.

After having listened to the whole text (e.g. explanations, song, story) children can demonstrate their understanding through one of the following comprehension activities:

- draw or choose a picture illustrating a text (e.g. find the pictures that corresponds to the weather forecast)
- sequence the text (e.g. putting pictures in the right order)
- complete a true/false table

- answer comprehension questions
- discuss the passages heard
- summarize the text
- act out the text (e.g. story)
- correct mistakes that the teacher has put into the text
- order scrambled sentences (e.g. children sequence pieces of paper on which lines of the lyrics of a song are written)
- do gap-filling exercises.

To develop language learning strategies, teachers can ask pupils to identify the strategies that enabled them to make sense of the text.

7.5 Developing speaking skills

Most educationalists would agree that the goal of language learning is communication. Many teachers use oral drills, problem-solving tasks and role-plays in order to stimulate interaction. Horwitz (2006) reminds us that these activities can *prepare* pupils for true communication but that they must not be confused with communication. She explains, 'Even when teachers are careful to ensure that structured communicative activities have a communicative context, these kinds of activities do not constitute "real communication"' (p. 92).

Structured communicative activities and authentic speech differ in a number of ways: predictability of language, authenticity, context, goal and choice. Teachers prepare structured drills to help learners practise vocabulary and grammatical structures. They have therefore pre-selected the content and the language to be used; there is no genuine exchange of information. In fact, most of the questions are display questions that aim to assess learners' knowledge and skills. In authentic situations, by contrast, the exchange of information is meaningful and purposeful and questions are asked out of interest. The language used is unpredictable and conversations can take unforeseeable turns.

The role of the teacher should be to create opportunities where pupils speak to classmates, teachers or native speakers inside and outside the classroom in order to practise and expand their existing language skills and to get new comprehensible input. In such activities the teacher should bear pupils' confidence and self-esteem in mind. According to Ericsson (1997) learners gradually build up self-esteem predominantly from the feedback they receive. earners with higher self-esteem are more likely to take risks and succeed. It is therefore crucial that teachers create a learning environment where pupils feel safe.

The following section looks at a range of ways to develop speaking skills. I suggest structured drills as well as ideas to enhance authentic communication.

7.5.1 Introducing learners to new words

Many research studies have looked into effective ways of teaching and learning vocabulary. Gu and Johnson (1996) found that reading and guessing words from context and looking up words in a dictionary are more effective ways of learning than memorizing words from a list. Paribakht and Wesche (1997) compared two groups of students. The first group read texts and answered comprehension questions that involved new vocabulary. They learned the new words in context and focused on meaning. The second group carried out vocabulary activities. Their findings showed that the first group remembered more than the second one.

Practitioners generally agree that it is difficult to learn words from vocabulary lists because the latter cannot completely render the meaning of a word. Pupils are more likely to understand and remember connotations and subtle nuances if they encounter the word in a meaningful context. In order to memorize new words, children need to consolidate the vocabulary and use it regularly. Therefore, teachers who recycle vocabulary and make learners use it in different contexts help children keep their vocabulary active.

The aims of teaching vocabulary are generally to help pupils learn the sounds, the pronunciation and the meaning of new words. Teachers need to use a range of strategies to ensure that they cater for their visual, aural and kinaesthetic learners and to keep children's interest alive. Typical semantic fields for beginner language learners comprise children, their families, friends, animals, food or toys.

In the next sections I suggest different ways in which teachers can help learners acquire new words and sentence structures.

Teaching vocabulary

Below are some examples of effective teaching strategies.

Pronounce words clearly	The teacher needs to pronounce words clearly. He/She can demonstrate and explain how an unfamiliar sound is produced and alert pupils to intonation patterns. He/She could, for example, gesture to express the intonation of a word. (If a word is particularly long, he/she can break it into syllables.)
Repeat the new words	The teacher repeats a new word several times, saying it in different voices, varying the speed of delivery and the pitch. This strategy ensures that pupils get enough input. To make the input comprehensible, the teacher can use visuals or refer pupils to a context in which they have heard the word before.
Encourage visuals links	The teacher helps pupils to form concepts and memorize new words by using visual resources (e.g. flash cards, books) or encourages pupils to associate the new words with mental images (e.g. the Japanese number *san* (3) with the word 'sunshine').
Encourage aural links	The teacher encourages the creation of aural links by asking pupils to associate the new words with familiar ones (e.g. the Japanese number *ni* (2) with the word English word 'knee'). If the new words are cognates, the teacher can point out the differences in stress, pitch and intonation between the new word and the English one. (Cognates are words that have a 'similar' etymological origin and the same meaning. Examples are the English and French words 'restaurant'.)
	The teacher needs to pay particular attention if words are false cognates, that is, words with the same etymological origin but different meanings. Examples

	are the German word *Gift* (poison) and the English word 'gift', or the French word *librairie* (bookshop) and the English 'library'. The more links pupils can make between the new word and already established concepts, the better the chance that they will remember it (Oxford, 1990).
Encourage kinaesthetic links	The teacher helps pupils to remember words by relating words and movements. For example, he/she could ask them to point to their knee when they say the Japanese number *ni*.
Mouthing	Mouthing a word (saying it without pronouncing a sound) makes pupils focus on sounds and the ways they are produced.
Ask pupils to repeat the words	Once the teacher feels that pupils have had enough opportunities to listen to the word, he/she can ask the whole class to repeat either a sound, a syllable of the whole word and to practise intonation and stress. Whole-class work has the advantage that less confident pupils can listen to the word once again, join in with particular sounds and build up their confidence. The disadvantage is that it is impossible for the teacher to assess whether individual pupils say the word correctly and to give them feedback. It is therefore important that the teacher thinks of working with both the whole class and individual pupils.
	Games such as Chinese whispers, where a word is whispered from child to child, and Mexican waves, where pupils repeat a range of words, are enjoyable ways of repeating words.
Revise words	The teacher revises words as he/she goes along.
Check children's understanding	The teacher points to pictures and labels them, sometimes correctly, sometimes incorrectly. Pupils are only allowed to repeat a word after the teacher if the label is correct (see also 7.4.3).
Play guessing games	Guessing games such as 'What am I thinking of?' (e.g. animal, toy) allow for a range of possible answers. This open question encourages many pupils to volunteer words without being afraid of being wrong.
Ask closed questions	Closed questions such as 'What is this?' allow for only one answer and are ideal to check an individual pupil's understanding and pronunciation.
	If the teacher teaches both question and answer forms he/she can ask pupils to practise in pairs. This gives pupils more opportunity to use the language and to practise without the watchful eye of the teacher.

The above strategies are typical of a teacher-centred approach. Below I present a more child-centred approach where pupils are more actively engaged in the learning process.

Helping children learn new words

One way of introducing new vocabulary in a foreign language is to ask pupils to list words related to a particular field and to present them to classmates. The task could consist of identifying the food items necessary for cooking a particular dish. Once pupils have agreed with the other members of their group on useful items they can use a range of resources to look up the words: a dictionary, story books, a simple cookery book in a foreign language or online resources. They present their list to the teacher who helps them pronounce the words correctly. The wish to present the new vocabulary accurately to classmates motivates pupils to practise the pronunciation. The presentation of the vocabulary items could lead to short conversations where pupils compare the words they identified as useful, express their opinions, likes and dislikes and share simple stories.

Task-based Instruction, a transactional approach, presented above has several advantages over a structured method:

- the activity is purposeful
- the words are meaningful because the original list comes from the pupils themselves
- the fact that the words are meaningful furthers memorization (Stevick, 1976: 118)
- pupils spend more time on a task, which helps them forge connections and learn words at a deeper level
- pupils feel ownership of the task and are therefore likely to be fully involved
- pupils use a range of authentic resources
- pupils use the new words in authentic situations of communication.

7.5.2 Practising vocabulary

In order to practise comprehension and encourage memorization of the new words, teachers can engage in some of the exercises described in sections 6.4.3, 7.4.2, and 7.4.3. If they have introduced the written word they can also look at sections 8.4.3 and 8.4.4.

Once teachers feel that the vocabulary is known, they can encourage pupils to use the vocabulary in whole sentences. Teachers who favour a structured approach will find *substitution exercises, sentence completion* and *sentence transformation exercises* useful.

Substitution exercises require learners to replace a particular word. The song 'Sur le pont d'Avignon' is built on that principle. It encourages singers to substitute the word *messieurs* by *demoiselles, militaires, musiciens*. Asking children to change some words or sentences in familiar songs, rhymes and stories is a useful starting point for creating their own text (Martin and Cheater, 1998; Skarbek, 1998; Cheater and Farren, 2001). If pupils see that they are able to express their ideas, they are likely to feel proud and successful. The progress can be a real catalyst for further language learning.

Sentence completion exercises can start with a phrase such as 'I went to the market and I bought . . .' (memory games, section 6.4.3). Teachers will ensure that pupils build up progressively longer and more complex sentences. For example, they can ask pupils to increase the length of a sentence by adding adjectives and adverbs, and by using conjunctions (e.g. I like milk and water but I prefer milk).

7.5.3 Expanding children's language skills

The aim of teaching vocabulary is to enable learners to eventually use the new vocabulary independently either orally or in writing. To this effect, it is important that teachers have created a supportive and risk-taking environment.

A good starting point is a daily routine such as taking the register. It provides children with an authentic opportunity to use a foreign language for a purpose. Teachers can slowly expand the language to make the rituals less rigid. They introduce new words or ask questions. The familiar context helps children understand the teacher. They guess the new words and can begin to use them. Children thereby learn that they can understand language through guessing, an important language learning strategy, and that they do not have to rely on translation (Haramboure, 2007).

Teachers encourage oral production when they ask children to share meaningful information with friends or pen-pals or to talk about their own opinions. It is important to create situations where children speak because they have something to say. If pupils feel that the teacher and their classmates are genuinely interested in what they say they will continue to share their thoughts and make the effort to learn the language in order to communicate. Teachers will need to listen carefully to utterances not just in order to show interest and respect, but also in order to expand and rephrase sentences if necessary. Needless to say, they need to be sensitive when correcting errors (see section 7.6).

The use of pair or group work can reduce anxiety levels but, above all, it increases opportunities to use the foreign language. Formulaic phrases and communication and compensation strategies (e.g. using gestures; using formulae to initiate and sustain conversation) help learners use the target language as much as possible.

Stories are an ideal way to expand children's language skills (see sections 6.5 and 7.4.4).

Using stories

Stories present learners with a meaningful context, authentic language, larger chunks of language and repetitive structures which enhance acquisition and memorization of new vocabulary items and structures. Below are some follow-up activities that are frequently used after learners have worked on text comprehension:

- retelling the story. A popular game to retell a story is *hot seating*: the pupil who sits in the hot seat starts telling the story. At a given signal, another pupil takes his/her place and continues (DfES, 2005a: 62)
- summarizing the story
- keeping the format and substituting some vocabulary items to create a new one
- creating an alternative ending
- discussing issues raised in the text
- relating the text to pupils' own experiences
- devising a short role-play
- acting out the story.

More activities are presented in Chapter 8 (sections 8.4, 8.5 and 8.6).

Encouraging pupils to create their own stories is a more creative and challenging way of expanding their oral skills. The Storyline approach (section 4.2.7), an example of task-based instruction and a learner-centred philosophy, is well suited to consolidating vocabulary and topics covered in other curriculum subjects. The method creates a meaningful context which provides an audience and a purpose for language use (Ehlers *et al.*, 2006). The teacher chooses a topic and designs the outline of the story while children fill in the details by developing the characters and the incidents. The learning process is more open and creative and therefore less predictable than traditional language teaching based on a structured curriculum (Fehse and Kocher, 2002: 199). An example of the storyline 'Zoo' (Bell, 1998) is presented in the box below.

The storyline 'Zoo'

The teacher presents the class with a blank poster representing the zoo (Bell, 1998: 10). In groups, pupils think of animals that live in this environment. Each group comes up with a list and presents it to the class. They then choose an enclosure for the animals on the poster and explain their choices. In the next step, they create the animals and, after some discussions, design the enclosures, paths for visitors and other services such as a kiosk or a restaurant. Next, they think about the people who work in the zoo and develop their biographies. Finally, pupils decide on possible *incidents*, a characteristic of each storyline. In this case, it could be the birth of an animal, feeding time, the escape of an animal or the opening of the zoo.

The teacher has many opportunities to work on language. He/She can ask pupils to describe the incident, create advertisements for the zoo, invent the dialogue for a drama or act out a role-play. This allows pupils to practise language orally and in writing in different forms (e.g. descriptions, reports, emails, articles). Word banks and dictionaries are helpful resources.

Pupils are particularly motivated because they can identify with the characters and feel some ownership of the story. They are actively engaged and learn to work independently. This is clearly illustrated in the following quotes from a teacher in Berlin and her pupils who explain what they liked about the approach while working on the storyline 'Castlehotel':

> The characters [we created]. It was like a second world where I lived as well. (Alia, 10)

> In this project the whole class has learned what nobody else will learn namely what it is like to work in a castlehotel. (Biko, 10)

> I have learned to work independently, to use English sentences and feel more familiar with the English language. (Tessa, 9)

> It is fascinating and motivating for me, as a teacher, to see how pupils working with the Storyline Approach grow – to see that they know and can do more than they thought and than I thought they could do. (K. Harder)

When planning a storyline teachers select a theme drawing on pupils' prior knowledge, the curriculum and cross-curricular activities. Teachers design possible sequences, choose an introduction, organize resources and plan key questions that help pupils develop their own stories. They carefully monitor and assess pupils' work and learning processes in order to identify the next steps. This method works best with confident and proficient language learners. Word banks and communication strategies help beginners use the foreign language.

Examples of the stories pupils in my Year 2 have created can be found in Chapter 8, section 8.5.2. I used another task-based approach called *Storying* which involves learners creating, telling, drawing, writing and acting out stories.

Many teachers believe that spontaneous conversations and *free speech* result in many errors. How to correct errors in an appropriate way is the focus of the next section.

7.6 Correcting errors

'Errors' need to be distinguished from 'mistakes'. Errors are 'consistent incorrect forms produced in speaking or writing' whereas mistakes are 'simple slips of the tongue' (Horwitz, 2006: 92). Apart from the behaviourist theory, most second language theories understand errors as normal steps in a learner's interlanguage (Chapter 3). Interaction theories even view them as positive in as much as they offer opportunities for negotiation and feedback which in turn help learners' progress.

Much research has been done on the impact of corrective feedback and the most recent studies have highlighted its usefulness (Savignon, 1972; Spada, 1997; Ellis, 1995, 2003; Stein, 2000a; Lightbown and Spada, 2003; Edelenbos *et al.*, 2006). Of particular interest to teachers might be the studies that focus on the learners' response to corrections. These have shown that learners react best if they spot an error and correct it themselves. This is called 'self-initiated self-repair'. Learners also find it acceptable to ask for help and to be corrected (self-initiated other-repair). They are less accepting if a person points out an error which they correct themselves (other-initiated self-repair), or if that person simply corrects the mistake (other-initiated other-repair) (Seedhouse, 1997: 34–9). Such findings remind teachers that they need to be highly sensitive when correcting mistakes and that they should offer learners opportunities to correct themselves.

Teachers can help pupils correct errors in the following ways:

- by giving pupils enough time to reflect on an answer and to correct errors
- by indicating that something is wrong (e.g. by frowning) and then waiting for the pupil to self-correct
- if that does not help, by indicating where the error is (e.g. by repeating the sentence and pausing before the error)
- by providing additional help by telling a pupil how to change a word or phrase (e.g. prompts such as 'use the plural' or 'pay attention to the tense').

Whether or not it is appropriate to correct a mistake depends on the focus of the lesson, the situation, the teacher and the learner (Klapper, 2006: 304). It is important to bear the following points in mind:

- pupils generally want feedback but this needs to be given sensitively
- pupils do not like to be repeatedly interrupted
- correct errors when they interfere with communication

- provide pupils with personal and relevant feedback that helps them overcome individual difficulties
- do not forget to point out pupils' strengths so that they can continue to develop them.

7.7 Main points to remember

In this chapter I have presented different ways in which teachers can develop children's listening and speaking skills at the level of sounds, words, sentences and texts. I have suggested structured activities akin to a 'presentation-practice-production model' as well as examples of Task-based Instruction which fits into a transactional approach. Some of the main characteristics of each model are listed below:

7.7.1 Structured drills in the PPP model

- Learning and teaching are understood as linear: the teacher *presents* new language items to the pupils who *practise* them with some help and eventually become able to *produce* the new language independently.
- Drills often take the form of question and answers, gap-filling or substitution exercises.
- Typical outcomes consist of vocabulary lists, knowledge of sentence structures and grammatical accuracy.
- The idea is to build up accuracy before fluency.
- The highly controlled settings are likely to help pupils develop confidence.
- The repetitive drills in which language structures are practised in isolation are relatively meaningless.
- The practice offered does not necessarily help pupils use language in authentic situations of communication. As Dulay *et al.* (1982) put it:

> Parroting activities, including most memorized dialogues and mechanical drills, appear to do little to encourage the development of fluent conversational skills.
>
> (p. 4)

- Drills are best used in brief, sharp bursts before the teacher moves on to real communicative tasks (Klapper, 2006: 300).

A good way to render drills more meaningful and relevant, and to make practice more efficient, is to use tasks.

7.7.2 Task-based Instruction, an example of a transactional approach

- Pupils use language for a real purpose (e.g. to solve a problem, to complete a task).
- Tasks represent real-life situations.
- Tasks are non-repetitive, meaningful and based on the pupils' needs.
- Tasks often require pupils to use all four language skills in a culturally appropriate way.

- The approach focuses on meaning and form, emphasizes the product and the process and is compatible with a learner-centred philosophy.

Educationalists distinguish between closed and open tasks. Closed tasks have a specific goal and outcome and are ideal at the beginning of a lesson. Open tasks are more loosely structured. They have a specific goal but an unknown outcome and resemble real-life situations. Closed tasks can be ideal for beginners. Klapper (2006: 299–301) proposes six different types:

- *listing*: brainstorming, memory games
- *ordering/sorting*: classifying things (e.g. the odd word out), sequencing pictures, rearranging jumbled sentences, collecting sets
- *comparing*: comparing pictures or texts to find similarities and differences
- *problem-solving*: answering open questions, guessing games, quizzes, puzzles
- *sharing personal experiences*: sharing meaningful information with friends, surveys
- *creative tasks*: doing role-plays, telling and acting out stories, using language outside the classroom and reporting back on the language used.

Compared to the more traditional drills, tasks have been described as non-repetitive and meaningful. They engage learners in authentic communications in the target language.

What type of model teachers choose depends on their philosophy of education; their understanding of how children learn best; their experience of learning and using foreign languages; their teaching experience; their own level of competence and confidence in the target language, the philosophy of the school and, above all, the pupils' needs. It seems clear, however, that a social constructivist approach such as Task-based Instruction is preferable to transmission models.

Developing Children's Reading and Writing Skills 8

Chapter Outline

8.1 Introduction

Young language learners are often eager to familiarize themselves with new scripts and to use the written word provided that they have a purposeful and secure learning environment. In this chapter, I present a rationale for the use of literacy with beginners and show that it supports the development of their language skills. After a short description of the bottom-up and top-down processes involved in reading and writing, I suggest practical activities to develop decoding, comprehension, spelling and composition skills.

Food for thought

- Imagine that you have to convince members of staff and parents of the importance of making young learners literate in the foreign language. What arguments would you put forward?
- According to theories of SLA, comprehensible input provided through listening and reading is essential to second language acquisition. What did you enjoy reading in a foreign language? In what ways has reading developed your language skills?
- According to cognitive theories of learning, writing offers opportunities for practice and, therefore, helps learners to automatize production. By contrast, interactionist theories value writing because it offers opportunities for feedback which learners can use to develop language. What have you written in your language classes? Can you think of writing activities that help primary school children both to practise vocabulary and grammar and express personal thoughts?

8.2 Rationale for the teaching of literacy

Introducing beginners to the written word often causes concen. Teachers fear that pupils might be confused, feel threatened or lose interest in learning the foreign language. Some think that learners might begin to mispronounce words they used to pronounce correctly. However, beginners can also mispronounce words when they read them the first time in their mother tongue. This can be the case, for example, when English pupils encounter the combination 'ough' as in 'through', 'thorough', 'cough' or 'bought'. This letter combination can be pronounced in seven different ways. The presentation of the written form can therefore make pupils aware of pronunciation and spelling patterns. In addition, it clarifies spoken language and focuses the learner's attention on aspects that are less apparent (e.g. cases in German, agreements in French). The following indicative example stems from Jones and Coffey (2006: 57, 58). They report that some children sang 'sunny semolina' instead of 'sonnez les matines' in 'Frère Jacques'. A visual support would have helped these pupils to learn the song correctly and would have reinforced their knowledge of vocabulary and grammar.

Some teachers in England appear to be concerned that the early introduction of literacy may have a demotivating effect. They fear that it diminishes the enjoyment of language learning and makes the lessons resemble the more 'serious' core subjects. Research studies have shown that eight-year-olds have developed a capacity for analytical thinking. As a result, they are more likely to enjoy language lessons with specific linguistic outcomes than mere 'interesting' fun activities (Sarter, 1997 in Wolff and Rueschoff, 2000: 122). If their needs are not met, their motivation is likely to decrease (Dewey, 1916; Graham, 1997).

From a linguistic point of view it is completely artificial to separate oral and written language. Most children are exposed to written language in everyday life through newspapers, advertisements, packaging, the internet or SMS. They know that they need to master all four language skills in order to communicate effectively. Learning to read and write in a foreign language is likely to enhance their interest in the *whole language* and to further their motivation to communicate. The absence of literacy in foreign language classes could make them feel that the foreign language itself is deficient and that foreign language learning is less 'serious' and important (Jones and Coffey, 2006).

It is generally agreed that 'the literacy skills of reading and writing are supported by and in turn reinforce, the development of oracy' (DfES, 2005a: 52). The earlier pupils learn to use the four skills the more likely they are to become successful communicators. Progress and achievement are likely to increase their motivation and their ability to further develop their language skills in both the foreign language *and* their mother tongue (Skarbek, 1998; Cheater and Farren, 2001). Pupils build on their first language (e.g. vocabulary, grammar) when learning a second. But through learning a foreign language, they reinforce their knowledge of language as a system which, in turn, enables them to develop their literacy skills (Martin and Cheater, 1998; DfES, 2005a; CiLT and Nacell, 2006).

Another argument in favour of the introduction of the written word at an early stage is the opportunity that foreign language resources offer to get insights into cultural aspects (e.g. the ways of life of other people) and to teach content in a different language. A final argument frequently mentioned is the teacher's duty to cater for a variety of learners with a range of learning styles. The written word is a valuable support for visual learners.

In many European countries the curriculum dictates at what age children are introduced to literacy in the foreign language. In England, teachers are free to judge when the time is right. The KS2 framework suggests that they base their decision on the following factors: children's age, literacy ability in English and previous learning experiences; the foreign language; the content and the competence and confidence of the teacher (DfES, 2005a, part 2: 40).

It is generally agreed that literacy learning should be purposeful and enable children to 'understand, make or do something' (Skarbek, 1998: 1). Therefore, teachers need to provide pupils with a wide range of appealing, appropriate and relevant reading materials (e.g. stories, songs, poems, jokes, recipes, menus, comics, letters, articles, emails, websites, articles, reports) and encourage different types of writing (e.g. captions, speech bubbles, invitations, lists, crosswords, instructions, poems, stories, reports) (Martin, 2002; DfES, 2005a).

In the early stages it is important to arouse children's curiosity and a real desire to start reading and writing in a foreign language (Skarbek, 1998). Teachers may try to do so in the following ways:

- writing the date in a foreign language
- writing the greeting used during the register on the board
- using multilingual labels on furniture and classroom resources
- displaying posters in foreign languages
- showing pupils rhymes, poems and songs in a written form
- having a foreign language noticeboard where pupils display postcards, letters, newspapers, magazines, labels, packages, instructions or leaflets in a foreign script.

Note that posters, labels or noticeboards need to be used regularly, for otherwise they risk not being noticed (Jones and Coffey, 2006).

In sections 8.4 and 8.5, I present different ways of developing reading and writing skills. In order to understand what type of activities is useful, I outline the main processes involved in reading and writing first.

8.3 The processes involved in reading and writing

In Chapter 7, I introduced the two techniques involved in processing oral input: the bottom-up and top-down processes (see 7.2). Learners draw on the same processes when working with written information.

- *Bottom-up processes*: learners use their knowledge of language (phonology, grammar, punctuation, cohesion, orthography) when they decode and make sense of a written text and, alternatively, encode an oral text (transforming sounds into text).
- *Top-down processes*: learners rely on their prior experience of reading and writing, their knowledge of the topic, their understanding of the intention of the author and their knowledge of writing conventions (formal schemata, genres and registers, knowledge of sociocultural and contextual background).

The following example shows how the pupils in my Year 2 class, seven- to eight-year-olds, used these processes when they read the French story *La souris gourmande* (MEN, 1986). The highly repetitive story is based on the structure '*le premier jour, la souris mange le pain*' (the first day the mouse eats bread) with the ordinals and the food items changing every day. The highlight comes on the seventh day when the mouse *éclate*.

The learners decoded the message: they sounded out letters (they matched the letters to the sounds) and they interpreted the sounds by assigning meaning to them. Grasping the story required pupils to understand food items and the key word *éclate*. A couple of months into learning French, children had acquired some food vocabulary but they had generally not come across the word *éclate*. Some pupils were able to decode the word correctly by sounding out each letter, but this did not help them with the meaning. Since their knowledge of language (bottom-up processes) did not lead to a successful interpretation, they had to use other strategies. Their knowledge of stories, in particular their understanding that many end with a climax, led some to speculate that something exceptional happened to the mouse. Although the children's general knowledge and their familiarity with stories helped them make sense of the text as a whole, they did not disclose the meaning of the unknown word. The children eventually found out that the mouse 'bursts' when they saw the illustration of that page of the story.

This example shows that proficiency in the foreign language plays a very important role in a learner's success in reading in a new language (Macaro, 2003). Though findings are not entirely conclusive, it would appear that strategy training can help students transfer reading and writing strategies from a first to a foreign language (Grenfell and Harris, 1993, 1994; Cohen, 1998; Chamot *et al.*, 1999; Macaro, 2006). Strategies can help the learners compensate for the bottom-up processes.

In the following sections I present some activities that teachers can use in order to foster the development of reading and writing skills.

8.4 Developing reading skills

Decoding and understanding a written word, sentence or text requires a range of skills and knowledge. Among them are the following:

- a knowledge of the ways in which sounds and letters are related (phoneme–grapheme correspondence)
- the ability to construct words out of sounds and syllables

- the ability to identify words
- the ability to understand the meaning of words, sentences and a text
- pronunciation and intonation skills.

In this section, I present exercises to help children practise their understanding of phoneme-grapheme correspondences, word recognition, text comprehension and pronunciation. Many exercises are inspired by those in SNE (2002a, b and c), MENFPS (2003) and DfES (2005a).

Educationalists working in a structural tradition tend to suggest a linear progression from reading sounds, single words and simple phrases to short texts. More advanced learners are expected to read unfamiliar sentences and a range of longer texts of different styles and genres independently (Satchwell and De Silva, 1995; Satchwell, 1997; DfES, 2005a). Teachers who favour a holistic approach tend to opt for a different direction: they start with a text, the meaningful whole, and work 'down' to the language items. They work on text comprehension and shift their focus to form whenever appropriate.

8.4.1 Working on the sound-letter correspondence

Example 8.1 illustrates children's ability to discriminate sounds and their eagerness to make sense of sounds and letters in a foreign language. It stems from a girl in my Year 2 class in Luxembourg. Like all pupils, Sandra had learned German in Year 1 and French, a second foreign language, in Year 2. Shortly after being introduced to French, she tried to read it. In order to know how to sound out the letters, she produced what she called a 'dictionary'. On the left, she wrote letters or letter strings and French words, on the right transliterations of these sounds in German. The note reminded her, for example, that she needed to read the letter 'u' in French in the same way as the letter 'ü' in German.

Example 8.1 Sandra's pronunciation rules, February 1997

u (tu)	⇔	ü
au (auto)	⇔	o
ou (nous)	⇔	u

Teachers help children associate and remember the correspondences between sounds and letters by pointing them out repeatedly and by creating 'word banks'. For example, they can explain that the German sound [ʃ] corresponds to the letter group 'sch' and then create 'phonic clouds' (Hurrell, 1999: 81). Each cloud presents a word with the sound [ʃ] (e.g. *Schiff*, *Schere*, *Scharf* and *Schal*). The clouds, suspended like a mobile, add to the decoration of the classroom.

Speaking about similarities and differences between sounds and letter–sound correspondences in the first and foreign language enables children to develop their knowledge about language. In the above example, they learn that the sound [ʃ] exists in both English and German but that the representing graphemes differ ('sh' in English, 'sch' in German). They will also learn that some languages have sounds that do not exist in others. For example, the French sound [ã] as in *dans* does not exist in English, and the English sound [θ] as in 'think' does not exist in French. This knowledge helps them recognize spelling patterns and develop simple reading and spelling strategies. This is especially useful with phonetic languages like German, Italian or Spanish (Cheater and Farren, 2001).

In order to further develop children's knowledge of sound–letter correspondences teachers can use sound/symbol identification exercises which require children to match sounds with the appropriate letters and vice versa. Working on the alphabet offers opportunities for practice (Skarbek, 1998; Cheater and Farren, 2001).

The alphabet
Mastery of the alphabet enables children to spell their own name and to use a dictionary to check the spelling, meaning and pronunciation of a word. Alphabet songs exist in most languages and are an enjoyable way of learning the ABC. Once children know some letters or the whole alphabet, they can engage in role-plays where they need to spell words. For example, they could phone an imaginary hotel and spell their name and address to the manager. They could then ask the manager to spell the name of the street.

Sorting words in alphabetical order develops pupils' knowledge of the alphabet and their dictionary skills. Children can use their first names and sort themselves into alphabetic order. Teachers increase the level of difficulty by using words that start with the same two, three or even four letters. A frieze of the alphabet on a wall is a useful resource.

Children can also create their own dictionary. They could illustrate each letter of the alphabet with a picture and a word. A German dictionary could start with *Affe, Bär, Chameleon, Dromedar*, etc. Next, children add new words in each section. This personalized dictionary visualizes the learning process and becomes a practical reference book to check spellings.

Teachers can offer further practice for the phoneme–grapheme correspondence with sound/symbol identification and segmentation exercises (see 8.4.2).

Sound symbol identification exercises
A simple identification exercise consists of giving children a list of words and asking them to highlight a particular sound or letter. A list that contains words with similar letter groups but different sounds ('ei' and 'ie' in Example 8.2), or different letter groups but same sounds (Example 8.3) requires children to really concentrate. In the first example, pupils need to discriminate between the diphthongs 'ei' and 'ie'. They learn that 'ei' can be at the beginning, middle and end of a word. In the second exercise, they need to 'listen' into the words and regroup *soleil* and *seau* and *parasol, au* and *eau* irrespective of their spelling.

Example 8.2 Identify the sound /aI/ (as in *mein*)

Ein, nie, ein, Eimer, in, Sieb, eilen, Knie, nein, Osterei

Example 8.3 Group words that start with the same sound

Soleil, feu, eau, sage, au, seau, peau

The exercise becomes more difficult if the teacher asks pupils to identify missing vowels or consonants (Example 8.4). This exercise requires a good lexical knowledge (vocabulary) and helps the pupils develop their spelling skills.

Example 8.4 Find the missing vowels in these animals (Italian)

c . . . v . . . ll . . .   g . . .tt . . .

8.4.2 Building words

Segmentation exercises encourage pupils to isolate or join up letters/syllables to form words. Examples 8.5 to 8.7 are 'anagram jigsaws' consisting of 'scrambled' words. Teachers can present the 'disintegrated' word as in Example 8.5 or ask the learners to combine the letters/syllables appropriately as in Examples 8.6 and 8.7.

Example 8.5 Follow the lines and discover three fruits in French
(Here: *une poire, une fraise, un abricot*)

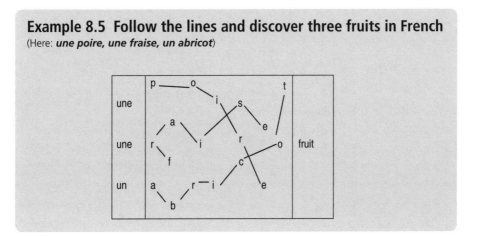

Example 8.6 Combine the letters and discover a fruit in Spanish (Here: *limón*)	**Example 8.7 Combine syllables to find three animals in German** (Here: *Krokodil, Känguru, Pandabär*)

n
       i
ó
       l
m
	Kro gu
	     bär da
	  ru dil
	         Pan
	  ko Kän

Exercise 8.5 forces pupils to read letters rather than to rely on the shape of words. This is a good way of developing children's bottom-up reading strategies. Exercises 8.6 and 8.7 require a good knowledge of vocabulary and help learners memorize spellings. The addition of pictures makes these challenging activities more accessible.

Rather than focusing exclusively on the 'right' words, teachers can encourage learners to create new ones. In Example 8.7 pupils could combine syllables in such a way that they produce non-existing animals such as a 'Krogubär' which has parts of a crocodile, a kangaroo and a panda bear. Such new formations are motivating reading exercises that provide insights into pupils' reading, pronunciation and comprehension skills.

8.4.3 Word recognition

The aim of word recognition exercises is to help children identify words. Example 8.8 focuses on the visual presentation only. Example 8.9 requires understanding and a good grasp of vocabulary.

Below are some possible exercises:

- identify words in mirror writing
- identify words that are partly hidden (e.g. Example 8.8)

Example 8.8 Identify the word
(Here: *topo, chat*)

- one and two-dimensional word searches (pupils are given a list of words which they have to find in a matrix filled with letters)
- divide a string of letters into meaningful words (e.g. Example 8.9)

Example 8.9 Can you understand this Italian sentence?
(Here: *Voglio giocare a pallone con i miei amici.*)

> Vogliogiocareapalloneconimieiamici.

8.4.4 Comprehension exercises

Listening and reading comprehension activities have many similarities. I therefore refer the reader to Chapter 7, section 7.4.3, for some guidance. Below are some additional examples.

Games can be an excellent way of practising reading and understanding. Teachers could play a form of treasure hunt. They organize pupils in small groups and give them a sheet with the names of the resources needed for a particular activity. The list, written in the target language, could include words such as scissors, glue, colours, paper, cupboard, shelves and drawer. The aim is to assemble all the materials as soon as possible. This activity is ideal for making pupils practise classroom vocabulary. Games that practise reading are ideal if they provide opportunities for immediate feedback. This is the case, for example, with Dominoes, Pelmanism or card games.

Some teachers and pupils prefer worksheets to games as they provide a record of the activity and can be taken home. Pupils like to show what they have learned to parents. Such worksheets are also ideal for homework. 'True/false' or multiple-choice exercises are easy to design and administer and can provide good evidence of children's knowledge and understanding.

'Draw according to instructions' is a popular exercise. In order to make children read the instructions carefully teachers can ask for unconventional things (e.g. colour a tomato in pink). When pupils are asked to colour in, draw or illustrate something, it is best to set them a time limit and to remind them to focus on the essential rather than details.

Classification exercises ('Classifying words into categories', Example 8.10) and identification exercises ('Identifying a misfit', Example 8.11) are other useful exercises for pupils to demonstrate reading and comprehension skills. The latter exercise can be done at text level. Teachers give children a text such as a recipe and include inaccurate information which the readers have to find. This exercise is ideal to develop scanning skills.

Example 8.10 Read the French words and regroup them in appropriate categories (Here: regroup the clothes and food)

chemise, pantalon, banane, lait, soulier, chocolat, eau, pullover

Example 8.11 Read the Italian words and identify the misfit (Here: *topo*)

pera, pomodoro, insalata, topo, limone

Matching words or sentences to pictures is another useful way of testing pupils' comprehension skills. The exercise in Example 8.12 can be made more challenging by adding some incorrect sentences that pupils can correct.

Example 8.12   Match the pictures and the sentence

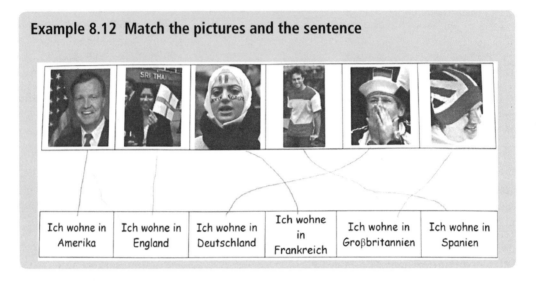

| Ich wohne in Amerika | Ich wohne in England | Ich wohne in Deutschland | Ich wohne in Frankreich | Ich wohne in Großbritannien | Ich wohne in Spanien |

A final effective means of testing pupils' comprehension of sentences or texts is through cloze tests. The latter are written passages where some words are deleted. The task consists of filling in the missing words (see Example 8.19).

8.4.5   Expanding children's language skills

Teachers can rely on a range of activities to further develop children's language skills. They can ask pupils to discuss issues raised in the text, relate the text to their own experiences, do a role-play or invent a different ending to a story. They can also use the text as a template to create their own. In the German poem presented in Example 8.13, pupils could be asked to fill in their own details.

Example 8.13   Read the German telephone conversation

Hier ist Peter.	*Here is Peter.*
Wer ist dort?	*Who is there?*
Leider ist mein Papa fort.	*Unfortunately my father is absent.*
Doch heute mittag um halb vier	*But this afternoon at half three*
Ist mein Vater wieder hier.	*He will be here again.*
Bitte schön, Herr Klingelmann	*Please, Mr Ringman*
Rufen Sie doch noch mal an.	*Would you call again.*

The text enables pupils to practise many of the words used in a basic conversation on the phone. It is also a suitable way of doing work on the diphthongs 'ei' and 'ie' and of developing knowledge about language, for example of the use of the formal *Sie.*

Working with a wide range of texts provides opportunities to develop composition skills. Focusing on the structure of a text helps pupils to learn about cohesive devices; focusing on the layout and the characteristic features of a text helps them to identify different types of texts such as instructions, recipes or weather forecasts (DfES, 2005a). The more types pupils are familiar with, the easier it will be for pupils to write a similar range of texts.

8.4.6 Pronunciation

Though difficult to read, tongue twisters encourage children to read carefully and to articulate sounds accurately. Pupils generally do not mind practising them alone or with a partner until they can read them correctly.

Teachers should be sensitive when correcting pronunciation mistakes, and try as much as possible to get children to self-correct their errors (see section 7.4.3).

When a longer text is being studied, the teacher can pick up on pronunciation once the pupils are familiar with the content. Teachers might need to remind pupils to read questions with a rising intonation and to draw their attention to punctuation and speech marks. As a result, children realize the differences between speech marks in different languages. For example, they learn that questions in Spanish have two question marks, an inverted one at the beginning of the sentence and a 'normal' one at the end.

Pupils can practise reading a text accurately, fluently and with expression, independently or with a classmate (Martin and Cheater, 1998; Cheater and Farren, 2001; Martin, 2002; DfES, 2005a). In order for children to learn from each other, it is important that the teacher has a good knowledge of children's pronunciation skills and groups pupils accordingly.

8.5 Developing writing skills

Writing is a complex activity as learners need to carry out a range of different tasks simultaneously such as: organizing ideas, thinking about spelling and grammar, choosing the right words, ensuring coherence and cohesion and considering the perspective of the audience. This list could suggest that writing in a foreign language can only be done by older learners. This is not the case as Examples 8.22, 8.23 and 8.14 show. They remind us that the purpose of writing is not (only) to memorize and practise vocabulary, spelling and grammar but also to express personal ideas. Writing therefore requires a purpose and an audience.

Many teachers distinguish between structured and communicative writing. The aim of the former is to help pupils gain control over the language items they have learned and prepare them for communication situations. To this effect, learners can do gap-filling or substitution exercises, or take spelling tests. The focus is on form.

By contrast, the aim of communicative writing is to express personal thoughts. Pupils can be asked to write stories, poems or reports. The task of the teacher is to help children express ideas coherently and accurately.

In Chapter 6 and section 8.4, I have shown how teachers can evoke interest in the written word. It is important to instil in children a real desire to write and to create a positive atmosphere where writing is valued and risk-taking encouraged. A good starting point is to 'experiment with words'. Children can write words in the air or on the back of the hand of a classmate. Guessing the word requires concentration and the ability to visualize words. Creative writing, particularly *shape-poetry*, is a similar enjoyable activity (Example 8.14). It consists of writing a word in such a way that it visualizes the concept it represents.

Example 8.14 Shape poetry

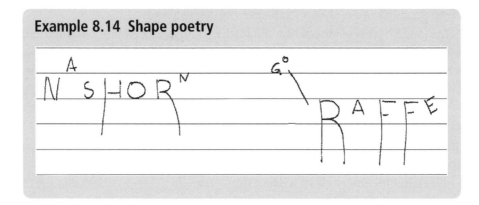

In the following sections, I describe different ways of developing writing skills thereby paying attention to vocabulary, spelling, grammar and composition. I give many practical examples; some are more akin to a structural approach and others fit better into a transactional approach.

8.5.1 Writing to practise vocabulary and spelling

Copy-writing (Example 8.15) is much used in primary schools in England as a way of remembering words and their spelling. Many pupils assume that copy-writing is easy and, therefore, don't always pay attention (Macaro, 2006). In order to avoid pupils making unnecessary mistakes it is best to draw their attention to the letters first as in the following exercises.

Example 8.15 Copy-writing body parts

Copia las palabras en el lugar correcto:

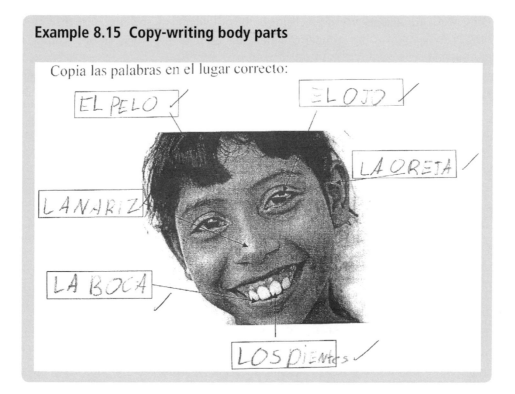

Word searches, crosswords, letter combination (Examples 8.5 to 8.8) and gap-filling exercises (Examples 8.4 and 8.16) draw children's attention to the individual letters and are therefore helpful for memorizing spellings. Exercise 8.16 offers an opportunity for auto-correction. Pupils choose the relevant letter(s) in each word and relate the respective numbers (here 2, 4, 9, 10, 15, 17). If they work correctly, a picture appears.

Example 8.16 Fill in the missing vowels and relate the relevant numbers. What shape can you see? (Here: Hexagon)

S, ss or β?

1. e ___en   s (1)   ss (2)   β (3)
2. Ei___   s (4)   ss (5)   β (6)
3. wei___   s (7)   ss (8)   β (9)
4. Gla___   s (10)   ss (11)   β (12)
5. Stra ___ e   s (13)   ss (14)   β (15)
6. da ___   s (16)   ss (17)   β (18)

			5 ×	7 ×	
		1 ×			
16 ×	2 ×			× 4	
					× 16
	17 ×			× 9	
3 ×					
14 ×					
8 ×		15 ×		× 10	6 ×
	18 ×				
				× 10	

Crosswords are an ideal way of practising both vocabulary and spelling. Since the number of boxes corresponds to the number of letters, the exercise also offers an opportunity for self-correction.

'Shape' exercises (Example 8.17) make pupils examine the letters and the overall shape of the word. They help children develop visual presentations.

Example 8.17 Which word fits into the box?

gato   perro

Example 8.18 requires knowledge of both vocabulary and spelling. Pupils are asked to identify a word by combining particular letters of the words represented by pictures. In the example below they are to find a profession in French by using the first three letters of the first word, the second and third letters of the following two words and the first and last letter of the fourth word. To complicate matters, they need to substitute the letter 'i' with 'a' in the word *tigre* and the letter 'o' with 's' in the word *lion*.

Example 8.18 Trouve la profession *(Here: garagiste; g a r – a g – i s – t e)*

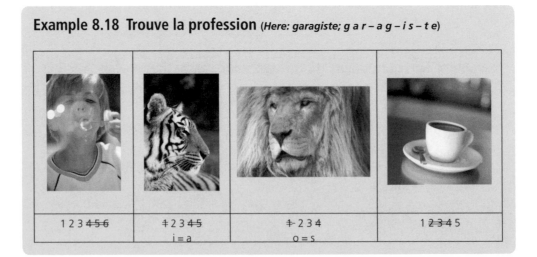

1 2 3 ~~4 5 6~~	~~1~~ 2 3 ~~4 5~~	~~1~~ 2 3 4	1 ~~2 3 4~~ 5
	i = a	o = s	

8.5.2 Writing to practise grammatical structures

In order to get pupils to practise the formation of coherent and grammatically correct sentences, teachers often choose sentence completion, sentence-formation/transformation and substitution exercises. Below are examples of each type.

After a few weeks of German the Year 6 pupils in Portway Primary School filled in the text in Example 8.19. The dialogue allowed for some creative and independent work. The pupils practised the dialogues with classmates and acted them out.

Example 8.20 is a sentence-formation exercise: learners are given word phrases, verbs and adjectives which they combine to create possible sentences.

Example 8.19 Complete the conversation in the market

_____ !
Bitte sehr.
Ich möchte _____ bitte.
Sonst noch etwas?
Ja, ich möchte _____ bitte.
Sonst noch etwas?
Nein danke, das ist alles.
_____ *Euro, bitte.*
Danke. Auf Wiedersehen.
_____ !

Example 8.20 Combine les éléments pour faire des phrases

(Example: *Je mange deux bananes.*)

Mon père	habite	deux bananes.
Les parents de Tim	va	au marché.
Je	mange	dans une grande maison.
La fille	vont	au bureau.

Substitution exercises ask children to replace particular words in order to create new sentences. The German poem in Example 8.13 is a substitution exercise at text level. Many teachers ask children to substitute words in books or songs to create new ones. For example, they could ask children to replace the food items in Carle's book *The Very Hungry Caterpillar*. It is important to make sure that these exercises are still creative and open-ended. They should not look like gap-filling exercises.

Example 8.21 is a more difficult substitution exercise because it requires text comprehension as well as mastery of vocabulary and grammar (agreements, syntax).

> **Example 8.21 Transforme la phrase**
> (Example: Les chats *mangent* des souris.)
>
> Le chien est *gentil.*   →
> Le *chat* est petit.   →
> Les chats *cherchent* des souris.   →

8.5.3 Developing communication and composition skills

A good way to develop children's composition skills is to make them study the features of different types of texts and to encourage them to write different genres (e.g. emails, recipes, stories, reports, articles).

In order to develop written communication skills it is important that teachers create a classroom environment where children are valued, respected and encouraged to take risks. Teachers need to be interested in what they say, create a purpose for writing and make sure that there is an audience. They also need to have realistic expectations of pupils and help children develop realistic expectations of themselves. This is important as many pupils want to write but could easily become frustrated if they see that they are unable to express themselves in the way they would like to.

Joint writing with a more experienced person (the teacher, a child, a parent) is a good way for children both to produce a written text and to learn how to produce texts. The 'expert' guides the learner in the writing process by helping them express their ideas, encouraging them to draw on their prior knowledge, expanding on their language, modelling how to use resources, offering words and structures, reminding them what they have written already, helping them read the text and keeping them calm and focused. With the help of the expert who offers scaffolding techniques (Wood, 1998; Cameron, 2001) pupils construct knowledge. They internalize the external model offered by the teacher and in the process acquire new language and develop their reading and composition skills. (See Chapter 3 on sociocultural approaches to language learning, section 3.4.)

Initially, children could dictate stories to the teacher, who acts as a scribe. These early stories might only be a sentence long. Because pupils remember the content and vocabulary they will find it relatively easy to read the text to classmates and parents. At a later stage, teachers can ask children to write texts in pairs or individually, assisted by word banks and reference books.

Below I describe Storying, a 'whole language approach' (Dìaz, 1990) which I used in my own classes to develop children's foreign language skills (Kirsch, 1996, 1997). A holistic approach considers language as an entity rather than an assemblage of rules and patterns, integrates work on the four language skills (listening, speaking, reading, writing) and encourages interaction with text and language, collaboration with other learners and communication for a given purpose within a meaningful context.

Storying encourages learners to tell, read, write, edit and perform their own stories. It draws on children's personal, social and linguistic experiences and offers many opportunities for purposeful language use (Britton, 1975; Dyson, 1997; Paley, 1992). Learners share experiences, negotiate meanings in authentic and meaningful learning contexts and construct new knowledge through collaboration. The finished product and their progress leave them with a sense of ownership, pride and achievement.

I used Storying in my own Year 1 and 2 classes. In Luxembourg, the six- to seven-year-olds learn German for eight hours in Year 1 and French, a second foreign language, for three hours in Year 2. When native Luxembourgish children enter primary school they generally have some knowledge of German through watching TV. This is also the case to a lesser extent with (on average) the 40 per cent non-nationals in a class.

Listening to, telling and playing stories helped all children develop their oral skills and inspired them to read and create their own. Example 8.22 stems from a six-year-old French native girl who did not speak German when she started school in September. Two months later she wrote a 'Maisy' story influenced by the many 'Maisy' books we had in the classrooms. Apart from practising the repetitive structure 'Maisy wants', she learned to use her newly acquired vocabulary meaningfully and to write a story in a logical and chronological order. Her achievements boosted her confidence and she was soon able to read fluently and to write more extensively.

Example 8.22 Mausi (Constance, Year 1, 20 October 1997)

Mausi will etwas essen.		*Maisy wants to eat something.*
Mausi ist fertig mit essen.		*Maisy has finished eating.*
Mausi will im Garten spielen.		*Maisy wants to play in the garden.*
Mausi will ins Haus.		*Maisy wants to go into the house.*
Mausi will nicht mehr im Haus bleiben.		*Maisy does not want to stay in the house anymore.*
Mausi will essen.		*Maisy wants to eat something.*
Mausi will auf den Baum.		*Maisy wants to climb a tree.*
Mausi will runter vom Baum.		*Maisy wants to climb down.*
Mausi will nach Haus.		*Maisy wants to go home.*
Mausi will ins Bett.		*Maisy wants to go to bed.*
Constance, 20.11.97		

Examples 8.23 and 8.24 stem from the same class in Year 2. Like Constance's story, the content of these texts reflects children's daily activities and personal experiences (e.g. playground, football); their likes and dislikes (e.g. feelings, favourite books); the influence of the media (e.g. Diddls popular at that time); the topics discussed in class (e.g. Maisy stories) and children's language proficiency.

Mandy and Sophie were below average learners. When writing the above story, they used familiar phrases as a framework. In this case, they had come across the structures of the sentences 1, 4, 5, 6, 7, 8, 9, 13, 18, 19 in stories written by their classmates. They appropriated these structures and 'filled' them with details (e.g. the names of the lobsters, the setting) to create a new story. They also drew on other children's stories, word banks and a dictionary and asked me several times for translations. The drawings are not mere illustrations of the story, they convey additional information. In this case, the two girls did not want to make their story more complicated by adding information about other animals. They therefore drew these animals rather than including them verbally.

Through a conversation with the girls and a comparison of their former stories I found, that through writing this story, they had memorized several new verbs, nouns and adjectives (i.e. *s'ennuie, triste, seul, balançoire, glissoire*) and learned to conjugate the verb *aller*.

Example 8.23 Les homards (Mandy et Sophie, 16 May 1999)

Les homards

1. Le homard s'appelle Hom.
2. Il s'ennuie.
3. Hom téléphone à Homi.
4. - Bonjour, c'est Hom.
5. - Bonjour, c'est Homi.
6. - Tu viens jouer?
7. - Non, ça ne va pas.
8. - Oooh. Au revoir Homi.
9. - Au revoir Hom.
10. Hom est triste.
11. Il joue tout seul.
12. Homi vient.
13. Il dit: Je joue avec toi.
14. Nous allons sur la balançoire.
15. Ils vont sur la balançoire.
16. Ils vont sur la glissoire.
17. Ils rentrent.
18. - Au revoir, Hom.
19. - Au revoir, Homi.

Fin
Mandy et Sophie 16 mai 1999

The story in Example 8.24 was written by two average pupils in June. Like the girls, they drew on some familiar structures which they expanded in their new story. While editing, they needed to write some plurals which gave me an opportunity to familiarize them with some rules about the agreement of verbs and adjectives. It became obvious that Christophe had learned these rules because he used some correct plurals in his next story.

All finished stories were displayed in the classroom or the corridors and those that were chosen by the children were published in our quarterly class journal. These journals served as reading material at home, at school and in the wider community. Children used them, for example, to read stories to nursery children, to older pupils at school and to patients at the local hospital. To increase the audience and get more feedback, pupils also posted some stories on our website.

Example 8.24 Les Diddls jouent au football (Chris et Christophe, 7 juin 1999)

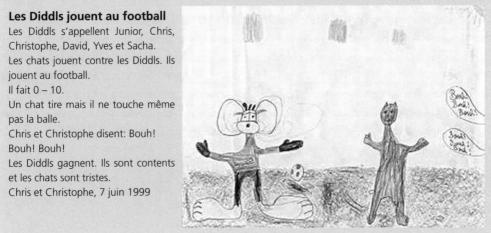

Les Diddls jouent au football
Les Diddls s'appellent Junior, Chris, Christophe, David, Yves et Sacha.
Les chats jouent contre les Diddls. Ils jouent au football.
Il fait 0 – 10.
Un chat tire mais il ne touche même pas la balle.
Chris et Christophe disent: Bouh! Bouh! Bouh!
Les Diddls gagnent. Ils sont contents et les chats sont tristes.
Chris et Christophe, 7 juin 1999

Stories like the above were usually not finished in a single lesson. Once children had completed a draft, they presented it to a group of children or the whole class in a 'writing conference'. They read out the story and asked some comprehension questions. This required careful preparation on their part: they knew that they could only catch and keep the interest of the audience by reading fluently, accurately and with some expression. Having listened to the story carefully, the audience made comments and suggested changes to make a passage more comprehensible, interesting or coherent. The comments focused on meaning and form, for example, on the use of particularly salient grammar or vocabulary items. The author(s) took account of the comments when editing the draft.

Dramatization or the acting out of the story is another useful way of enhancing children's language skills. First, the author read the text and allocated the roles. Then the cast (a group of children) discussed the text in the light of the performance. They invented dialogues and thought about the setting. In the process they often became aware of parts of the story that were incoherent or incomprehensible. The cast suggested changes which the author often integrated into the original text after the performance.

The discussions about the texts during the writing conferences, and before and after the performances, enhanced children's self-esteem and confidence in their own abilities and contributed to their learning and language learning in a range of ways. First, they developed children's social skills and desire to communicate. By listening carefully to each other, the teacher and the pupils show respect for each other and indicate that what someone else has to say is valuable and important (Wells in Barnes *et al.*, 1986).

Second, the discussions furthered the pupils' language development. The authentic situations of communication were invaluable sources of language input. Pupils acquired new vocabulary and grammatical structures both from their classmates and from me and practised language in a meaningful way.

Third, the discussions increased children's awareness of the creative process of writing. The findings of a study by McNamee *et al.* (1995) have shown that dramatization enhances the storytelling ability of preschool children. Preschool children who were used to acting out stories invented more complex and coherent ones than those who were unfamiliar with this practice. I found that dramatization and conferencing enhanced the pupils' ability to reflect on the structure and content of stories. The seven year olds learned that a text needed to be comprehensible and have the right balance between action, suspense, surprise, humour, dialogue and description. Some examples, translated from Luxembourgish into English, illustrate the point:

> CK: What qualifies as a good story?
>
> Cynthia: One has to make sure that the story is comprehensible; so one has to think of how one writes. We cannot write 'The ball is broken, there is a hole' and then, in the next sentence 'we blow it up'. (The story has to be logical.)
>
> Anne: There has to be some action. One should not have dialogues the whole time. One has dialogues, some action and one explains a little bit.
>
> Arno: You should not always use the words 'go' and 'say'. You have to think of other words such as 'walk' or 'run'.
>
> Interviews, May 1999

The many discussions about text made the children aware of the need to write comprehensibly, clearly and accurately. They learned to choose appropriate genres to captivate their audience and were prepared to spend the necessary time on improving their lexis, spelling and grammar. The discussions therefore acted as a 'mediator for the learning process' (Gretsch, 1992). Children internalized a model of writing which they could use in the future. Storying therefore also enabled them to work more independently.

The ability to think about language and language use is a very important metalinguistic skill. It contributed to the success of these children's stories and to their language development. The ability to critically reflect on language and to increase one's metacognitive and metalinguistic skills takes time to develop. At first, children tend to make banal comments but the teacher's feedback serves as a model. Pupils learn to make pertinent comments and to present them in a constructive way. They learn to argue, take and defend a position as well as accept constructive criticism and build on it (Celce-Murcia and Olshtain, 2000).

Though Storying can be a very efficient, this holistic, child-centred and transactional approach is challenging and demanding for teachers. It requires a lot of preparation and organization, good monitoring skills and a willingness on the part of the teacher to step back and to give pupils some responsibility for and control over their learning.

Note that the method is possible in any context, not just in multilingual Luxembourg. It is true that children in other countries are subjected to less language teaching but the story 'Les Diddls jouent au football' was produced by Year 2 pupils after roughly 50 hours of learning French. This means that other children could write it in their second or third year, depending on the time allocation for foreign languages.

8.6 Main points to remember

Pupils can become easily anxious, nervous or frustrated while listening to or reading in an unfamiliar language or when asked to produce language orally or in writing. I close this chapter with some implications drawn from chapters 7 and 8, which can help you develop a productive language learning environment.

- Develop realistic expectations of what pupils can achieve.
- State your expectations (for example, pupils should know that they are not expected to express themselves as fluently and accurately in their second language as in their first).
- Help pupils develop realistic expectations of what they can achieve.
- Discuss your expectations with children and parents. Their view of what reading or good writing is might differ from yours.
- Create a friendly and risk-taking classroom environment that allows for dialogue and meaningful and purposeful communication in authentic situations.
- Be interested in what pupils say and give feedback.

8.6.1 General considerations for planning

- Try to use a *whole language approach*. It integrates work on the four language skills and encourages authentic communication.
- Use a multimedia approach. Pupils can listen to and read things at the same time (CD-ROMs, internet).
- Define appropriate learning objectives.
- Define a task to frame your lesson (e.g. find a reason why pupils should read a text).
- Choose activities that are appropriate for the pupils' level of comprehension, their interests, needs and age.
- Plan key questions and key vocabulary in the foreign language.
- Prepare appropriate resources (big books, OHPs, whiteboard, reference books).
- Plan assessment opportunities (e.g. plan when and how you assess if pupils have learned what you want to teach them).
- Define appropriate follow-up questions and follow-up activities.

8.6.2 Planning oral and written activities

When planning listening and reading activities, you should also consider the following points:

- Choose a meaningful text (e.g. story, song, poem) that suits the cognitive and linguistic needs of pupils. Repetitive texts facilitate listening and remembering.
- Choose appropriate and authentic materials whenever possible (e.g. CD, CD-ROM, internet). If you use audio resources, make sure that the text is comprehensible (e.g. appropriate accent and pace).
- Familiarize yourself with the text.
- Analyse the topic and pupils' familiarity with it. You might need to give pupils some background information.
- Decide whether the text offers pupils enough clues to determine its meaning. You might need to pre-teach some vocabulary.
- Be aware of cultural references that pupils might be unfamiliar with (e.g. references to people, places, traditions, customs. To give an example, pupils who are unfamiliar with the concepts 'bedtime story' or 'tooth fairy' will not be able to predict these words and might need help in understanding their meaning).

If you want pupils to communicate in a foreign language with you, classmates and people outside school you must create a classroom climate that encourages dialogue. When planning speaking and writing activities, you should consider the following points in addition to the ones raised above:

- Listen carefully to your pupils and have regular conversations with them about things they are interested in (in the first language).
- Plan opportunities where pupils can use language for a communicative purpose with a range of speakers or writers (e.g. pupils in other classes, pen-pals, journals).
- Expand pupils' use of language (e.g. rephrase what they say, use a wider range of vocabulary, ask follow-up questions).
- Praise pupils for their efforts.
- Use structured oral and written exercises in brief sharp bursts before moving on to real communicative tasks.
- Be sensitive when you correct errors (e.g. you can correct those that interfere with the communication).

Developing Knowledge about Language 9

9.1 Introduction

Knowledge about language (KAL) and *language awareness* feature in most language learning programmes. The underlying assumption is that pupils can improve their proficiency if they have some understanding of how languages work. As seen in Chapter 3, theories of SLA differ in their opinion on this. While Krashen (1982) holds that teaching grammar does not aid acquisition (and might even hamper it), theorists working from an information-processing perspective maintain that a focus on form can improve language learning.

Food for thought

- Reflect on your own language learning experience. How have you learned to spell words correctly? How did teachers introduce you to gender or agreements?
- How have you learned to adapt speech to the particular situation at hand (e.g. to choose an appropriate style)?
- Do you think that your 'knowledge about the language' has helped you become a better language learner or language user?

In this chapter I define KAL and language awareness, explore the role of KAL for the acquisition of foreign languages and offer some practical ideas of ways of developing KAL. I close with some considerations on the relationship between KAL, language awareness programmes and learner proficiency.

9.2 Knowledge about language and language awareness

The concept 'knowledge about language' goes back to Chomsky (1965) and the distinction he made between 'competence' and 'performance'. Knowledge about language is related to a person's competence which develops, in Chomsky's view, more or less automatically under the right conditions. He believed that children are born with a *Language Acquisition Device* (LAD) which has evolved over time to acquire the UG (see 3.3.1). The UG makes it possible for children to discover linguistic rules and to generate language on the basis of the fragmentary input from interlocutors. As a result, they acquire their first language with practically no instruction or error correction.

Chomsky believed that this competence or knowledge about language comprises knowledge of phonology, morphology, syntax and semantics. Other linguists would add other fields to this list, for example sociolinguistic and pragmatic knowledge.

9.2.1 Chomsky's concept of knowledge about language

It is worth defining the four different types of knowledge that an infant draws on during the language acquisition process.

Phonological and phonetic knowledge	Phonetic knowledge enables children to recognize and produce sounds and to identify boundaries between units. For example, they know that the sounds [ð] and [ə] form the word [ðə] ('the') and are able to identify that [mou] is the first syllable of the last word in the sentence [ðə Kăt Kăch'ĭz ə mous] (the cat catches a mouse). Phonological knowledge makes children understand which sounds can legally follow others. Children know that the sound [ə] can follow [ð] in English but not in German where this sound does not exist.
Knowledge of morphemes	Knowledge of morphemes helps children join morphemes in the right order and pronounce them correctly. (A morpheme is the smallest linguistic unit that has semantic meaning.) For example, children know that they have to add the morpheme 'y' to the word 'hunger' in a such way that they create the word 'hungry' rather than 'hungery' or 'yhunger'. They also know that they need to pronounce the letters 'ed' in 'closed' as a [t] and the 'ed' in painted as [əd].

Syntactic knowledge	Syntactic knowledge helps children put the constituents of a sentence in the right order and understand the role that these constituents play. They say 'The hungry cat catches a small mouse' rather than 'The cat hungry catches a mouse small', and know that the cat is the actor (subject) and the mouse the one to which the action applies (object).
Semantic knowledge	Semantic knowledge helps children relate objects to meanings.

According to Chomsky speakers 'know' grammatical rules and therefore 'know' that of the two sentences below, only A is grammatically correct.

    A: They regularly watch TV.
    B: They watch regularly TV.

Chomsky (1986) explained that this 'knowledge' is largely 'tacit' and therefore generally inaccessible to consciousness. This explains why many native speakers are not able to explain their preference of sentence A over B. Some might know that there is a grammatical rule that forbids inserting an element between a verb and an object. Only those who are familiar with the principles and parameters of a particular language (see section 3.3.1) are likely to know the precise rule which states rather abstractly that the value for the case assignment parameter in English is strict adjacency. Although not everybody 'knows' the accurate rule, speakers can learn and understand them. The relationship between knowledge about language and proficiency has been extensively researched.

9.2.2 Teaching knowledge about language

Hawkins (1999) relates the inability to read in the mother tongue to one's knowledge of how language works. Reading (as well as listening) requires pupils to predict words and structures. Poor readers lack this syntactical knowledge and therefore do not know what words are likely to follow others. Pupils who read in a second language have the same problem initially: they cannot anticipate because they do not know what words are likely to follow others.

Educationalists and linguists generally agree that pupils draw on their mother tongue and their knowledge of how this language works when they learn a foreign language. They can thereby consolidate their knowledge about language. Hawkins (1999) gives concrete examples that show how French and English students who learned Spanish drew on their first language. The French speakers expected nouns to be marked by gender. They even assumed that they had the same gender as in French. They thought, for example, that the words for 'silence' and 'group', masculine in French, were also masculine in Spanish. The English students had no such expectations and found the matter of gender confusing and difficult to grasp. (Nouns are not marked by gender in English.)

Findings from the early Primary French pilot project in England (Burstall *et al.* 1974) also pointed to a link between KAL and foreign language learning. The researchers found that the boys fell behind after two or three years of learning French. They explained this problem by their lack of understanding of how language works. As Luc (1992: 28, mentioned in Hawkins, 1999: 130) wrote:

> as soon as the child goes beyond common places and stereotypes . . . greetings, introductions, expressing preferences . . . where he does not have to construct a sentence but only to repeat what has been learned as a chunk, great difficulties appear . . . either the child cannot say anything . . . or else he models what he wants to say precisely on the way it would be said in (the mother tongue) . . .. What he lacks essentially is a correct idea of how the foreign language works, *notably of how it relates to the mother tongue, which, for most children brought up in a monolingual environment, offers the only possible reference point.*
>
> (Hawkins' translation and emphasis)

Many teachers and students make similar comments. Pupils apparently find it difficult to generate new sentences since they lack an understanding of the underlying structure of the language. For example, they might 'know' a set phrase such as *'J'ai un frère'*, but they might be unable to form the sentence *'J'ai une sœur'* or to deduce the meaning of *'J'ai'*. Many educationalists therefore suggest teaching pupils explicitly how a foreign language works. The popularity of this idea has changed over time.

John Locke's (1690) statement 'French should be talked into the child. Grammar is only for those who have the language already' influenced much foreign language teaching (Lock, mentioned in Hawkins, 1999: 131). A similar idea was voiced 200 years later by Gouin (1894), the father of the 'natural method'. He observed his two-and-a-half-year-old nephew acquire his mother tongue without any instruction and concluded that the best way to learn a second language was to do it in a natural way, like a child. A colleague corrected him and explained that comparing foreign language learners to children meant not acknowledging the wealth of knowledge that adults bring to the learning process. Nevertheless, the belief spread widely that foreign language teaching consisted largely of providing input which learners eventually use to produce language. This assumption was revived by Chomsky's concept of LAD that did not make formal learning or feedback a necessary condition for learning a first language. Though Chomsky did not speak about foreign language learning, many educationalists believed that the LAD plays some role in the process of learning a second language. Talking about the language and teaching grammar were therefore excluded in Communicative Language Teaching (see section 4.2.5).

When Hawkins, the 'father' of language awareness, proposed adding time for explicit reflection on the mother tongue and on foreign languages to the school curriculum, his ideas were considered heresy. Many educationalists feared that this meant a return to the old-fashioned teaching of grammar such as in the Grammar-Translation method. However, Hawkins had no such thing in mind.

9.2.3 Language awareness

Language awareness has been loosely defined as 'a person's sensitivity to and conscious awareness of the nature of language and its role in human life' (Donmall, 1985: 7). Language awareness programmes sensitize pupils to the nature, purposes and structure of languages by making explicit the knowledge they implicitly possess through their experience of language use. They 'educate the ear' (Hawkins, 1987) and offer 'a forum where language diversity can be discussed' (Hawkins, 1984: 4). Most programmes emphasize affective and cognitive aspects: they encourage the development of positive attitudes to languages and language learning and foster knowledge about language. Pupils' reflections on the use of language strengthen their understanding of the structure and concept of that language, improve basic literacy and enable them to transfer knowledge from one language to another. The reflections on language strengthen pupils' understanding of the structure and concept of language, promote basic literacy and enable them to transfer knowledge from one language to another. As such the teaching of the mother tongue and of foreign languages complement and enhance each other (Johnstone, 1994).

Hawkins's (1999) *Language Awareness Model* has five essential elements and is broader than *knowledge about language*:

- mastery of the mother tongue
- examination of how languages work and are used in society
- education of the ear (e.g. developing listening skills)
- awakening to languages (i.e. creating positive attitudes, considering differences as interesting and not threatening; opening up of new and culturally diverse experiences in and outside the classroom)
- learning how to learn the foreign language.

Most practitioners would now agree that knowledge about language and grammar are an integral part of a language and that it therefore makes little sense to do away with this aspect in language lessons (Jones and Coffey, 2006: 32). This new understanding helps explain the implementation of KAL and language awareness in many curricula, for example in the KS2 framework for languages (DfES, 2005a).

Below I outline different aspects of KAL that can be taught at primary school.

9.3 Different aspects of knowledge about language

According to Mariani (1992), knowing about the nature of language means realizing that a language is both a formal system with rules and a flexible means to communicate. This knowledge enables learners to speak accurately and appropriately, thus to choose utterances that take account of the interlocutors and the situation at hand. Like many others,

Mariani suggests that teachers should develop the learners' understanding of language as a system, of language use and of the learning process. These elements are included in Hawkins's 'language awareness' programme.

9.3.1 Learning languages and understanding the learning process

At a time when learner autonomy and independence pervade the majority of documents on FL teaching, many language programmes aim to help pupils develop some understanding of the language learning process, for example of the ways in which they interpret and produce language. This knowledge helps them realize that they can make sense of a text even if they do not understand every single word.

Many practitioners highlight the importance of strategy development. Research findings have highlighted the relationship between effective strategy use and 'good language learners'. In Chapter 11, I present activities and teaching approaches that promote the development of language learning strategies.

9.3.2 Language variation according to the context, the user and time

To communicate effectively, pupils need to master some sociolinguistic and pragmatic elements. They need to realize that people who speak the same language can differ because of their accent or dialect and that those who speak different languages might also use different scripts. They will learn that speakers make deliberate choices in terms of styles, registers and genres in order to communicate in socially and culturally appropriate ways. For example, they respect conventions and the use of the formal '*vous*' and the informal '*tu*'.

Teachers help pupils understand how language use varies according to the context and the user by introducing them to texts in a range of styles, registers and genres and by helping them to correctly identify the type of text and the critical features characterizing it.

There are several ways in which teachers can foster pupils' understanding of the variations of language use over time. A comparison of similar words and analyses of their etymology can initiate some knowledge of language families. This work, in turn, could open up the possibility of cross-curricular links with History and Geography (e.g. on migration). An illustration of change in progress is the creation of new words (e.g. *texting*, *CD-ROM*) and the use of borrowed words (e.g. *un mel*, French for email). More advanced learners could compare the vocabulary used in texts written in different centuries, for example plays by Shakespeare and Harold Pinter.

9.3.3 Language as a system

Pupils need to develop their understanding of language-specific rules and to learn to apply these rules when producing new language. The KS2 framework for languages (DfES, 2005a) outlines the following learning objectives. All pupils should learn:

- to identify sounds and letters which are similar to and different from English in spoken and written forms
- to discriminate vowels and consonants
- to identify syllables
- to reflect on phoneme–grapheme correspondences
- to learn some basic spellings
- to classify words into word classes
- to understand and use question forms and negatives.

In addition, pupils in Year 5 and 6 should strengthen their knowledge of word order; recognize some basic aspects of agreement (e.g. gender, singular/plural, pronoun/verb) and come to understand the role of intonation and punctuation.

In chapters 6 and 7, I have given examples of activities that teachers can carry out to help pupils practise spelling and develop their understanding of sounds, syllables and the sound-letter correspondence. In the following sections I concentrate on vowels and consonants, word classes, gender, agreement of nouns, verbs and adjectives and syntax.

9.4 Teaching knowledge about language

As seen in Chapter 4, neo-communicative approaches emphasize form-focused teaching in an overall meaning-based context. In other words, teachers generally focus on meaning but they turn pupils' attention to form, for example, when they encounter difficulties with spellings or grammatical structures in interactions. This idea has been expressed as follows in the training handbook for teachers: 'Children's growing understanding of how language works will develop from interaction with and in the new language. It will arise through reflection and observation during the course of language learning activities' (CiLT and NACELL, 2006: module 3, p. 27).

The comparison of words, structures and sentences in the foreign language and mother tongue is an ideal starting point to help pupils see and discuss similarities and differences in the ways languages work. When teachers draw pupils' attention to grammatical points and introduce simple grammatical rules, they will need to define a relevant and meaningful context. For example, they could introduce possessive pronouns with pets as in *mon chat/ ma chienne/mes poissons*, elicit their meaning, ask pupils to hypothesize about the reasons behind the variations and explain the changes. Once they have introduced the grammatical points and given many examples demonstrating the use of rules, they provide pupils with a range of opportunities to apply them and to generate new sentences. It is important that they praise pupils for their attempts at production, their spontaneous use of grammatical rules and their reflection on language use.

Next I look at ways of developing pupils' knowledge of vowels and consonants, word classes, gender, agreements and syntax.

9.4.1 Working on vowels and consonants

The concept of vowels and consonants should already be clear to pupils from their lessons in the mother tongue but work in the foreign language offers an excellent opportunity to revisit and reinforce the concept.

Poems or songs in the foreign language that are about consonants or vowels are an ideal starting point. The French poem 'Voyelles' (Example 9.1) revisits vowels and practises the sound–letter correspondence in an efficient way. The poem in Example 9.2 encourages the reader to think about associations between sounds and colours. Pupils can use it as a template for writing their own poem.

Example 9.1 'Voyelles'	**Example 9.2 'Voyelles', Rimbaud (MEN, 1986: 35)**
Voyelles	**Voyelles**
A, E, I, O, U	A noir
A, A, A, j'ai du chocolat	E blanc
E, E, E, je vais le manger	I rouge
I, I, I, il est trop petit	U vert
O, O, O, j'en veux un plus gros	O bleu
U, U, U, y en a déjà plus!!!!	Voyelles

Example 9.3 is a German song that asks singers to substitute all vowels with one particular one, for example with 'a', so that the song sounds 'Chinese'. This highly enjoyable and creative activity is ideal to practise sound–letter correspondences. It can be done as a reading exercise but is even more challenging without any visual support.

Example 9.3 'Drei Chinesen mit dem Kontrabass:' Change all vowels in the song to the same one

Drei Chinesen mit dem Kontrabass

Drei Chinesen mit dem Kontrabass,
saßen auf der Straße
und erzählten sich was.
Da kam die Polizei:
Ja was ist denn das?
Drei Chinesen mit dem Kontrabass.

Other possible exercises to reinforce vowels and consonants are identification exercises (Chapter 7, section 7.4.1) or quizzes. For example, the teacher could say: 'I am thinking of a French word for an animal with four legs. It is tall and can run fast. The word has four consonants and two vowels, "e" and "a". Who knows which word I am thinking of?' (The word is *cheval.*)

Teachers should draw on pupils' knowledge of consonants and vowels when they explain rules. For example, pupils are less likely to forget or misplace the apostrophe in *j'habite* or *l'éléphant* if they know that a word ending in a vowel cannot be followed by a word beginning with a vowel or the letter 'h'.

9.4.2 Word classes

Pupils should be familiar with verbs, nouns, adjectives, adverbs or prepositions from their lessons in the mother tongue. In order to help pupils understand and memorize word classes, teachers could encourage the creation of visual, aural and physical associations. For example, they can ask pupils to represent concrete or abstract nouns with pictures or symbols and verbs with actions. In order to reinforce the knowledge, many teachers ask pupils to classify words into word classes (e.g. through colour-coding). In Example 9.4 pupils must select the path consisting only of adjectives (path 2). The exercise is challenging since it requires a good knowledge of vocabulary and agreements (e.g. *Fraise* is not the feminine form of *frais.* Like *feu,* it is a noun).

Example 9.4 Le chat se promène uniquement sur un chemin plein d'adjectifs. Comment arrive-t-il chez la souris? (The puzzle is inspired by Jouannetaud (2002a))

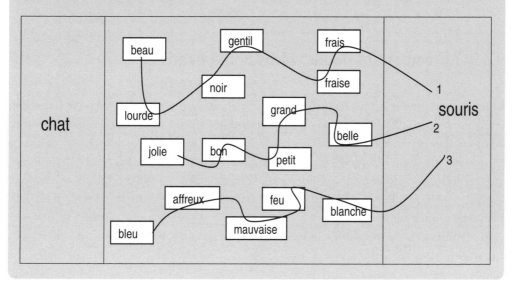

9.4.3 Gender

In order to understand the principle of agreement pupils have to understand the concept of gender and know the gender of nouns (i.e. in the French language adjectives agree with the gender of the noun they qualify). Some languages such as German have three genders (masculine, feminine and neuter); others such as French have only two. Genders are attributed randomly and can therefore be different in different languages. Pupils who have learned that the word 'sun' is masculine and 'moon' is feminine in French, Spanish and Italian might be astonished to hear that it is the opposite way round in German (e.g. *le soleil, die Sonne, la luna, der Mond*).

The concept of gender can be difficult to grasp especially when pupils' first language is not marked by grammatical gender. This is the case, for example, for English.

> **Example 9.5 Relie les noms et les articles**
>
> | | autobus |
> | un | vélo |
> | | moto |
> | | avion |
> | une | locomotive |
> | | wagon |
> | | auto |

Traditionally, pupils learn genders in vocabulary lists with articles put in front of words. Some teachers colour-code the words to help pupils memorize the article. To practise gender, pupils can find the article of particular words or do classification exercises (Example 9.5).

9.4.4 Agreement of nouns, verbs and adjectives

Nouns

Knowledge of gender is a prerequisite to learning about agreement. To encourage reflection, teachers can focus pupils' attention on word endings. Pupils generally know what plurals are and how they are formed in their mother tongue. The formation of plurals for nouns in French seems to be easy to grasp for English children: as in English many nouns (though not all) end with an –s. However, the phoneme [s] in 'dogs' is clearly audible while the 's' in *chiens, chats* or *tigres* is not. Pupils learn some pronunciation rules: in French, the letter 's' at the end of a word is often silent.

It becomes slightly more difficult in Italian where singular masculine nouns end in 'o' in the singular and in 'i' in the plural (e.g. *il ragazzo, i ragazzi*) and where singular feminine nouns ending in 'a' end in 'e' (e.g. *la ragazza, le ragazze*). The formation of plurals is more complex in inflected languages like German where the ending of nouns in the plural depends on the case (For example, *Die Pferde sind im Stall. Ich gebe den Pferden Heu.* The horses are in the stable. I give the horses some hay. Comparing the formation of plurals in several languages reveals that not every language functions in the same way (Cheater and Farren, 2001).

In order to practise plurals, teachers can suggest the following exercises:

- discriminate between singulars and plurals, for example by underlining the words in different colours
- match words in the singular with those in the plural
- find the plural (or the singular) of words (Example 9.6)
- complete a gap-filling exercise (Example 9.7).

The level of complexity of these four exercises increases each time. The pupils recognize plurals and singulars in the first two types but have to produce the correct forms in Example 9.6. In Example 9.7 they need to read and understand the sentence, decide on the meaning of the missing word, know the spelling of it and find the correct plural. This cognitively demanding exercise requires a good grasp of language and an almost automatic processing of plural formation.

Example 9.6 Trovare il plurale

Trovare il plurale

il cavallo _____   il gatto _____
il cane _____   il maiale _____

Example 9.7 Trouve les mots

Trouve les mots

Le matin, j'ai faim. Je mange deux _____ et je bois deux _____ de lait.
Je vais à l'école. Je lis deux _____ et j'écris des _____.
A la récré, je joue avec mes _____.

Verbs

Children need to know verbs in order to 'do' something with nouns and to begin to express themselves in a meaningful way. Teaching pupils verbs can be more complicated than teaching nouns.

Comparing the use of verbs in different languages makes pupils realize that different languages express the same ideas in different ways. English people say 'My name is James', the Italians '*Mi chiamo Alberto*', the Germans '*Ich heiße Anna*' and the Japanese '*Watashi wa Akira desu*'. Through such examples pupils understand that things cannot always be translated literally from one language into another.

Teachers tend to introduce pupils to the first-person singular and then the second and third singular. The latter are helpful to form questions. This enables pupils to practise questions and answers in short structured dialogues such as:

¿Cómo se llamo?
Me llamo Juan.

In Years 5 and 6 many teachers introduce pupils to one or more tenses, generally a past and a future tense.

Pupils seldom conjugate verbs in primary schools. Teachers tend to offer some practice through structured dialogues, gap-filling or sentence transformation exercises. Below is the sequence that a secondary German teacher used to teach relevant verbs to a Year 5 class in West Hill Primary (Chapter 5). Note that pupils learn to use the verbs in questions and answers from the beginning.

- First lesson: pupils learn 'Ich heiße . . . ' and 'Wie heißt du?'
- Second lesson: 'Ich wohne in'; 'Wo wohnst du?'
- Third lesson: 'Ich bin . . .' ; 'Wie alt bist du?'
- Fourth lesson: 'Ich wohne in'; 'Wo wohnst du?' and the three questions above in the third person.
- Fifth lesson: Ich habe . . . Schwestern . . . Brüder . . . Vater . . . Mutter; Du hast . . . ; Er/Sie hat . . .
- Sixth lesson: Pupils revisit all questions in the third person in a written text.

In the sixth lesson she presented a text about Bart Simpson which was based on the same vocabulary. The text was written in the third person and pupils had to change it into the first person, as seen in Example 9.8. Pupils had to change the pronouns and verbs (which the teacher had underlined) and to copy-write all other words. The secondary teacher designed a poster with the sentence structures and vocabulary mentioned above in order to create a resource for the primary teacher.

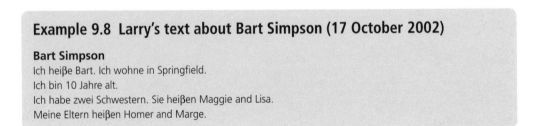

Example 9.8 Larry's text about Bart Simpson (17 October 2002)

Bart Simpson
Ich heiße Bart. Ich wohne in Springfield.
Ich bin 10 Jahre alt.
Ich habe zwei Schwestern. Sie heißen Maggie and Lisa.
Meine Eltern heißen Homer and Marge.

The class teacher decided to draw on this text and made pupils write an autobiographical account. Pupils substituted names, ages, numbers and added the appropriate information about siblings and parents. They then sent their text to their Swiss German pen-pals.

The fact that they were able to produce some meaningful writing in German six weeks into their German lessons made all the pupils proud. They agreed that it was challenging but worth the effort.

Adjectives

'Big' and 'small' seem to be among the first adjectives taught to beginning learners. Several reasons explain why these words can be easy to learn: these adjectives are placed in front of the noun in English, French, Spanish or Italian; they are regular and most endings are clearly audible (e.g. *une grande poupée*). Inflected languages like German pose some problems since the agreements depend on the gender and the case. Teachers use a number of drills to practise adjectival agreements; these include matching, gap-filling and sentence transformation exercises.

9.4.5 Syntax

Pupils learn that word order is language-specific. In Latin, for example, the subject does not have to be at the beginning of a sentence and the verb can be placed in any position. They also learn that most adjectives are placed after the nouns in French unlike English.

Pupils are likely to learn to produce negative and interrogative sentences. Teachers should not issue simple rules bereft of explanation. For example, when working on the structure of negative sentences in French, they should not simply state that the words *ne* and *pas* are placed before and after a verb but they should furnish pupils with the correct rule: *ne* comes after the subject (e.g. noun or pronoun) and *pas* after the verb (auxiliary) (e.g. *il n'a pas voulu venir*).

When speaking about interrogative sentences teachers can draw the pupils' attention to the language-specific punctuation. Pupils discover, for example, how questions marks are used (e.g. in Spanish) and how direct speech is indicated by speech marks. They should be taught to recognize how punctuation helps articulate meaning and shape intonation.

Typical exercises used to practise word order, negative and affirmative sentences consist of the following:

- games (e.g. produce the longest sentence you can think of by adding adjectives, adverbs or conjunctions)
- sentence transformation exercises
- scrambled sentences (Example 9.9).

Example 9.9 Mets les mots dans le bon ordre

? ami joue que basket Est-ce l' de au Paul

9.5 Impact of teaching knowledge about language

The question remains whether the teaching of KAL makes pupils better language learners and users. Some research has been done on the effectiveness of language awareness approaches. As seen in 9.2.3 KAL is a part of these programmes. In the 1970s, language awareness was introduced in foreign language teaching in secondary schools. The model was discarded in the 1990s because the benefits were 'too slight to justify the time spent on the course' (DfEE, 1990: 16).

More recently, a language awareness programme called Evlang (*Eveil aux langues*/ Awakening to languages) was introduced to 160 primary schools in France (including Réunion Island), Austria, Switzerland, Italy and Spain from 1999 to 2001. The structured programme resembled the language awareness approach implemented in England in the 1970s. It was also based on Hawkins (1987) but focused more on attitudinal outcomes and cultural awareness, and less on KAL. Evlang was underpinned by social constructivism and boosted with high expectations.

Candelier *et al.* (2003) found that Evlang was not entirely successful. It had some of the expected effects on the development of metalinguistic and metacommunicative skills but pupils did not transfer their skills to the first language. The curriculum increased pupils' motivation but had only a limited impact on their attitudes. It had a positive effect on their sense of linguistic and cultural diversity but there was no evidence that pupils developed new perspectives on target languages and cultures. These researchers concluded that Evlang has not been entirely successful in its aim to develop language awareness and positive attitudes. Genelot and Tupin (2001), on the other hand, reported that pupils had developed their knowledge about language. In particular, they had learned to recognize different languages and to identify differences between languages; understood that alphabets and gender differ according to the particular language; discovered that languages borrow words from each other and, finally, had improved their knowledge of how to learn languages.

I conclude that it seems clear from a theoretical perspective that there is a relationship between knowledge about language, mother tongue and foreign language. It is reasonable to assume that pupils who have developed some understanding of how a foreign language works find it easier to produce meaningful and accurate utterances.

9.6 Main points to remember

Developing pupils' knowledge about language means developing their:

- understanding of the language-learning process
- understanding that language varies according to context, time and users
- understanding of language as a system.

You develop pupils' understanding of the learning process when you help them reflect on how they learn and develop language learning strategies.

You develop their understanding of language use when you present them with a range of meaningful contexts where they can use the foreign language.

You develop their understanding of how the foreign language 'works' when you help them:

- identify and discriminate sounds and letters
- identify and discriminate vowels and consonants
- identify phoneme–grapheme correspondences
- practise basic spellings
- recognize verbs, nouns, adjectives (and other word classes in a second instance)
- understand and practise agreements of nouns, verbs and adjectives
- produce affirmative, negative and interrogative sentences.

Some useful types of exercise are: identification; classification; sentence completion; sentence formation and transformation; structured dialogues and gap-filling. Note that these drills are best in sharp spurts and that one should focus on form in a meaningful context.

10 Developing Intercultural Competence

Chapter Outline

10.1 Introduction

Until 30 years ago, language learning meant the development of communicative competence (see Chapter 4). Pupils learned some basic skills that they could use, for example, as tourists, in casual encounters with 'foreigners'. With the development of global markets, many people have to live abroad for work purposes. Schools need to teach students to become competent and sensitive social actors in a multilingual and multicultural society.

Many people agree that one cannot be competent in a language without understanding the culture that has influenced it. Jones and Coffey (2006) describe language as 'a cultural code which embodies specific world-views and historically shaped behaviours and preferences' (p. 138). The following example illustrates the relationships between language and culture. Some Indian languages have a variety of words for the concept 'cousin'. The correct choice depends on the position of this person in relation to other family members implicitly mentioned in a conversation. The fact that the choice depends on the family relationship is evidence of its importance in these cultures. If one understands language as social practice, then culture becomes the very core of language teaching (Kramsch, 1993).

In the 1970s the European Council recommended the incorporation of an intercultural perspective in education in order to increase pupils' awareness of their own culture and identity; to develop awareness of and respect for cultural diversity and to promote openness, empathy and tolerance (Hélot and Young, 2005). Many people hold that primary school children are more open to, and have less fixed ideas on cultural differences. It is therefore a good time to introduce pupils to different cultures at an early age.

Intercultural learning involves helping pupils make relationships between their own and the target culture by drawing their attention to similarities and differences and by giving them the opportunity to express their views, however stereotyped. Stereotypes can be a good starting point for discussions about cultures and reflections on one's perspective, which can in turn foster cultural awareness.

Food for thought

- How do you define 'culture'?
- Think about your own experience of learning languages. What importance was given to intercultural learning? What, if any, aspects of culture were you introduced to?
- What effect did this 'intercultural learning' have on your beliefs, values and behaviour?

In this chapter, I define the concept 'culture', outline Byram's (1999) concept of intercultural competence and present concrete and authentic activities that can be used to develop pupils' understanding of linguistic and cultural diversity and their knowledge of cultural artefacts, traditions and social practices.

10.2 Culture and intercultural competence

It is important to clarify the meaning of culture before defining what it means to be 'interculturally competent'.

10.2.1 What is culture?

The word 'culture' comes from the Latin root *colere*, to inhabit, cultivate or honour. The word refers in general to human activity (Wikipedia). Jenks (1993) provides four different definitions of 'culture'.

1. A culture can be synonymous with a particular country, region, religion, civilization or nationality or can correspond to several of these. In that sense, it is an 'embodied and collective category' and invokes a state of intellectual or moral development. An example is the early Mayan civilization.
2. Culture can be understood as a person's cognitive state of mind (e.g. 'the cultured person').
3. Culture can be interpreted as a descriptive category relating to the collection of arts and intellectual work (e.g. literature) within any one society.
4. Culture, understood as a 'social category', describes the way of life and a set of social practices shared by the members of a group. These members shape and are shaped by particular habits, attitudes, beliefs, values and behaviours.

These different interpretations are related: a civilization is composed of cultured individuals who express their beliefs and customs through social practices, art, philosophy or literature.

Some people distinguish between Culture with a capital C, and culture with a lower case c. Culture with a capital C refers to the first three definitions, hence, to historical and national events, famous figures and artefacts (Jones and Coffey, 2006: 141, 2). Celebrating these national emblems brings people together and provides them with a sense of shared identity and collective consciousness.

Culture with a small c corresponds to the day-to-day habits and routines of the members of a group, such as eating, dressing or greeting rituals. This definition corresponds to Jenks's fourth interpretation. Most of these habits have only been created recently but give the illusion of longstanding traditions which have bound people or a group together. Pupils need to understand that practices and customs are not 'natural' happenings or 'innate characteristics of a group'. Rather, they have been constructed for particular purposes. Understanding the historical, social, political and geographical dimensions of cultural constructs encourages them to question their own beliefs and helps them understand where they come from. This, in turn, enables them to develop a more centred sense of self and to define their position in the world in relation to their own cultural context.

10.2.2 Intercultural competence

Intercultural competence needs to be distinguished from cultural awareness and cultural competence.

Developing *cultural awareness* means raising people's awareness and developing an understanding of their own culture and those of others. It does not imply the ability to operate effectively cross-culturally.

Cultural competence goes beyond cultural awareness and usually involves a change of one's attitudes and values. It is a relatively recent term mainly used in the United States in the fields of social work, health care and education. It refers to a person's sensitivity to ethnic, linguistic, religious and class differences which enables them to function effectively in different cultural contexts and to provide effective services to people of another culture. Culturally competent people accept and respect differences between and within cultures and understand the dynamics of difference.

In the field of education it means, for example, that teachers understand how reading habits vary between cultures. In England, story books are traditionally read to and with children who are not competent readers. This is not the case in other cultures. Gregory (1996, 2008) tells the story of a Chinese boy whose grandfather refused to give him a book on the grounds that he could not read it yet. He explained that one can only possess books once one has mastered the skill of reading. Teachers who understand habits of their own culture and those of others react appropriately in such situations.

Most people relate *intercultural competence* to the work of Byram (1999, 2002) who has defined this competence as a set of *savoirs*:

1. *savoir être* refers to 'attitudes'. Pupils learn to abandon ethnocentric attitudes towards other cultures and develop curiosity, openness and some interest in other languages and cultures. They show some understanding of the differences and relationships between their own and other cultures. They accept another person's perspective as normal and their own as strange when seen from the other's perspective.
2. *savoir* refers to 'knowledge'. Pupils need to familiarize themselves with the practices and cultural artefacts that natives use as a system of reference to communicate and to share beliefs and meanings. These insights into the way of life of the target culture enable the pupils to act socially and culturally appropriately.
3. *savoir apprendre/comprendre* refers to the 'skills' of observing, enquiring, analysing and interpreting which are required to understand events (or documents). Pupils need to suspend value judgements based on their own cultural background, detach themselves from their own culture and understand how people of another culture perceive and experience their world (Beacco and Byram, 2003).
4. *savoir faire/s'engager* is the ability to draw on the other three *savoirs* and to use them in authentic interactions with people of other languages and cultures. It requires a critical awareness and understanding of one's own and other cultures, and an ability to negotiate a new object that is acceptable to both cultures, hence an 'intercultural' object.

The development of intercultural competence enables pupils to increase their understanding of their own culture and 'cultural selves' as well as those of others. This understanding can help them act sensitively and culturally appropriately. Intercultural competence thus goes beyond a body of knowledge. It includes a set of practices requiring knowledge, attitudes and skills such as:

- observing and identifying
- comparing and contrasting
- dealing with or tolerating ambiguity
- accepting difference
- decentring and taking the perspective of somebody else
- interpreting messages and limiting the possibility of misinterpretation
- defending one's own point of view while acknowledging the legitimacy of those of others.

10.3 Developing intercultural competence

Byram and Doyé (1999) hold that primary school children are able to develop *savoir être, savoir* and *savoir faire*. It requires pupils to distance themselves from their own culture, to reflect on it, to share their interpretations with people of other cultures and to define appropriate means of acting. Intercultural competence is therefore constructed in interactions with people from other communities, and through reflection on experienced similarities and differences (Haramboure and Bonnet-Falandry, 2007). In primary schools, such interactions can occur with both actual and virtual members of another community, for example with classmates from diverse sociocultural backgrounds, or with pen-pals in another country. They can happen in and outside school, on a regular basis as well as on special occasions such as a concert, a festival or the European Day of Languages.

Acknowledging language diversity in a school through ad hoc references to words and cultures and tokenistic celebrations of festivals are important initial steps to raise children's *awareness* of other cultures and languages, but they are not enough to help them understand their own cultural selves. The development of intercultural competence is challenging and requires teachers to develop a structured programme with relevant and appropriate contents and activities that enable pupils to discover a range of perspectives and to develop a critical and analytical understanding of their own and other cultures. Teachers need to develop children's knowledge as well as their attitudes and skills. The component *savoir* seems to be easier to develop than *savoir être* and *savoir comprendre*. This is reflected, for example, in the objectives of the KS2 framework for languages (DfES, 2005a): pupils in Years 3 and 4 are to familiarize themselves with linguistic diversity, to come to know celebrations and festivals and to reflect on different languages and cultures. (These objectives seem to turn around the development of cultural awareness.) Only the older pupils are to work on attitudes (e.g. prejudice) and skills (e.g. interpreting messages).

In the following sections, I give concrete examples of ways in which primary teachers in different countries have raised pupils' awareness of language and cultural diversity, developed their knowledge of culture (both with a capital C and small c) and began to work on their *savoir être* and *savoir comprendre*.

Case study: The Didenheim Project

Hélot and Young (2005) report on an innovative project in a small rural school in Didenheim (Alsace) with an intake of 37 per cent of pupils of non-French origin. Their lack of motivation to learn German and an increase in racist incidents at school led teachers to start a programme on 'Languages and Cultures' for the first three year groups. The objectives were formulated as follows:

> to bring the children into contact with other languages and to sensitize them to the use of languages, to familiarize the children with other cultures through the presentation of festivals, traditions, costumes, geography . . . and last but not least to promote the acceptance of differences, to learn about others and to attempt to break down stereotypical misconceptions.

Pupils were introduced to 18 different languages including among others Arabic, Polish, Alsatian, Malay, Mandarin, Serbo-Croat and Sign Language. Sessions were mostly led by parents who had prepared them in collaboration with teachers. The presenters talked about geography, history and lifestyles; presented their personal histories of migration; taught simple phrases and songs; told traditional stories or prepared typical food.

Hélot and Young (2005) indicate that the project was beneficial for pupils, parents and teachers. Pupils reacted enthusiastically. Their confidence and self-esteem increased and they became more open towards other cultures. They learned some words in new languages and, by comparing these words with words in their own language, developed some knowledge about language. Teachers made closer links with the local communities and parents from different backgrounds came to know each other. The former gained a greater understanding of the linguistic and cultural background of their pupils and developed a deeper understanding of bilingualism. Sustained dialogue with parents and support of the home languages helped the teachers reduce the distance between home and school culture. They developed a global vision and found their own pedagogical solutions to intolerance.

Not every school has the means to set up a project like the school in Didenheim. But teachers can tap into the mix of language and cultural resources of their own class, invite native speakers into the classroom or rely on television programmes, books, newspapers or websites to familiarize children with other languages and cultures and develop some understanding of their own culture and that of others. In the next sections I describe some of the *savoir*, attitudes and skills that teachers can begin to develop with pupils in primary schools.

10.3.1 Discovering linguistic and cultural diversity

In order to raise *cultural and linguistic awareness* teachers should start with the pupils in their own classroom. Thanks to the daily (authentic) contacts with their classmates or opportunities to meet children of other cultures on holiday, pupils experience various cultures and slowly learn what it means to be a member of a different culture (Haramboure, 2007). Apart from taking an interest in different habits, pupils might also share their experiences of learning and using languages. They might discuss what language they speak to whom and explain why and how they have learned particular languages. Teachers can assist pupils in the construction of their knowledge by encouraging such conversations, comparisons and reflections.

When working with children aged 7 to 11, I made pupils think about learning, knowing and using a language by giving them a sheet with pictures of computers of different sizes. Each computer represented a language. It was fascinating to see how they matched their languages to the computers. Many automatically linked the biggest computer to their mother tongue; others associated it with the language used most which was not necessarily their first language. Some used the smallest computer to indicate that they knew a few words of a language; others refused to mention languages in which they did not have some minimum proficiency. The idea of using computers (as representing different parts of the brain) led to interesting discussions on pupils' perceptions of how languages are learned.

Once teachers have explored the language and cultural backgrounds of the pupils in the classroom, they can move on to the linguistic and cultural diversity in the whole school and the wider community. As seen in Chapter 2, the teachers in Portway Primary School foster tolerance, respect and friendly relationships in a range of ways.

A welcome poster (Figure 10.1) compiling the range of languages spoken at school and a display of original costumes provide a feeling that language and cultural diversity are appreciated and celebrated (see Chapter 2, Figures 2.4, 2.5 and 2.6).

Signposts in community languages are displayed anywhere in the school. The aim is to familiarize children with different languages and scripts. Teachers help pupils learn some greetings and numbers in community languages, particularly those spoken by their classmates. To help them do this, they put up posters in each classroom with simple phrases of the 'language of the month' (e.g. Lithuanian, Bengali).

Teachers need to ensure that pupils understand that associating a language with a country may be correct but only in part. French, for example, is spoken in Francophone Africa, and is only one of many other languages spoken in France itself. As a result, pupils understand that France is both multilingual and multicultural and do not automatically relate 'the' French to white Europeans.

Cross-curricular work

Learning about languages and countries provides the teacher with rich opportunities for cross-curricular work. Below I give an example of how the teacher can explore a topic in Geography and make links with ICT and Mathematics.

A task in a Geography lesson could consist of organizing a visit to the target country in a 'good' season. Pupils would need to find ways of travelling from England to that country. This requires them to locate it on a map, familiarize themselves with the geographical features of the country (e.g. rivers, mountains, seaside), discover the main cities and identify airports and ports.

Pictures, books, travel guides and the internet give pupils access to information about the agriculture, architecture, national products and climate, which in turn provide them with an incentive for the visit. Keeping a record of the weather and discussing its consequences on the inhabitants and the agriculture help pupils find a possible period for the visit but, more importantly, enable them to view the country from the perspective of the locals. In addition, collecting and representing weather records reinforces the pupils' knowledge of drawing charts.

Anagrams are a good way of revising the names of countries, rivers or capitals. The exercise can be challenging but the teacher makes it easier by keeping to particular themes such as towns and regions as in the example below.

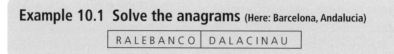

Example 10.1 Solve the anagrams (Here: Barcelona, Andalucia)

RALEBANCO | DALACINAU

10.3.2 Investigating the link between language and culture

The etymology of words can be a useful starting point to help pupils relate languages and cultures. An example, taken from Jones and Coffey (2006), illustrates the point. The Year 5

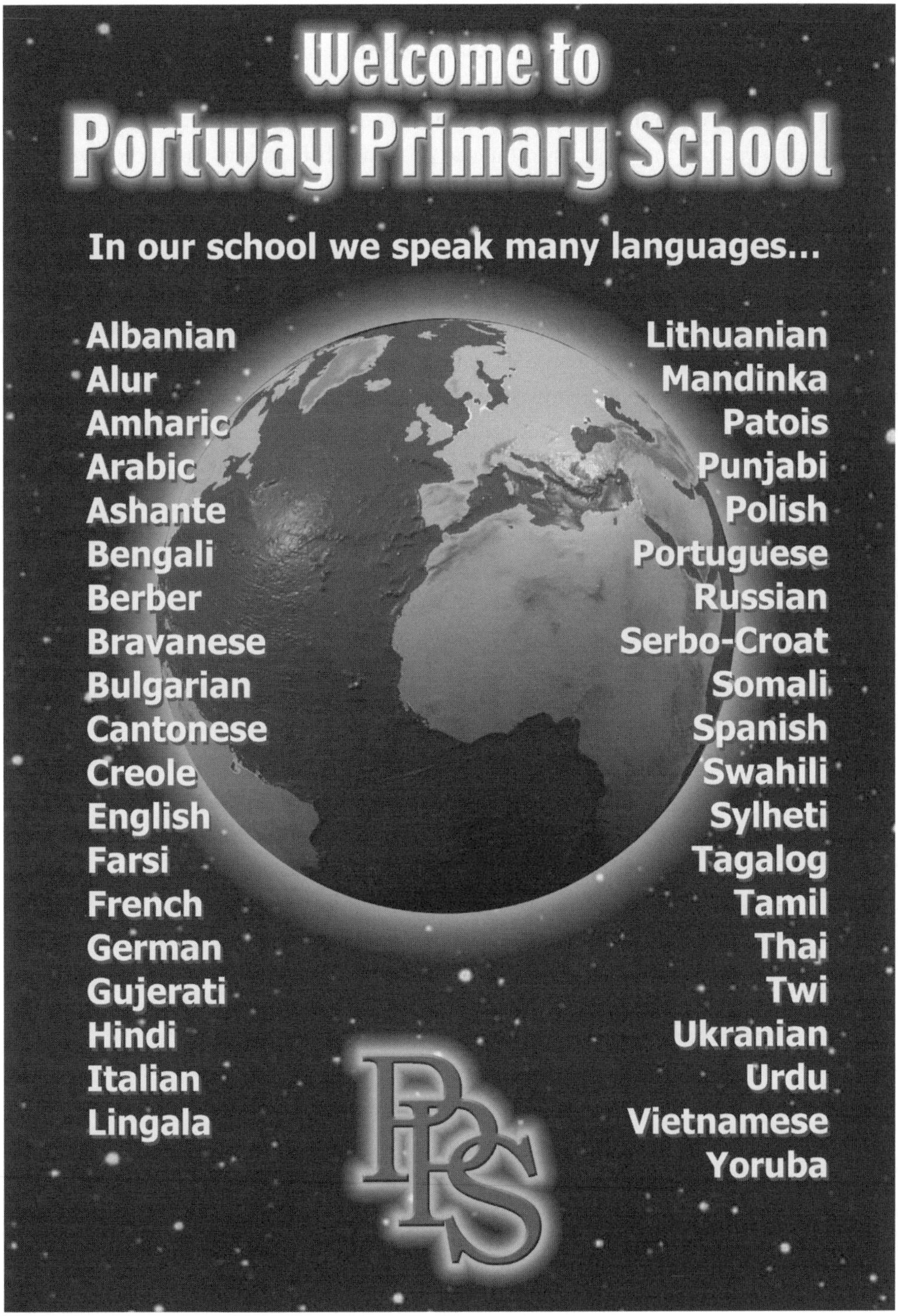

Figure 10.1 Languages poster.

pupils in a school in the West Midlands explored the origin of some Spanish words. They found that many words such as *algodón* (T-shirt), *arroz* (rice), *azucar* (sugar), *canela* (cinnamon) or *naranja* (orange) are derived from Arabic and go back to the expansion of Islam (711 to 1492) when the Arabs introduced these objects to Spain.

Becoming aware of the Moorish influence on Spanish food and products gives pupils an insider's perspective on the language and culture. They understand some aspects of the collective identity of 'Spanishness' and learn how Spanish people (possibly) perceive their language and culture. In terms of *intercultural competence*, they develop some *savoir être savoir* and *savoir apprendre*.

Using etymology and drawing pupils' attention to cognates has other advantages. The German teacher at West Hill Primary School (see Chapter 5) often encouraged children to find the meaning of a word by comparing the English and German versions. She believed that pupils' understanding of the common origins of words fostered an 'I-can-do-this' attitude. Apart from increasing their knowledge about languages and developing a good language learning strategy, pupils learned to draw on their linguistic skills and developed the feeling that language learning gets easier as the number of languages learned increases.

10.3.3 Discovering cultural artefacts

Many teachers aim to familiarize children with the Culture of a country. As seen in section 10.2.1, this includes national and historical events, famous people and artefacts or symbols which represent the country (e.g. local products, the language).

Some songs or poems have the potential to raise the pupils' cultural awareness. The song 'Sur le pont d'Avignon' (Example 10.2) draws on a distinctive feature of the town Avignon in France: the medieval bridge St Bénézet, originally 900 metres long, which has collapsed several times during floods and has not been repaired since 1668.

Example 10.2 'Sur le pont d'Avignon'

Sur le pont d'Avignon On y danse, on y danse, Sur le pont d'Avignon On y danse tous en rond.	*Children hold hands and dance in circle.*
Les messieurs font comme ça. Et puis encore comme ça.	*They stop and boys bow politely.* *They bow once again.*
Les demoiselles font comme ça. Et puis encore comme ça.	*Girls do a curtsy.* *Girls do another one.*
Les militaires/musiciens/etc.	*The soldiers salute, the musicians use their instruments etc.*

Project work and pen-pal links are ideal ways to make pupils think about their own culture and let them discover arts, crafts and products. Teachers and pupils can develop projects about particular cultural aspects and exchange information through letters, emails and videoconferencing. The children in West Hill Primary School exchanged writings, drawings and typical artefacts with a school in Japan. The presents they received from the pen pals (e.g. a Japanese fan, books, cards and paintings) were displayed in the corridors of the school (see Figure 6.1, p. 82).

The classes of Years 1 to 3 in Portway Primary School worked on a Performing Arts project with a Spanish school. The exchange of information and artefacts enabled pupils to develop their knowledge of both their own cultural heritage (e.g. paintings, dances and song) and that of the Spanish children. The comparisons about art and traditional music and dance led to discussions about similarities and differences in scripts, the use of musical instruments, the choice of colours and tools.

In Cardwell Primary School in London classes are named each year after sets such as writers, musicians, artists or explorers. This provides pupils with the opportunity to learn something about well-known people and their sociocultural and geographic background. In 2005/6, all classes were named after countries. The class of the language coordinator was the 'China class'.

Pupils learned about the geography, customs and languages; went on a trip to the Royal Academy to see the 'Three Emperors' exhibition; visited the Greenwich Observatory to learn about Chinese astrology; adopted a panda through the WWF and did a class assembly about Chinese New Year for the rest of the school. This included making and dancing in a lion

Figure 10.2 Chinese display.

costume. Each class did an assembly about their country and put up displays to share what they had learned.

Introducing pupils to national events (e.g. the French Revolution, Independence Day) is another popular way of developing their knowledge about another culture. These national 'emblems' convey a feeling of pride, identity and shared consciousness. Children learn when, how and why they are celebrated and discuss the similarities and differences between the ways in which people celebrate.

Experiencing festivals such as Diwali (Hindu), Id (Muslim), The Day of the Dead (Mexico) or Chinese New Year with all senses makes pupils feel that they have been part of them (Spielmann, 2000). As a result, they are more likely to develop intercultural competence. However, teachers need to make sure that they go beyond tokenistic celebrations of festivals.

10.3.4 Learning about routines and traditions

Next I turn to culture with a small c, and give some examples of how teachers can develop pupils' understanding of everyday routines, practices and festivals.

Pupils are generally eager to find out about the ways of life of children of the same age in other countries. They are interested in their hobbies, families and eating and dressing habits.

Links with other countries

Pen-pal links are once again an ideal method of developing *savoir*, *savoir être* and *savoir apprendre*. They provide pupils with an insider's perspective of the lives of their pals. This information satisfies their curiosity and, more importantly, can lead them to question their views on 'others'. This is necessary if they are to develop tolerance and respect. Depending on the location, pupils and teachers might even be able to visit each other.

The following example sheds some light on the insights that ten-year-old pupils attending a class in Luxembourg (Year 5) and West Hill Primary in England (Year 4) gained through their communications.

The first exchanges helped children to get to know each other and to build up a relationship. The pals asked each other questions about hobbies, favourite colours, books, sports and siblings and exchanged pictures of themselves at home and at school. Then they began to collect information about the rulers, flags, geographical features and sports facilities in their respective countries. They made all sort of comparisons, for example of nursery rhymes. The pictures of the classrooms were of particular interest and led to further inquiries about resources (e.g. position of desks, number of boards, use of ICT) or the school uniforms as shown in the examples below. The answers of the Luxembourgish children (translated into English) are displayed in italics.

Mike (UK): Why don't you wear uniforms? Because we do.
Patrick (Luxembourg): *Everything is different in England. People drive on the other side of the road, they have a different currency and do different things. That's why children might also wear uniforms there. (translation)*

| Larry (UK): | Why don't you hang your up bags with your coats on the hooks outside? |
| Yves (Luxembourg): | *Because the hook would break! Our bags are too heavy. But also because we need everything in the classroom at any time and we cannot leave the classroom each time we need to get a textbook or book.* |

The English pupils were particularly interested in their counterparts' bulky satchels. The Luxembourgish pupils justified the size by saying they had to carry home their textbooks, exercise books and files to do homework. The English pupils carefully studied the design of the classroom and discovered that there was room for a satchel to stand next to the desk. The fluorescent stripes seemed to indicate that children used to walk to and from school when it was dark. This led to more questions related to transport.

This example of the satchel shows that even a single object, when carefully studied, can provide pupils with many interesting perspectives into the life of children in other countries.

The children of both countries were interested in the daily school routines and classroom language. Through their German lessons, the English pupils knew that there is a formal and an informal way of addressing people in German and French. They learned that conventions and forms of politeness were similar in Luxembourgish.

A pen-pal exchange not only enables pupils to compare aspects of everyday life in different countries; it also helps them to reflect on their perceptions of their own culture and that of the 'other' culture. The developing understanding helps them review stereotypes. Excerpts of the conversations indicated that the Luxembourgish children seemed to believe that in England all buses, telephone boxes and postboxes were red and all taxis black. They thought it weird that steering wheels were on the *wrong* side and wondered whether all English children *really* had eggs and bacon for breakfast. One boy seemed to believe that English people liked wars. The questions asked, some of them displayed below, made the Luxembourgish children review their own perspectives and see England from the perspective of the English children.

Laura (Luxembourg):	*Why is the steering wheel on the right side in English cars?*
Anne (UK):	Because it is easier if you drive on the other side of the road to have the steering wheel on the other side of the car.
Yves (Luxembourg):	*Do you see a lot of airforce planes in the air?*
Larry (UK):	You see a lot of normal planes but only a few army planes. It is because people in England are always going on holiday. There are lots of normal planes because there are four airports in London alone. There are about 20 in England.

Letter exchanges such as the ones above illustrate both the perceptions that pupils have of their own culture and those they have of 'other' people. The exchanges can highlight stereotypes children hold, tensions or dislikes. Pupils might even reject parts of a culture. As such, pen-pal links offer excellent opportunities to encourage pupils to analyse the origins of their beliefs, to review their ideas and to discuss links between stereotypes, tensions, prejudice and racism.

Pupils can also discuss the type of stereotype images other people have of them. Such discussions help them see their own culture from a different perspective. The analysis of pupils' beliefs and ideas is the starting point for them to develop some acceptance of other views, tolerance, open-mindedness and respect.

Another way in which pupils benefit from pen-pal links is that they can improve their language competence, intercultural competence and ICT skills (e.g. email, webcam). The fact that they use (and are able to use) language for a real purpose might act as a catalyst to learning a language. In addition, pen-pal links and projects with other countries help pupils to develop their knowledge of geography, history, art and music.

To be effective, pen-pal links require a lot of hard work as well as:

- good relationships between the partner institutions
- involvement of the head teachers or some senior teachers (to give the project some stability)
- vision on the part of the people in charge
- clear planning from motivated teachers
- good management skills
- an appropriate time frame
- flexibility.

Initial contacts can be created through the British Council, the European Schools Net set, foreign embassies, cultural and educational departments or websites.

Pen-pal links are, of course, not the only way to help pupils gain insights into the ways of life and traditions of other cultures. Teachers should first tap into the mix of language and cultural resources of their own class. They can also invite native speakers into the classroom or rely on authentic material resources. The German teacher at West Hill Primary, for example, made the Year 5 class listen to the German 'Top ten' to make them realize that people in Germany have a musical taste not unlike the English.

Rhymes, poems and songs

Traditional rhymes, poems and songs related to particular customs and festivals are another popular way of developing intercultural competence. For example, the traditional French song 'Petit Papa Noël' (Example 10.3) and of the poem 'Nikolaus' (Example 10.4) provide some insights into the ways in which Christmas and December 6 are celebrated in France and Germany.

Example 10.3 Traditonal French Christmas song

Petit Papa Noël

Quand tu descendras du ciel,	*Father Christmas, when you come down from heaven*
Avec des jouets par milliers.	*with your millions of toys, don't forget my little shoe.*
N'oublie pas mon petit soulier.	

> **Example 10.4 German poem for Santa Claus (6 December)**
>
> **Nikolaus**
>
> | | |
> |---|---|
> | Heute stell' ich meine Stiefel raus, | *Today I put my boots outside* |
> | Denn morgen kommt der Nikolaus. | *Because St Nicolas will come tomorrow.* |
> | (Peschel, 2006) | |

By comparing the poems with each other as well as with English traditions, pupils learn the following:

- young children get presents on different days in different countries (6, 24 or 25 December)
- the 'person' who offers the gift is different (Santa Claus, Father Christmas)
- children in France, Germany, Austria or England traditionally put out some footwear; either boots, shoes or stockings depending on the country.

I refer to chapters 6 to 8 for ideas on how to use such songs, rhymes and poems to develop pupils' language skills. Suffice it to say that pupils can memorize simple meaningful phrases used in these poems or songs and use them when making cards for these special occasions (Tierney and Hope, 1998; DfES, 2005a). Below are messages and symbols that can be used on Portuguese Christmas cards.

> **Example 10.5 Children learn what they can write in Portuguese and what pictures they can draw on their Christmas cards**
>
> | O que é que se escreve nos cartões? (captions to write on cards) | Que motivos têm os cartões? (pictures to put on postcards) |
> |---|---|
> | Boas Festas (literally Good Feast) | A árvore de natal (A Christmas tree) |
> | Feliz Ano Novo (Happy New Year) | Os sinos (bells) |
> | Bom Natal/Bom Nata (Merry Christmas) | O Pai Natal (Father Christmas) |

When talking about Christmas, teachers might like to make links with religion and show pupils how illustrations and symbols vary according to local and cultural contexts. Jones and Coffey (2006) give the example of a Roman Catholic church in East Anglia where pupils compared representations of Jesus. They looked at pictures of an early Byzantine Jesus, an Italian Renaissance Jesus, an Ethiopian black Jesus and a blue-eyed white Hollywood Jesus. Through such examples, children learn how symbols and products present cultures and how interpretations vary according to social, historical and geographic contexts. It is important that children do not only learn that people do things differently. They also need to understand the contextual reasons behind these differences (Jones and Coffey, 2006).

Tales, fables and stories

Some teachers like to familiarize pupils with traditional tales, fables and stories. Many fables (e.g. Aesop's *The Ants and the Grasshopper*) and stories (e.g. *The Hare and the Tortoise)* have been translated and are available free of charge on the internet.

Working with traditional stories allows teachers to work at many different levels. They can focus on language, look at the ethical and moral dimension (e.g. fable) or work on cultural aspects. Teachers can ask pupils to identify and discuss similarities and differences between stories of their own and the target country, reflect on the values and beliefs portrayed in the story or analyse the different ways of telling and representing stories.

Figure 10.3 is part of a display made in 2002 by pupils in West Hill Primary School when they worked on Aborigine stories. They highlight the pupils' excellent work and testify to the great enjoyment they gained from doing the topic.

Parents of different cultural backgrounds are an invaluable resource to mine and explore the meaning of traditional stories. The teachers of the school 'Las Lomas' in Almería, a multi-ethnic school, ask parents to record or write down traditional stories of their country of origin. All the stories are filed in the library. Teachers use the stories to explore different ways of life and to work on the underpinning cultural values and beliefs.

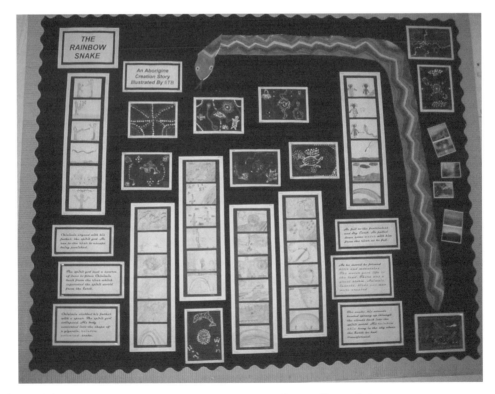

Figure 10.3 'The rainbow Snake', an Aborigine Creation story illustrated by pupils in Year 6.

This school runs another exciting project. The aim is to develop pupils' knowledge of the countries of origin of their classmates, to foster the integration of all pupils and to develop close relationships with parents. Pupils and parents are asked to write a story of a pet's travels to their country of origin. This story is passed from family to family like a baton in a relay race and is enriched at each leg with accounts and pictures of the pet's travels in each country. The final product is a storybook and a photo album.

The fact that the stories stem from their classmates makes them attractive reading materials. The teachers of this school have found that the collective story-writing project increased pupils' understanding of each other's countries and ways of life and fostered tolerance and respect for each other.

10.4 Main points to remember

What you need to know about culture and intercultural competence:

- The aim of language learning has shifted from an almost exclusive focus on linguistic competence to communicative competence and now intercultural competence.
- The concept of culture encompasses the notions of civilization, historical and national events, artefacts, tradition and ways of life.
- Intercultural competence consists of knowledge, attitudes and skills. It enables people to understand their own culture and cultural selves and those of others, to abandon ethnocentric attitudes and to act sensitively and culturally appropriately.
- Discovering linguistic and cultural diversity is a good way of increasing pupils' awareness and understanding of other cultures.

You foster the development of intercultural competence when:

- your teaching goes beyond the development of knowledge of, for example, a culture's artefacts and ways of life, and includes a focus on attitudes and skills.
- you encourage interactions with other people. Pen-pal links with other countries are an ideal way of achieving this.
- you help pupils understand their own culture from both their own perspective and that of others.
- you develop pupils understanding of the target culture.
- you encourage pupils to think about their own perspectives, recognize the origin of their cultural values, beliefs and attitudes and review stereotypical images

Developing Language Learning Strategies

Chapter Outline

11.1 Introduction

In the last 20 years, learner autonomy became an essential educational aim (Holec, 1988, 1992; Dam, 1995) and the Council of Europe (2004) encouraged countries to adopt a more learner-centred approach. A number of factors contributed to this increased interest in learner independence and self-directed learning: cognitive sciences with their focus on learning processes; humanistic approaches to language learning with their emphasis on the 'whole' learner; studies on individual learner differences; research into the 'good language learner' with a focus on efficient language learning strategies; social changes and, finally, changes in the labour market requiring flexibility and the ability to retrain oneself (Mariani, 1992).

Teachers who encourage learner autonomy take on the role of facilitators and helpers. They make pupils aware of their potential and needs; encourage them to take responsibility for their learning; involve them in decision-making; support their reflection and involve them in assessment (Donato and McCormick, 1994). In order to be able to organize their work efficiently, learners need to have some understanding of the nature of learning and of the demands of the tasks. They also need to be able to identify their personal needs and skills, to choose appropriate learning strategies, to evaluate their own learning and to address factors that impede the learning process (Mariani, 1992; Klapper, 2006).

The development of learner autonomy and the ability to use language learning strategies efficiently do not happen automatically. In fact, even settings and tasks that foster autonomy do not automatically make learners develop and use appropriate strategies (Grenfell and Harris, 1993; Oxford and Leaver, 1996 and Kirsch, 2006b). In this chapter I focus on different ways in which teachers foster the development of learner strategies. Learner autonomy and the use of learning strategies are essential components of education at all levels of schooling. For example, language learning strategies are one of the five strands of the KS2 framework for foreign languages (DfES, 2005a).

Although much of the research reported in this chapter has been carried out with students attending secondary school, the findings are of equal importance for teachers and pupils at primary school. This is evident in the case-study (section 11.2.3) where I describe the language learning strategies of the six English children you met in Chapter 5.

> **Food for thought**
> - What strategies have you used successfully in the past to learn foreign languages?
> - What helped you develop your own strategies? (Think of people and situations.)
> - Why is it important to develop your pupils' learning strategies?

I begin this chapter with a definition of learning strategies and a presentation of the different types. I then outline the differences between successful and unsuccessful learners in their choice of strategies and give concrete examples of the range and development of the strategies of six nine-year-old children. Finally, I describe some principles for efficient strategy training.

11.2 Language learning strategies

Language learning strategies have been defined as specific actions, behaviour patterns or techniques undertaken by learners to enhance their learning (Scarcella and Oxford, 1992: 63). In Oxford's words (1990):

> Learning strategies are operations employed by the learner to aid the learning, storage, retrieval, and use of information . . . [They] make learning easier, faster, more enjoyable, more self-directed, more efficient and more transferable to new situations.
>
> (p. 8)

Learning strategies are problem-oriented and task-dependent tools for active and self-directed involvement. The choice of efficient strategies depends on the task, the learning situation, the pupil's prior learning experience and some pupil variables such as age, gender, cultural background, needs, learning style and level of proficiency. The use of appropriate strategies facilitates learning and fosters proficiency and self-regulation (Chamot *et al.*, 1999;

Oxford *et al.*, 1996; Cohen, 1998). Most theorists agree that they involve some element of consciousness but the precise degree of awareness has been debated (Bialystok, 1981; Pressley and McCormick, 1995; Hsiao and Oxford, 2002).

Findings of research studies show that the efficient use of strategies shortens the learning processes, facilitates learning, results in improved proficiency and constitutes an important step towards autonomy (Oxford, 1994; Chamot *et al.*, 1999; Cohen, 1998; Grenfell, 2000). Most of the research projects reported in this chapter have been carried out with adolescents (hereinafter students) or adults.

11.2.1 Different types of strategies

Successful language learners use a range of strategies. Below is a list of techniques that they use in oral tasks:

- planning (deciding what to listen out for)
- carefully listening out for gist and detail
- inferring
- checking their understanding of what has been said (monitoring)
- indicating when they have not understood a piece of information
- asking people to speak more slowly or to clarify an utterance
- using mime or gesture
- paraphrasing
- checking whether something they have said has been understood (evaluating)
- adjusting messages
- changing communicative goals.
  (Mariani, 1992; Celce-Murcia and Olshtain, 2000; Klapper, 2006; Macaro, 2006)

Researchers have grouped these strategies into different categories. Different taxonomies have been suggested but most researchers would agree with a broad classification into *cognitive*, *metacognitive*, *social* and *affective* strategies (Cohen *et al.*, 1995). Examples of strategies are provided in Table 11.1.

Cognitive strategies are the ones most commonly used. They operate directly on incoming linguistic information and manipulate it so that it enhances rehearsal, organization and

Table 11.1 Classification of strategies and concrete examples based on O'Malley and Chamot (1990) and Oxford (1990)

Type of strategy	Examples
Cognitive	Practising; analysing and reasoning; inferring; memorizing
Metacognitive	Paying selective attention, checking comprehension
Social	Asking questions; cooperating with others; emphasizing
Affective	Encouraging oneself; lowering one's anxiety

elaboration processes (O'Malley *et al.*, 1989; Chamot *et al.*, 1987; Oxford, 1990). Memorizing and practising are among the most popular cognitive strategies. Making mental representations and using mnemonic devices, to name two *memorizing* techniques, both help store and retrieve information. Practising can be divided into *formal practice* and *functional practice*, also called *naturalistic practice* (Fillmore, 1985; Oxford, 1990). Examples of the former include practising and revising; having private lessons; using computers and working with dictionaries. Examples of the latter are listening to music or to people talking; watching television; playing games; conversing; reading and writing. Functional practice maximizes input and interaction and enables students to use the language efficiently in real and authentic situations of communication. Rubin (1975), Bialystok (1981), Fillmore (1985) and Oxford (1990) have illustrated the importance of such techniques in developing proficiency. It is therefore unfortunate that strategies encouraging functional practice are rarely used by students (Nyikos and Oxford, 1987). The failure to use these strategies has been related to the lack of opportunities for functional practice in classrooms, students' inability to transfer this skill to out-of-school contexts and their lack of awareness of the usefulness of this strategy.

Metacognitive strategies involve thinking about the learning process and help students to regulate their own cognition, plan, monitor and evaluate. They enable them to analyse the demands of a task, to pay attention to particular points, to evaluate the efficiency of strategies and to coordinate the learning process. Metacognitive strategies play the most important role in determining the efficiency of the learning process, but students only use them sporadically and without appreciating their value (O'Malley *et al.*, 1985; Chamot, 1987; Oxford, 1990).

Social and *affective strategies* are used least (Chamot *et al.*, 1987; Oxford, 1990). *Social strategies* provide learners with enhanced interactions and opportunities to develop empathetic understanding. *Affective techniques* support the regulation of emotions, motivations and attitudes which enables learners to engage successfully in learning tasks and, in turn, to develop confidence and perseverance (Oxford, 1990; O'Malley and Chamot, 1990).

The different categories of strategies have been much debated, particularly the overlap between metacognitive and cognitive techniques. Nevertheless, this classification scheme, initially developed for ESL (English as a Second Language) students, was validated in the 1990s with students learning foreign languages and is still used today.

11.2.2 Differences between successful and unsuccessful learners

Early research studies have investigated the strategy use of successful and less successful language learners. Chamot *et al.* (1990) found that 'successful students use language learning strategies more frequently, more appropriately, with greater variety, and in ways that help them complete the task successfully' (Chamot *et al.*, 1990). Many researchers agree that the number of strategies is unimportant; rather, it is the manner and the combination in which they are deployed that determines success. Successful learners use a variety of strategies in efficient combinations whereas less successful learners use strategies in a desperate and random way.

Research findings also show that students differ in the type of strategies used. Successful learners tend to devote more energy to practising and to create more opportunities for practice outside the classroom (Stern, 1975; Naiman *et al.*, 1978; Graham, 1997). They also use more metacognitive strategies than unsuccessful students who use comparatively more cognitive ones.

The use of metacognitive strategies distinguishes successful from unsuccessful learners. Students vary in their ability to monitor task completion and efficient strategy use and performance (Naiman *et al.*, 1978; Nisbet and Shucksmith, 1986; Chamot *et al.*, 1990). Unsuccessful students are inconsistent in their monitoring (Graham 1997, 2006). They tend to look for surface errors without checking for general meaning, and to infer words without assessing the overall sense of their interpretation. When they know that they have made a mistake they are uncertain how to correct it. Students also differ in their ability to assess their achievements. Successful students are able to evaluate their learning environment, their use of strategies and the learning outcomes accurately.

Once practitioners had identified efficient strategies, it seemed sensible to make learners aware of 'good' strategies, to increase their repertoire and to foster successful use of strategies. The idea of teaching strategies was born.

Before outlining the principles of efficient strategy training, I give concrete examples of the language learning strategies used by some nine-year-olds. The case-study illustrates that even beginners have developed language learning strategies, are aware of them and are able to reflect on language learning. The following section therefore provides a useful background for the discussion on the teaching of strategies.

11.2.3 Case study: children's language learning strategies

In 2002, I carried out a longitudinal study with six monolingual English children. My aims were to identify their language learning strategies, to follow the development of their strategic thinking over the course of the calendar year and to understand the reasons behind this development (Kirsch, 2006a). Below is a brief description of their language learning strategies. I refer to Chapter 5 for an explanation of the context of this study, in particular their opportunities to learn languages at home and at school.

Children's strategy use

I asked children at the beginning and the end of the year about the strategies they used to improve their linguistic competence. The excerpts below give a flavour of the interviews. In brackets are the codes I use in Figures 11.1 and 11.2.

Excerpt 11.1 Interviews on 17.10.02, 11.11.02, 07.11.02 and 25.02.02

CK (researcher):	What do you do to get better in French?
Anne:	Trying to remember. *(Memorizing)*
CK:	What helps you remember?
Anne:	When you look back on all your things. Doing stuff like playing games and maybe afterwards I teach somebody words like 'hello' and 'good-bye' in German. *(Revising, playing games, teaching/speaking)*
CK:	What can you do to learn more French?
Mike:	Stay in at lunch time and ask if he [the teacher] can teach me any more words. *(Getting help)*
CK:	What do you do with these words?
Mike:	I repeat them and try to remember them. *(Memorizing)*
CK:	What exactly do you do to learn German?
Jane:	I listen and speak. And I could buy German tapes and listen to them. *(Listening, speaking)*
CK:	Who could you speak to?
Jane:	Uh, I speak to my teachers. To German people, I would go to Germany and meet people. *(Speaking, finding native speakers)*
CK:	Do you consider going to Germany then?
Jane:	Yes, that helps learn the language. I could stay with the family and see what they do and talk. I do what they do.
CK:	What can you do to improve your Japanese?
Larry:	I would go back to the Japanese Festival in Greenwich. Last year, there were a lot of Japanese people, you could see what they had, eat different food. And there were Japanese writings as well, they were written in big letters and below, you had English in smaller letters. I did not understand anything. But one can work it out by looking at the food and reading the English. So I would go back to this festival and talk to different people. *(Finding native speakers, studying artefacts, reading, inferring meaning)*

All six children were aware of their strategies and able to articulate them, a finding in line with studies by Chamot (1987), Low *et al.* (1993, 1995), Chamot *et al.* (1999), Chamot and El-Dinary (1999) and Yongqi *et al.* (2005). They listed strategies in several languages but I restricted my analysis to French, German and Japanese since they used these languages at home, at school and, sometimes, on holiday.

The excerpts above show that the children referred to two different categories of strategy: those that they used at the time of the study (Anne, Mike) and those that they imagined using in the distant and more distant future (Jane, Larry). Generally, the strategies that were intended for the future comprised formal study (e.g. studying at secondary school) and travelling to the target country to meet native speakers.

Figure 11.1 shows the 17 different strategies reported by the six children as a group. The strategies were similar across languages with the exception of 'studying cultural artefacts' which is restricted to Japanese, a culture that the children were least familiar with. This

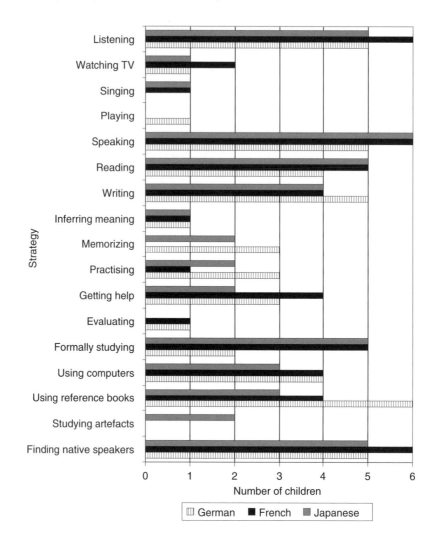

Figure 11.1 Children's language learning strategies across languages in December 2002.

suggests that children perceived some 'universals' in the methods of learning languages even though the languages themselves differed considerably. One could argue that such a holistic view is beneficial at this early stage of language learning since it encourages pupils to tackle any language.

Children mostly referred to social and cognitive strategies, particularly to the cognitive strategies labelled 'formal or functional' practising by Fillmore (1985) and Oxford (1990). Among their highly efficient strategies for functional practising were listening to native speakers, speaking, singing, watching TV, reading and writing. The strategies subsumed under formal practice comprised practising, having private lessons and studying a language at secondary school. Only a few children reported practising at home as an efficient strategy, but several complained about the lack of worksheets at school which made further practice impossible. Having private lessons and studying a language at secondary school are practices that can become useful in the future.

I found only one metacognitive technique used by the children: evaluation. Paul explained that he told his cousins 'how much he knew' which helped them 'try to improve' (interview, 04.11.02). In other words, he drew on metacognitive skills to assess his skills and needs and then planned the necessary 'language input'.

My data suggested that children tried to balance formal and informal learning settings. Most children reported that they relied on a mix of family members (e.g. parents, siblings, grandparents, cousins), teachers (primary, secondary or private teachers), classmates and holiday acquaintances. One child even mentioned chatting to people on the internet. The material resources they indicated were a good mix of resources allowing for functional practice in informal settings (e.g. tapes, radio and television programmes, internet, newspapers, labels, signposts) and for formal practice at school and at home (e.g. textbooks, dictionaries, computer programmes). Neither the facilitators nor the diverse and multifunctional resources were language-dependent. The number of strategies and human and material resources mentioned are shown in Figure 11.2.

A comparison between my findings and the study done by Chesterfield and Chesterfield (1985) shows that the nursery and first-grade Mexican American children studied by the American researchers and the English children in my study used very similar strategies. Most of the strategies listed in both studies resemble general activities rather than specialized techniques. The English children have only just begun to think of more specific strategies such as inferring meaning (what Larry called 'working it out'). This finding is in line with research on the developmental nature of strategies. Brown *et al.* (1983) and Chesterfield and Chesterfield (1985) claimed that strategies start off as task-specified activities that develop

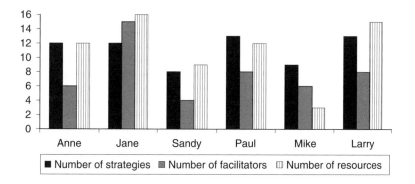

Figure 11.2 Number of different strategies, facilitators and resources that children deployed independently of the language (interviews in December 2002).

into vague and unfocused techniques before they finally become more distinctive, concrete, flexible and specific as pupils get older and more experienced.

Development of children's language learning strategies

Over the course of the calendar year, all the children developed their concept of strategies and increased their understanding of how particular learning activities further language acquisition. In February, for example, the six pupils only made a 'superficial' link between writing and learning languages. They explained that writing helped them build up a record of phrases that they could use and revisit at a later stage. In December Anne, Jane and Larry claimed that writing furthered memorizing, facilitated practising and enhanced their knowledge of language by providing insights into spellings.

Children's strategies also became more precise, concrete, efficient and appropriate as a result of being adapted to their immediate needs and the particular circumstances of their settings. Two examples, representative of many others, illustrate the point. In February Sandy expressed her strategy for learning Japanese as follows:

> 'You could go to the library and pick out nearly all the books of Japanese and then get a teacher to come and teach you.'

> (interview, 18.02.02)

This technique is an idea of a plan that is unlikely to happen rather than a concrete strategy. It is expressed in the second rather than the first person, and the conditional instead of the present. In December Sandy still mentioned reading because she believed in the efficiency of the strategy but she had found a way of making the strategy work. She focused on labels of packages and frequent words in her Japanese primers because she had discovered that these words were easier to read, understand and memorize.

In February Paul defined memorizing as 'putting things in one's head'; in December he understood that this strategy entailed listening, repeating and even reading and writing.

On a quantitative level, all the children increased the total number of strategies they used by adding 'new' strategies and transferring efficient ones across languages. For example, Jane mentioned in February that attentive listening to the French being spoken around her on a day trip to France had helped her pick up some words. In December she reported that she found listening a useful way of improving her language skills and therefore used this strategy in all three languages she was learning. All the children had developed their strategies gradually over the calendar year, but differences remained in December as shown in Figure 11.2.

The development of these strategies triggered an investigation into the reasons behind the change. My findings revealed that the six children developed strategies through observation, imitation and, most importantly, reflection on the efficient strategies they used while they participated in a range of language learning activities. They did not receive explicit instructions, but the Year 5 teachers played an important role. They provided children with a productive learning environment that encouraged autonomy and reflection and fostered the development of metacognitive skills. My examples, representative of others, stem from lessons in PE and Mathematics. (These teachers also taught some languages, but most of the language teaching was done by secondary teachers.)

The PE lesson described below is a good example of the ways in which Mrs Freeman encouraged children to plan their learning and to evaluate their achievements. In this particular lesson, she wanted children to learn a range of movements. She explained several movements and asked children to have a go. She carefully observed pupils' performance, assembled the class and invited children to explain how they got on. Mrs Freeman then asked some children to perform the movement again and the others to watch them. In the subsequent discussion, pupils analysed what their classmates had done in order to perform the movement successfully and what they could do to improve their performance. Mrs Freeman observed them perform once more and gave them individual feedback.

Apart from developing a new skill, the pupils learned how to learn thereby drawing on Anderson's (2000) five metacognitive skills: preparing and planning; selecting; monitoring; orchestrating strategies; and evaluating. In the PE lessons, all pupils:

- prepared and planned for learning: they decided what they wanted to achieve
- selected strategies from their own repertoire and chose those deployed by their friends
- monitored their strategy use: they checked if they and their classmates were doing what they intended to do
- orchestrated various strategies: they tried out a range of possible strategies
- evaluated their learning and strategy use: they assessed whether the strategy was efficient.

Mrs Freeman adopted a similar focus on learning to learn in her maths lessons. After introducing a complex algorithm for multiplying, she asked pupils to work in pairs. One was to calculate aloud and the other to check whether the classmate followed all the steps and, if necessary, to remind the friend to observe the procedure. This 'reciprocal teaching' (Palincsar and Brown, 1984; Rosenshine and Meister, 1994) ensured that pupils monitored and evaluated each other's strategy use. I found similar examples in Mrs Moore's maths and English lessons. This type of teaching helps pupils to develop metacognitive skills.

In my study I showed that the six children's emerging analytical powers, developed in a range of subjects, enabled them to assess the efficiency of learning strategies, to transfer strategies specifically to language learning and to refine their use of language learning strategies. In other words, although children did not receive any explicit instruction on how to develop language learning strategies, they had developed them. This is not to say, however, that they would not have benefited from explicit guidance.

11.3 Teaching language learning strategies

In this section, I present what is called 'strategy training' (Cohen, 1998) in the States, or 'learner training' (Dickinson, 1995) in Europe, explain strategy-based instruction and outline some principles for efficient training.

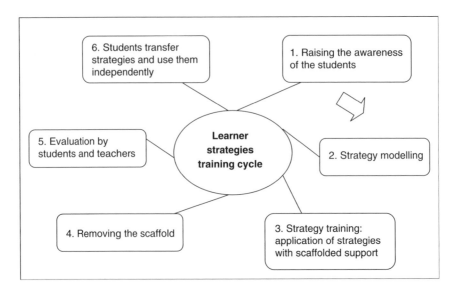

Figure 11.3 Learner strategies training cycle, adapted from Erler (2006) and Macaro (2006).

11.3.1 Strategy training

Research findings have shown that efficient strategy training helps students in four ways:

- it raises their awareness of the learning process
- it increases their strategy repertoire
- it improves their understanding of strategy use and of the learning process
- it facilitates transfer of strategies across languages.

This new knowledge helps students regulate their behaviour in order to meet their personal, linguistic, communicative and sociocultural needs, and, eventually, makes them independent learners (Dam, 1995; Oxford *et al.*, 1996; Cohen, 1998; Grenfell and Harris, 1999).

The training itself is based on a behavioural approach which prescribes a particular sequence of steps as shown in Figure 11.3. Ideally, the responsibility shifts from the teacher who explains and models strategies to the student who begins to use them independently in the course of the training.

1. In the preparation period, teachers provide pupils with opportunities to activate their background knowledge and to identify strategies. These group conversations make pupils aware of strategies and encourage them to compare and to reflect on strategy use.
2. Teachers give supplementary information on strategies and demonstrate their efficient use through modelling or think-aloud procedures.

3. Pupils practise the new strategies with their teacher and possibly classmates in 'reciprocal teaching' (Cotterall, 1993). Teachers provide support and give extensive feedback.

4. While teachers may remind pupils of strategy use at the beginning of the training period, they phase out the reminders towards the end. Teachers help pupils monitor their strategy use and set targets.

5. In the evaluation stage, teachers and pupils evaluate the usefulness of strategies. Pupils learn to plan, monitor and evaluate their learning which fosters the development of metacognitive strategies and self-directed learning.

6. Many teachers offer pupils opportunities to apply their new skills in new situations. This enables pupils to transfer strategies and to take control of their learning. Teachers continue to monitor how pupils use strategies independently.

Oxford (1990), Wenden and Rubin (1987) and O'Malley and Chamot (1990) report that many training cycles unfortunately leave out the crucial 'control-step' and are heavily teacher-centred. Teachers are in charge of selecting strategies and materials, modelling them and helping students practise, evaluate and transfer them. This teacher-centred training runs counter to the whole idea of learner autonomy. It might even reduce learner independence, its very aim, and lead to dependency rather than self-regulation (Klapper, 2001).

There is much evidence of the positive effect of strategy training, particularly on the pupils' performance in reading, writing and problem-solving in the first language. Research on strategy instruction in second and foreign languages has begun to appear but provides mixed results: some positive, some partially successful and some negative. Reviewing literature, Chamot *et al.* (1996) conclude that 'the specific conditions that lead to good strategy use are not yet completely understood in second language learning though advances in efficient strategy instruction in first language contexts indicates that such instructional procedures have been identified' (p. 180).

Nevertheless, many educationalists are confident that strategy instruction, if done properly, can enable language learners to take greater control of their language learning and to enhance performance (Chamot and Rubin, 1994; Oxford and Leaver, 1996).

Many educationalists now prefer a model such as strategy-based instruction that combines strategy training and language learning. In the past, strategy training was taught separately from language learning. This might explain why students found it difficult to transfer their new skills to other contexts.

11.3.2 Strategy-based instruction and learning programmes with a focus on learning strategies

Strategy-based instruction is a learner-centred approach to teaching where learning strategies are embedded in the learning tasks. One of the most popular models is the Cognitive Academic Language Learning Approach (CALLA) developed by Chamot and O'Malley (1994). In Canada and the States teachers use it in primary schools with pupils learning

English (as a second language) and foreign languages. The model has three integrated and interrelated components: content area (school subjects such as Mathematics), English language teaching and direct strategy instruction. Pupils learn and use strategies while studying a range of subjects. After testing the model, Chamot and O'Malley (1994) maintained that students improve their understanding of the target language, increase their motivation and become more responsible and active learners.

Strategy instruction and strategies-based instruction are currently not general features of classroom instruction, although some textbooks include a focus on strategies. Some curricula propose strategies as one strand of language learning, among them are Dam's 'Flower model' (Dickinson, 1987), and, in England, the KS2 framework for languages (DfES, 2005a) and KS3 (DfES,2003).

The aims of the KS2 framework in relation to language learning strategies are as follows:

- to make pupils aware of how they learn
- to give them regular opportunities to identify and apply language learning strategies
- to plan the use of specific strategies (DfES, 2005a: 9).

The document suggests familiarizing pupils with six categories of strategies and proposes concrete activities as shown in Table 11.2.

It is interesting to relate my findings on children's learning strategies to the KS2 framework. The six pupils were already familiar with most of the strategies mentioned in the above document and, apart from the metacognitive ones, made good use of strategies though not always consciously. For example, the six children knew about the importance of memorizing, but it took them a while to discover the best way of memorizing. Some needed to repeat words, some to write them down, others to use them in full sentences, still others to revise them continuously on their own. These six children would not have been helped if their teacher had told them only that memorizing improves their competence, or, worse, made them remember words without telling them explicitly that remembering is an efficient strategy. These children would, however, have benefited from explicit, concrete and individ-

Table 11.2 Language learning strategies in the KS2 framework for language (DfES, 2005a)

Language learning strategies	Activities	Year group
Planning, analysing and evaluating	Analyse what they need to know in order to carry out a task	4, 5, 6
Practising language	Say new words aloud	3, 4, 5, 6
Applying prior knowledge	Apply grammatical knowledge and prior knowledge to make sentences	5, 6
Memorizing	Remember rhyming words	3, 4, 5
Using dictionary skills	Use a dictionary or ICT source to look up spellings and check for meaning	4, 5, 6
Communicating	Ask someone to clarify/repeat	3, 4, 5, 6

ualized advice as to 'how' to memorize. Similarly, they would have benefited from guidance on how to develop metacognitive strategies and how to transfer strategies across situations.

The identification of principles for efficient instruction was a useful outcome of the research into the efficiency of training.

11.3.3 Principles for efficient training

Strategy training needs to be *direct, overt* and *explicit*. Teachers must make learners aware of the purpose and the potential of learning strategies. Pupils are unlikely to develop strategies if they do not understand how the teaching activities contribute to their learning. This means that teachers need to tell pupils, for example, that giving a physical response such as answering questions with their thumbs up is a communicative strategy.

Training should be *individualized* and *take account of pupils' experiences, beliefs, attitudes, motivation and goals*. If strategy training is to make sense to pupils, be of interest to them and be efficient, teachers need to start where pupils are. They need to acknowledge the learners' strategies, consider their prior experience and introduce new strategies carefully 'without whisking away pupils' "security blankets"' (Harris, 2003: 11). For example, learners who believe that it is essential to understand every single word or who have misunderstood information because of wrong predictions might be reluctant to use the strategy 'predicting' which the teacher has introduced to the class. They will only use this new strategy if they see the value of it and develop confidence in their ability to use it.

Learner training should be *collaborative* and *offer opportunities for reflection*. Sharing experiences offers pupils opportunities to reflect on their learning process, to encounter new strategies, to compare them and to assess their efficiency. If the discussions are carried out in the target language, pupils have additional opportunities to improve their communicative skills. Even if they do not use the target language because their knowledge is too limited, it helps them use metacognitive and metalinguisic skills and thus develop their knowledge about how the language works.

Moreover instruction should be *integrated* into regular language lessons, a principle realized in strategy-based instruction. It should also be delivered over a *long period of time* to give pupils enough time to develop a range of strategies and to learn to use them independently.

Research studies have shown that students who want to learn a language *create opportunities for functional practice inside and outside the classroom* (Graham, 1997: 53). The wish to learn and to communicate leads students into situations where they need to develop strategies to cope with the demands of the setting. This means that teachers promote strategy development by creating an environment where pupils can use their newly acquired language skills in purposeful ways.

Primary school teachers are in an excellent position to develop a 'strategic classroom' (Coyle, 2000). They need to take a consistent approach and provide pupils with multiple and continuous opportunities to take control of their learning, and reflect on their progress in a range of subjects. This will enable pupils to develop learning skills and strategies, and to transfer them to tasks in other subjects. The classroom climate that Mrs Freeman created, reported in section 11.2.3, is an example of such a 'strategic' classroom.

It is crucial that pupils have control and responsibility if they are to maintain high levels of motivation, grow in confidence in their own abilities, develop metacognitive skills and become independent learners (Holec, 1981; Chamot and O'Malley, 1987; Oxford, 1990; Graham, 1997; Anderson, 2000). Some activities, such as carousel activities, seem to foster independence because they include an element of choice (e.g. the order in which tasks are done; the organization of the work), but in reality teachers often decide on the content of the tasks and influence the way in which problems are solved. In order to foster learner independence teachers need to give pupils opportunities to set targets, negotiate aims, create tasks and materials, find methods that work and reflect on appropriate learning strategies.

11.4 Main points to remember

Pupils differ in their use of strategies.

- Language learning strategies have been classified into four different categories: cognitive, metacognitive, social and affective.
- Metacognitive strategies are a prerequisite for pupil autonomy. They help learners plan, monitor, evaluate and regulate their own learning.
- Successful learners differ from others in the type and range of strategies they use and in the way they combine them. Successful learners use more metacognitive strategies than their peers.

Language learning strategies develop gradually:

- Pupils change initially vague and unfocused activities into precise strategies that meet their needs.
- Pupils develop their strategies through observation and imitation, transfer, reflection on the efficiency of their strategy use, and explicit strategy instruction.

Learning strategies can be taught as follows:

- Strategy training familiarizes pupils with new strategies and offers opportunities for practise, reflection and independent use. The teaching of strategies is entirely dissociated from language learning.
- Strategy-based instruction embeds the teaching of strategies into language learning. Pupils learn, identify and apply strategies and reflect on the impact of the strategies while they learn and use a language.

You help pupils develop strategies when you:

- familiarize them with new strategies in an explicit way thereby taking account of their backgrounds, experiences, beliefs and personalities
- explain the usefulness of a strategy
- provide opportunities for scaffolded practice (e.g. the teacher or a pupil observes a pupil use a strategy and offers assistance when needed)

- provide them with opportunities to take control of their learning and select strategies appropriate to them
- provide opportunities for learners to reflect with their classmates on the efficiency of the strategies used and on their learning progress
- talk about learning and learning strategies on a regular basis in all subjects
- provide a learning environment where pupils want to learn and use a foreign language. If they want to communicate they will find a way to do so.

12 Assessment and Transition to Secondary School

12.1 Introduction

The Council of Europe's Common European Framework on learning, teaching and assessment is widely used throughout Europe. It offers language learners the opportunity to document their progress and assess their achievements on six different levels. Primary school children generally achieve the first two levels of the European Language Portfolio (ELP). Language learning is perceived as a life-long process and the contribution of primary school to the early language learning process is explicitly valued (Haramboure, 2007). The ELP has both a recording and a pedagogic function. The assessment points highlight key areas of learning that primary teachers can address to support the young learners. The document facilitates transition to secondary school: it informs the secondary teachers of the students' level of achievement and provides some insights into the content of the early language learning programmes. Secondary teachers can take account of this invaluable information when they design their language syllabus.

In England, some teachers use the *Languages Ladder* to assess pupils' achievements. The teachers at Portway Primary School, for example, assess pupils' level of achievement at the end of each term with the Languages Ladder. They use this information to set pupils in ability groups and to write reports for parents at the end of the year. At the end of Year 6, teachers pass on the evaluations to the secondary schools. In 2006 most pupils achieved the level 'Intermediate'.

Although educationalists agree that assessment is necessary to ensure progress and continuity, many teachers in England questioned in 2004 and 2005 were opposed to the assessment of foreign languages, a non-statutory subject (Driscoll *et al.*, 2004; Muijs *et al.*,2005, OFSTED, 2005). They stated that assessment could cause anxiety in learners, spoil their motivation in this 'special subject' and 'kill the fun' (Bolster *et al.*, 2004: 37). Others pointed out that assessment cuts into valuable teaching time. Still others were unsure how to assess children's developing attitudes, skills and levels of linguistic and cultural awareness. Teachers acknowledged that the dearth of assessment was an issue, particularly at transition from primary to secondary school, and that improvements needed to be made (Driscoll *et al.*, 2004; OFSTED, 2005).

Food for thought

- Think about your own experience of learning foreign languages. How did you feel about being assessed? How were your knowledge, skills and attitudes assessed?
- Do you think that assessment helped you improve your language skills?
- Were records of your achievements passed on from one teacher to another? If so, in what ways did the teacher(s) take account of and use this information?

In this chapter, I review why, what and how pupils' skills and attitudes should be assessed and show how teachers can use daily activities or formal tests to do so. I outline characteristics of efficient assessment and introduce tools such as the national level descriptors, the Languages Ladder and the European Language Portfolio. I close this chapter with some suggestions on how to facilitate the transition from primary to secondary school.

12.2 Assessment: why, how and what

Assessment is an integral part of learning. Many of the activities that teachers carry out prompt pupils to demonstrate their knowledge, understanding and skills. Teachers observe, listen to, interpret and judge their pupils' responses in the light of their prior knowledge, the curriculum and the national attainment targets.

In the following sections I give some reasons why assessment is necessary and outline different ways to assess and record pupils' understanding, skills and attitudes.

12.2.1 Planning for progression and continuity

Assessment and feedback are essential for progression and continuity. Drummond (1993) explains that '[T]he process of assessing children's learning – by looking closely at it and striving to understand it – is the only safeguard against children's failure, the only certain guarantee of children's progress and development' (p. 15).

Research findings have shown that pupils achieve more if they are fully engaged in their own learning process. Without a firm understanding of their achievements and of possible ways to address gaps they can neither improve nor develop into independent learners. The feeling that one's work is not valued and that one does not improve has a demotivating effect. Thus, the *lack* of valuable feedback on individual achievement rather than assessment as such can hamper pupils' positive attitudes as well as their progress. The English pupils interviewed by Muijs and his team (2005) generally felt that they did not receive any feedback in foreign languages even though the teacher kept some records of their work. They explained that they did not know how they were getting on and that they would like to be told how to improve. Pupils are likely to enjoy foreign language learning if they know they are making progress and have their achievements recognized. That will increase their confidence and their motivation.

Assessment enables teachers to inform their own planning (e.g. to plan differentiated lessons) and to evaluate the efficiency of their teaching. In addition, it facilitates the transition from class to class and, particularly, from primary to secondary school. The information gathered through observation, record-keeping and formal tests can be passed on to teachers of the next year group. It provides these teachers with relevant information on the content covered and the pupils' achievements which, in turn, inform the planning of a relevant curriculum and the choice of appropriate methods of teaching. A record of pupils' achievements can be passed on to their parents. They have a right to know what their children learned in their lessons and will certainly be pleased to hear about their child's progress.

Finally, assessment gives foreign language lessons the same status as other subjects (Jones and Coffey, 2006). Foreign language learning should not be seen as merely consisting of fun activities and perceived as lacking rigour. Rather, it needs to be acknowledged as a 'real' subject and taken seriously.

12.2.2 Formative and summative assessment

Both formative and summative assessment is appropriate in foreign language lessons. Formative assessment, or assessment for learning (AfL), is useful in raising pupils' achievements. Teachers inform pupils of the ways in which they can make progress. This type of assessment is based on the understanding that every pupil is able to improve their knowledge and performance if they understand what to learn, where they are in relation to the learning objectives and how these can best be achieved (QCA, 2005).

Summative assessment, or assessment of learning, usually happens at the end of a unit, year or Key Stage to 'sum' up the learners' achievements and to show the level of understanding or competence attained at a particular point in time. Teachers come to these decisions by measuring pupils' learning against particular criteria. In England, the criteria stem from the national level descriptors. The Standard Attainment Tests (SATs) in English, Maths and

Science are an example of summative assessment. They allow for comparisons of pupil achievement across an age group, region, nation or even the world.

There are many ways of assessing pupils and there are many resources on the market, but it is the teacher's responsibility to choose the resources and methods appropriate to their own pedagogy. They can base their jugements on conversations with pupils (e.g. notes of comments they made), observations (e.g. pupils' engagement in lessons; their participation in pen-pal exchanges) and documents (e.g. samples of work).

12.2.3 Assessing knowledge, skills and attitudes

There are a number of ways in which teachers can assess pupils' knowledge and skills. Among them are 'performances' (e.g. singing a song, reciting a poem, participating in a role-play, reading a text) and written work (e.g. worksheets, displays, homework). The examples presented in chapters 7 to 9 can be used both for practice and as a basis for assessing achievements more formally. Below is a list of some of the different types of exercises presented earlier:

Comprehension
- Relate pictures and words/sentences
- Follow instructions
- Identify misfits
- Order jumbled sentences
- Answer comprehension questions

Spelling
- Identify the missing letter
- Find the mistake
- Do a spelling test

Vocabulary
- Identify words
- Label pictures
- Classify words
- Substitute words

Composition skills
- Gap-filling exercises
- Form sentences
- Transform sentences
- Write a short text

Grammar
- Classify words
- Transform sentences
- Conjugate verbs.

As shown in Examples 12.1a and b, such exercises can form the basis of a formal test. The excerpts are drawn from a test that the Spanish teacher in Portway Primary School carried out to evaluate the Year 5 pupils' knowledge of vocabulary, composition skills, spelling, listening comprehension and knowledge of the geography of Spain at the end of a unit of work. This is an example of summative assessment.

Examples 12.1a Excerpts from a 'formal' test used in Year 5 at Portway Primary School

c. tres en la cuerda faldas hay rojas (*There are three red skirts on the washing line*)

En la cuerda hay tres faldas + rojas   2

d. puesto lleva azul un gorro (*He is wearing a blue cap*)

Puesto lleva puesto un gorro azul.   2

$\frac{7}{8}$

4. **Encuentra el error en la ortografía de estas palabras y luego escribe la palabra correcta a su lado.**

Naranga: Naranja ✓

Vlusa: Blusa ✓

Norrte: Norte ✓

$\frac{3}{3}$

5. **Rellena los huecos en estas frases.**

a. Me gusta el ___Norte ✓___ y el ___oeste ✓___ de España.

b. Me duele el ___manzana mano___ y la ___mano la oreja ✓___

c. Mis frutas favoritas son el ___manzana___ y la ___naranja ✓___

$\frac{4}{6}$

6. **Escribe lo que oigas:**

la manzana roja	Un gorro negro	En el Sur	El pico y la mano	los ojos
3	3	3	5	2

16

Examples 12.1b Excerpts from a 'formal' test used in Year 5 at Portway Primary School

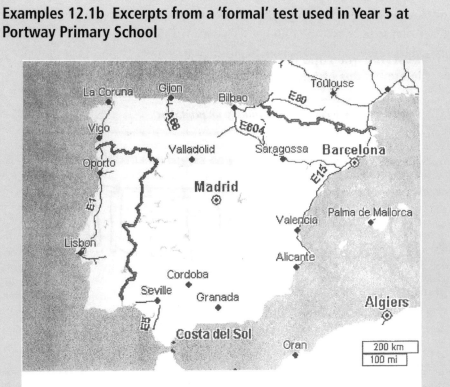

7. **Mira el mapa de España y contesta las preguntas usando 'norte, sur, este u oeste'.**

Ejemplo: *Sevilla está en el sur de España*

¿Dónde está Granada?   2

Granada está en el *sur de España* ✓

¿Dónde está Gijón?   2

Gijón está en el norte de España ✓

¿Dónde está Valencia?   2

Valencia está en el este de España ✓

¿Dónde está Vigo?   2

Vigo está en el oeste de España ✓

While teachers might find it relatively easy to assess language skills and knowledge, they will need a more holistic approach to evaluate changing attitudes and levels of awareness. They can base their judgements on conversations with children (e.g. notes of comments children made) and observations (e.g. pupils' engagement in lessons; their participation in pen pal exchanges).

12.3 Characteristics of efficient assessment

English practitioners have described the key characteristics of efficient assessment as follows (QCA, 2005; Jones and Coffey, 2006):

- sharing learning objectives and assessment criteria with pupils
- discussing learning strategies
- using efficient questioning techniques
- giving appropriate feedback
- involving pupils in assessment.

The different principles are outlined below.

12.3.1 Sharing goals and assessment criteria

Pupils are more actively engaged in their learning process if they know the objectives, the reasons behind particular activities and the assessment criteria. It is important that teachers explain the objectives and success criteria in such a manner as to encourage responsibility. They need to choose appropriate vocabulary and give relevant examples. If pupils understand the demands of the tasks and are able to identify appropriate strategies to achieve the target they are likely to succeed.

12.3.2 Discussing learning strategies

By constantly reminding pupils of the range of learning strategies they can use throughout the lesson, teachers keep pupils on task.

12.3.3 Efficient questioning techniques

Efficient questioning techniques enable teachers to establish what pupils know, understand and can do and what misconceptions they need to address. Questions that only require a yes/no answer do not provide a deep insight into pupils' understanding and skills. The so-called 'wh' questions (what?, who?, why?, when?) are generally better at revealing pupils' thinking. For example, the question 'Does *joli* in *la jolie fille* end with the letter 'e'?' provides teachers with limited information about a pupil's understanding of agreement. A slightly more sophisticated question calls on children to use their metalinguistic skills to justify their reasoning. The question 'Can you explain why *jolie* in *la jolie fille* ends with the letter 'e'?' could trigger the following comments: articles and nouns in French display gender; *la* is the feminine form; adjectives agree with gender; this particular adjective changes from *joli* to *jolie*.

12.3.4 Giving appropriate feedback

Comments and marks affect the pupils' confidence and enthusiasm. Giving constructive, relevant and specific feedback requires teachers and pupils to build a learning environment based on trust and respect. Pupils need to feel confident about asking for feedback and about classmates or teachers commenting in a sensitive and constructive way.

12.3.5 Involving pupils in assessment

Feedback is most efficient if it is given regularly, focuses on progress and product and encourages comparison of achievement over a period of time. Teachers will need to make time to engage pupils in a discussion about a particular performance or about the progress made during a whole term. Rather than indicating an area for development and suggesting remedies, teachers should help pupils to identify their own strengths or weaknesses and to define strategies to address them. This minimal support can help pupils perform better the next time. Assessment that works within the learners' zone of proximal development (see p. 46) therefore encourages learning and fosters motivation.

Teachers may want to use peer or self-assessment in addition to teacher assessment. Involving pupils in the assessment process has the advantage that they reflect on their strengths and weaknesses, identify ways to address possible gaps, refine thinking skills and develop metacognitive and metalinguistic awareness. For peer and self-assessment to be efficient teachers need to develop the pupils' ability to listen carefully, to identify their own needs and those of others, to define ways to address strengths and weaknesses and to use appropriate language to express constructive criticism (Ehlers *et al.*, 2006). Pupils as young as six are capable of self-assessment with appropriate guidance (Krajnovic and Djigunovic, 2006 mentioned in Edelenbos *et al.*, 2006).

Peer assessment can be done on a one-to-one basis or involve a group of children. It needs to be managed carefully and sensitively because pupils who compare themselves with more successful learners could lose their motivation. Good peer-assessment has the potential to create a classroom culture of support. As with peer-assessment, self-assessment requires honesty, sensitivity and self-confidence as well as knowledge and an understanding of learning intentions and of the assessment criteria (Klapper, 2006).

Tools for self-assessment

Self-assessment gives teachers feedback on what pupils have learned and helps them plan the next steps. During or at the end of a lesson teachers often revert to the 'traffic light', 'smiley faces' or a 'thumbs up' system: a green dot, a smiley face and a 'thumbs up' indicate that pupils have fully understood a concept. 'Can do' statements inspired by the European Language Portfolio are particularly efficient after a longer unit of work. Pupils read phrases such as 'I can count up to ten in French' and colour them in green, amber or red to show their level of competence.

To involve pupils in Years 3 and 4 in the assessment procedure, the teachers at Portway Primary School asked pupils in Years 3 and 4 to write their own 'can do' statements and to colour them in. Older students filled in a table similar to the one presented in Figure 12.1. To complete the table they had to think about their achievements, the aspects of the lessons they particularly enjoyed or found especially difficult and to set themselves targets.

A very popular way of getting pupils to record achievements is the 'two stars and a wish' system. They identify two positive achievements (two stars) and set one target (the wish).

In the next section different ways of comparing achievements on a national and even international level are presented.

12.4 Measuring achievements

The Council of Europe's Common European Framework makes it possible for learners to document achievements, to self-assess knowledge and skills and to compare competencies across Europe. In England, some teachers use the Languages Ladder, influenced by the European framework. This highly versatile document allows for self-assessment, formative and summative assessment. Studies have shown that schools in England also use self-assessment in the form of 'smiley-face-sheets' or 'can-do-statements' and pupil-friendly versions of the National Curriculum level descriptors (Muijs *et al.*, 2005; OFSTED, 2005). Details of each document are given below.

My record of achievement for languages					
Date	My achievements 	Did I understand the work? 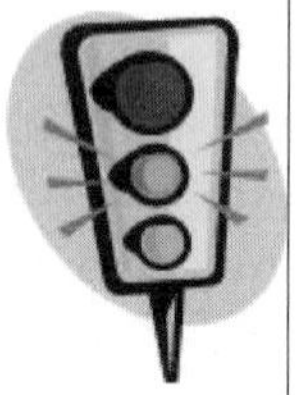	What I enjoyed most 	What I found difficult 	To improve I need to . . . 

Figure 12.1 Self-assessment by pupils in Year 5 and 6 at Portway Primary School.

12.4.1 The national level descriptors

The Attainment Targets (AT) of the National Curriculum set out the 'knowledge, skills and understanding which pupils of different abilities and maturities are expected to have by the end of each Key Stage' (as defined by the Education Act 1996; DfEE (1999c)). The ATs consist of eight level descriptions of increasing difficulty plus a description for exceptional performance. Each level description defines the types and range of performance that learners working at that level should demonstrate. Below are two examples:

> *Writing, Level 3*:
> Pupils write two or three short sentences on familiar topics, using aids (for example, textbooks, wall charts and their own written work). They express personal responses, (for example, likes, dislikes and feelings). They write short phrases from memory and their spelling is readily understandable.
>
> *Speaking, Level 4*:
> Pupils take part in simple structured conversations of at least three or four exchanges, supported by visual or other cues. They are beginning to use their knowledge of grammar to adapt and substitute single words and phrases. Their pronunciation is generally accurate and they show some consistency in their intonation.
>
> (www.nc.uk.net/prog_study.html)

At the end of Key Stages 1 and 2, teachers judge the pupils' performances against these targets and choose a 'best fit'. The chosen level descriptors do not represent everything pupils can do but provide a 'rough' picture.

Where primary schools provide well for foreign languages the DfES expects most pupils to reach Level 4 at the end of KS2 and bilingual children to exceed this. But these levels are high and pupils are more likely to attain between Levels 2 and 4. Pupils who have been taught foreign languages well in primary school are expected to reach Level 4 at the end of KS2. Bilingual children might be able to exceed Level 4. These levels are relatively high and children are more likely to attain between 2 and 4.

12.4.2 The Languages Ladder

One of the main aims of the National Languages Strategy (DfES, 2002b) was the implementation of a voluntary recognition scheme to complement the Common European Framework and the existing national qualifications such as GCSE, A level and NVQs (vocational qualifications). The idea was to give learners credit for their language skills in one or more languages learned and used in a range of contexts such as home, school or the wider community. The first three levels of the Languages Ladder have been available in 24 languages since 2006, Gaeilge, Japanese and Urdu being among them. Additional languages and phases are to be developed in 2008.

The Ladder comprises six stages: Breakthrough, Preliminary, Intermediate, Advanced, Proficiency and Mastery. Each of the first four stages is divided into three smaller steps or grades. Primary school children are expected to reach the first three stages (DfES, 2005b and c). Using 'can do' statements such as the one below, they assess their competence in one or all four language skills:

> Stage1 (Breakthrough)/Grade 2/reading: I can understand familiar written phrases (Asset Languages, 2005).

> Stage 2 (Preliminary)/Grade 4/speaking: I can take part in a simple conversation and I can express my opinions (e.g. discussing a picture with a partner) (Asset Languages, 2005).

Pupils can use the Languages Ladder for self-assessment but teachers can also use it as a basis for formative and summative assessment. Learners can have their attainments externally accredited and 'officially' recognized through the external agency 'Asset Languages'.

12.4.3 European Language Portfolio

The European Language Portfolio (ELP) is part of the Council of Europe's Common European Framework on learning, teaching and assessment. More than 31 of 45 States are currently engaged in piloting and implementing it (CiLT and NACELL, 2006). The English Junior version of the ELP was revised in 2006 by CiLT, the National Centre for Languages, to take account of the KS2 framework (DfES, 2005a) and the Languages Ladder.

The ELP comprises three sections:

- biography
- language passport
- dossier.

The *biography* encourages pupils to reflect on their language learning experience and their achievements. They compare their skills to 'can do' statements in relation to listening, spoken interaction, spoken production, reading and writing. Below are some examples of statements (Council of Europe, 2004):

> A1/ listening/Grade 3: I can understand the main point(s) from a short spoken passage (e.g. a short rhyme or song) (Council of Europe and CiLT, 2006: 23)

> A2/ writing/Grade 6: I can write a simple text (e.g. letters) (Council of Europe and CiLT, 2006, 2006: 9)

> B1/spoken production/Grade 6: I can tell a story or relate the plot of a book or film and give my opinions on it (e.g. a film I have recently seen) (Council of Europe and CiLT, 2006: 26).

A1 (Breakthrough), A2 (Waystage) and B (Threshold) are the first three of the six reference levels commonly used across Europe. Primary school children generally reach A1,

A2 or possibly B1. In the English Junior ELP, learners use the 'can-do' statements of the Languages Ladder.

In the *language passport* pupils summarize their achievements and linguistic experiences and indicate the reference level they have reached. In the 'dossier' they collect documents, pictures or recordings to illustrate their achievements and experiences with other languages and cultures.

The ELP provides the teacher with a holistic picture of the pupils' experiences, understanding and skills and takes account of all the languages learned in a range of contexts. It is up to children to complete the ELP, but teachers are encouraged to help them assess themselves against the levels and to update the *dossier* with more recent documents.

The use of portfolios promotes reflection and contributes to learner autonomy (Holec, 1981; Dam, 1995) and can have a positive impact on pupils' self-concept and confidence (Tsagari, 2005).

The pupils' ELP and their assessment against the Languages Ladder or the national level descriptors can be passed on to the Year 7 teachers to facilitate the transition from primary to secondary school.

12.5 Facilitating transition

In this section I present some transition issues and outline some arrangements that make transition more efficient.

12.5.1 Transition issues

Continuity of foreign language learning across different levels of schooling has been identified as a problem throughout the world. In Europe, Blondin *et al.* (1998: 28–30) have identified five common issues:

- a communication gap between senior managers and teachers involved in primary and secondary school
- a lack of fine-tuning and compatibility between aims
- differences in approach and type of curriculum
- reluctance in secondary schools to acknowledge and draw on what pupils had learned at primary school
- shortcomings in initial teacher education and continuing professional development to address the problems mentioned above.

The lack of liaison between primary and secondary schools has proved to be an obstacle to children's learning. In England, Burstall *et al.* (1974) explained Year 7 pupils' inability to build on their primary school experience in terms of the inadequate liaison between primary and secondary schools, the lack of continuity in foreign language teaching across the schools and the lack of differentiation of secondary teachers.

Bolster *et al.*'s study (2004) confirmed many of these findings. They found that pupils with an early language learning experience started secondary school with confidence, good accents, fluency in communication and good listening comprehension. However, apart from their positive attitudes, they were unable to sustain these advantages until the end of the year. The researchers' investigation revealed inadequate assessment procedures and a lack of liaison between the primary and secondary schools. Pupils' achievements were not assessed at the end of Year 6 which meant that the Year 7 teachers had no information about their performance and the curriculum they had covered. The secondary teachers did not make any extra provision but aimed to have all students at the same stage at Christmas, irrespective of whether or not they had any previous language learning experience. The teachers' tendency to downplay and ignore prior achievements contributed to the disillusionment of some students. The trend to expect beginners to catch up rather than make provision for more advanced learners has also been described in other studies (Hill *et al.*, 1997; Kipp, 1996).

Research findings reported by Driscoll *et al.* (2004) and OFSTED (2005) point to a similar lack of transition arrangements between the primary and the secondary sector. They show that many primary schools did not adequately communicate the pupils' achievements to secondary schools. Only a small minority of secondary schools, for the most part Specialist Language Colleges, modified their provision in Year 7 usually through differentiation, setting and fast-tracking. Many Year 7 students spoke of their frustration at repeating what they had already been taught at primary school.

Making efficient transition arrangements and planning for continuity is a challenge for teachers in all subjects but it is particularly difficult for foreign language teachers in England where MFL will not be a compulsory subject until September 2009. As a result, secondary schools currently have to accommodate pupils who have learned different languages (or none at all) for different purposes, over different time spans, with different pedagogical approaches and different curricula. Once the subject has got a definitive place in the timetable, pupils are likely to have a similar learning experience, which, in turn, should facilitate transition arrangements, collaboration and differentiation.

The choice of language in relation to transition has been much discussed. Some educationalists state that transition would be eased if every primary school taught the same language, probably French, so that secondary teachers can build on pupils' prior knowledge. (Industries would disapprove.) Others maintain that pupils do not necessarily need to learn the same language in each sector. They still benefit from their early language learning experience because they develop transferable language learning skills.

12.5.2 Pupils' perspectives on transition

Jones and Coffey (2006) investigated pupils' attitudes on transition. Asked about their expectations of foreign language learning at secondary school, all Year 6 pupils said that 'it will get harder' and that they will cover more literacy in the target language. Most feared that they would be unable either to understand the language used in the classroom and or to do the homework. Some pupils described the textbooks they had come across as 'scary'.

The authors found that students had good ideas about how to create continuity in their language learning experience. They wanted more opportunities to write at primary school to prepare them for the emphasis on literacy at secondary school. They also suggested having more opportunities to work on their oral skills, for example through using the language to members of staff and through taping some speaking activities. They also asked for more independent study and project work and activities which involved them researching cultural information. Some wanted more homework, others wanted their teachers to show them typical resources used at secondary school. All the pupils hoped that the secondary teachers would take account of their prior learning experience and needs.

12.5.3 Making efficient arrangements

In order to achieve a smooth transition, primary teachers should start by addressing the problems that Blondin *et al.* (1998) have identified at the level of schools: information gap between staff, difference in aims, approaches and curricula, and lack of provision for advanced learners.

Regular dialogue

The regular dialogue between primary and secondary teachers helps them to: share aims; exchange documentation, policies and schemes of work; discuss each other's pedagogy and curricula; examine resources and develop some understanding of the ways in which pupils learn languages. Their phase work must focus on the development of communicative and intercultural skills, knowledge about language and language learning skills to ensure continuity.

Lesson observations and team teaching

Both primary and secondary teachers benefit from hosting each other and working along side each other. Secondary teachers who attend foreign language and literacy lessons at primary schools familiarize themselves with the curriculum and see how primary teachers build up knowledge about language and language learning skills. When they observe lessons in other subjects they become aware of the variety of ways in which class teachers can integrate foreign languages into the curriculum and embed them in the daily life of the school. The regular visits make them realize how much primary children can learn.

Lesson observations and team-teaching enable primary teachers to model their pronunciation vocabulary and grammar on those of the secondary teachers. In addition, they come to know what is expected of the Year 7 students in terms of skills, knowledge and pace.

Bridging units

Bridging units (QCA, 2007) can be used with Year 6 pupils to prepare them for secondary schools and with Year 7 students to smooth the transition.

Assessment documents

The efficacy of transition depends largely on the quality of the transfer documents used to inform secondary teachers of the achievements and progress of the Year 6 pupils. Teachers of both sectors should agree on documents that are useful for each sector. This could be a report, samples of work and attainments. In England, it is recommended that these documents include either the ELP or the Languages Ladder. Some primary teachers add a list of topics covered in their FL lessons, for example, numbers, pets and family members. This list is particularly useful if teachers explain what pupils can *do* in their new language. Secondary teachers like to know if pupils can use this vocabulary in sentences and read these words. Primary teachers should therefore concentrate on pupils' language, skills and, especially, the transferable skills. Secondary teachers will find it useful to know, for example, that pupils have understood the concept of gender and agreements. They will be in a good position to help pupils draw on their knowledge about language. This is especially important if pupils begin to study a different foreign language from the one taught at primary school.

Planning for progression and continuity

The transfer documentation facilitates planning for progression and continuity. It provides teachers with an opportunity to consolidate and build on pupils' prior learning. They can set challenging targets, provide new and exciting material and use different methods to revisit vocabulary and structures covered earlier. If they teach the same topic they can expand it. For example, when speaking about families, they can speak about families in different cultures. They can build on students' experience of literacy in a foreign language and introduce a wider range of genres. Grammar is often taught implicitly in primary schools. Secondary teachers have an opportunity to teach it more explicitly thereby developing students' metalinguistic and analytic skills.

Personalized learning

Secondary teachers can differentiate their teaching by setting students in different ability groups. They can fast track the advanced linguists so that they can take their exams at an earlier stage and set up booster classes for students without any prior language learning experience. In classes where only a few students have learned a foreign language, a buddy-system could work well. Sometimes the more experienced students teach the less experienced. Both students benefit from this arrangement: the more advanced reinforce their knowledge and the beginners develop some language skills. However, teachers should not forget to provide special tuition for the more experienced learners so that they can continue to develop their skills.

Student visits

The process of transferring to secondary school is made less daunting if the Year 6 pupils have an opportunity to visit a secondary school, have a look at some resources and make contact with current Year 7 students and teachers. They appreciate taster lessons taught by a secondary teacher either at their own or a secondary school. Alternatively, Year 7 students could visit their former primary schools and brief the Year 6 pupils on the activities, teaching approaches and levels of achievement expected at secondary school.

Good transition makes pupils feel that the secondary teachers value and take account of their prior learning. As a result, they are likely to continue to develop confidence and competence (Jones and Coffey, 2006; CiLT and Nacell, 2006).

12.6 Main points to remember

Both formative and summative assessment is appropriate in foreign language lessons. Teachers can use a variety of activities to assess the pupils' knowledge, understanding and skills. They need a more holistic approach to assess the pupils' developing attitudes. The pupils' understanding of language learning and their language learning strategies become apparent in the course of discussions about their learning process.

Assessment is efficient if it:

- contributes to pupils' learning and increases their motivation
- encourages reflection and highlights the progress they have made
- promotes the development of metacognitive and metalinguistic skills
- makes pupils reflect on their strengths and weaknesses.

You should:

- share learning goals and assessment criteria with pupils
- discuss learning strategies
- use efficient questioning techniques
- give appropriate feedback
- involve pupils in assessment.

To facilitate and improve transition, to develop a shared understanding of language learning and to share responsibility, primary teachers may:

- use the European Language Portfolio, the Languages Ladder or the national level descriptors in their class and pass the documents on to secondary schools
- organize regular meetings with secondary colleagues
- exchange documentation, policies and schemes of work with secondary colleagues
- observe secondary teachers and team-teach

- collaborate with secondary teachers to develop units of work that take account of and expand students' prior learning
- arrange for Year 6 pupils to visit a secondary school
- organize opportunities for Year 6 and Year 7 pupils to meet and share experiences.

Secondary teachers facilitate and improve transition if they:

- make good use of the assessment documents of the primary pupils
- differentiate, set students and organize fast-tracking opportunities
- organize a buddy system and booster classes for beginner language learners
- collaborate with primary teachers and engage in the activities mentioned above.

Bibliography

Allwright, D. (2000) *Interaction and Negotiation in the Language Classroom. Their Role in Learner Development'*. Available from: www.ling.lancs.ac.uk/groups/crile/docs/crile50allrigh.pdf, accessed on 3 January 2000.

Andalo, D. (2007) 'All primary schools to teach foreign languages by 2010'. *The Guardian, 12 March.*

Anderson, J. R. (1983) *The Architecture of Cognition.* Cambridge, MA: Harvard University Press.

Anderson, J. R. (1985) *Cognitive Pyschology and Its Implications.* New York: Freeman.

Anderson, N. J. (2000) *The Role of Metacognition in Second Language Teaching and Learning.* Available from: www.eric.ed.gov/ERICWebPortal/recordDetail?accno=ED463659, accessed on 5 February 2000.

Anning, A. and Ring, K. (1999) *The Influence of the Socio-cultural Context on Young Children's Meaning making.* Available from: www.leeds.ac.uk/educol/documents/000001177.htm, accessed on 6 July 2000.

Armstrong, P. W. and Rogers, J. D. (1997) 'Basic skills revisited: the effects of foreign language instruction on Reading, Math and Language Arts', *Learning Languages,* 2: 20–31.

Arndt, P. and Effgen, G. (2005) *Encouraging a Curiosity for World Cultures.* Available from: www.education.com/reference/article/Ref_Curiousity_World/, accessed on 14 January 2008.

Asher, J. J. (1972) 'The learning strategy of the Total Physical Response', *The Modern Language Journal,* 56: 133–9.

Asher, J. J. (1979) *Learning Another Language through Actions.* San José, CA: AccuPrint.

Asset Languages (2005) *The Languages Ladder Can-do Statements.* Available from: www.assetlanguages.org.uk/UserFiles/File/specialists/cando_sept2005.pdf, accessed on 4 September 2005.

Ausubel, D. (1964) 'Adult versus children in second language learning: psychological considerations', *Modern Language Journal,* 48: 420–4.

Baker, C. (1997) *Foundations of Bilingual Education and Bilingualism, 2nd edition.* Clevedon, Avon and Sydney: Multilingual Matters.

Barnes, D., Britton, J. and Torbe, M. (1986) *Language, the Learner and the School.* London: Penguin.

Bayley, R. and Schecter, S. R. (Eds) (2003) *Langue Socialisation in Bilingual and Multilingual Societies.* Clevedon, OH: Multilingual Matters.

BBC News (2006) 'Schools "ignored" languages edict', 1 November. Available from:.http://news.bbc.co.uk/go/pr/fr/-/1/hi/education/6442837.stm, accessed on 1 November 2006.

BBC News (2007a) 'Schools to get £50m language help', 12 March. Available from: http://news.bbc.co.uk/go/pr/fr/-/1/hi/education/6442837.stm, accessed on 12 March 07.

BBC News (2007b) 'Seven-year-olds to take languages', 12 March. Available from: http://news.bbc.co.uk/go/pr/fr/-/1/hi/education/6435885.stm, accessed on 12 March 2007.

Beacco, J. C. and Byram, M. (2003) *Guide for the Development of Language Education Policies in Europe: From Linguistic Diversity to Plurilingual Education.* Main version. Strasbourg: Council of Europe, Language Policy Division.

Bell, S. (1998) *Storyline Scotland.* Available from: www.storyline-scotland.freeserve.co.uk, accessed on 5 June 2002.

Bialystok, E. (1981) 'The role of conscious strategies in second language proficiency', *Modern Language Journal,* 65: 24–35.

Block, D. (1996) 'Not so fast: some thoughts on theory culling, relativism, accepted findings and the heart and soul of SLA', *Applied Linguistics,* 17: 63–83.

Blondin, C., Candelier, M., Edelenbos, P., Johnstone, R., Kubanek-German, A. and Taeschner, T. (1998) *Foreign Languages in Primary and Pre-school Education: Review of Recent Research within the European Union.* London: CiLT.

Bloomfield, L. (1933) *Languages.* New York: Holt.

Bolster, A., Balandier-Brown, C. and Rea-Dickins, P. (2004) 'Young learners of modern foreign languages and their transition to the secondary phase: a lost opportunity?', *Language Learning Journal,* Winter: 35–41.

Branaman, L. and Rhodes, N. (1999) 'Foreign language instruction in the United States: a national survey of foreign language instruction in elementary and secondary schools', Available from: www.cal-online.survey@cal.org, accessed on 9 March 2003.

Britton, J. (ed.) (1975) *The Developing of Writing Abilities 11 to 18.* London: Macmillan.

Brooker, L. (2002) *Starting School – Young Children Learning Cultures.* Buckingham: Open University Press.

Brown, A. L., Bransford, J. D., Ferrara, R. A. and Campione, J. C. (1983) 'Learning, remembering, and understanding', in J. H. Flavell, and M. Markman (eds), *Carmichael's Manual of Child Psychology.* New York: Wiley.

Brumfit, C. J. (1984) *Communicative Methodology in Language Teaching.* Cambridge: Cambridge University Press.

Brumfit, C. J. (1994) 'Understanding, language, and educational process', in G. Brown, K. Malmkjaer, A. Pollitt and J. Williams (eds), *Language and Understanding.* Oxford: Oxford University Press.

Brumfit, C. J. (ed.) (1995) *Language Education in the National Curriculum.* Oxford: Blackwell.

Bruner, J. S. (1986) *Actual Minds, Possible Worlds.* Clevedon, Avon and London: Harvard University Press.

Bruner, J. S. (1990) *Acts of Meaning.* Cambridge, MA: Harvard University Press.

Bruner, J. S. (1996) *The Culture of Education.* Cambridge, MA: Harvard University Press.

Burstall, C., Jamieson, M., Cohen, S. and Hargreaves, M. (1974) *Primary French in the Balance.* Slough: National Foundation for Educational Research.

Bush (2006) *National Security Language Initiative.* Available from: www.ed.gov/about/inits/ed/competitiveness/nsli/index.html, accessed on 4 May 2007.

Byram, M. (1999) *Language Learning in Intercultural Perspective.* Cambridge: Cambridge University Press.

Byram, M. (2002) 'Foreign language education as political and moral education – an essay', *Language Learning Journal,* 26: 43–7.

Byram, M. and Doyé, P. (1999) 'Intercultural competence', in P. Driscoll and D. Frost (eds), *The Teaching of Modern Foreign Languages in the Primary School.* London: Routledge.

Cameron, L. (2001) *Teaching Languages to Young Children.* Cambridge: Cambridge University Press.

Canale, M. (1983) 'From communicative competence to language pedagogy', in J. C. Richardsand R. W. Schmidt (eds), *Language and Communication.* Harlow: Longman.

Canale, M. and Swain, M. (1980) 'Theoretical bases of communicative approaches to second language teaching and testing', *Applied Linguistics,* 1: 1–47.

Candelier, M. (ed.) (2003) *L'éveil aux langues à l'école primaire. Evlang: bilan d'une innovation européenne.* Brussels: De boeck.

Carless, D. R. (2003) 'Factors in the implementation of task-based teaching in primary schools. Elsevier 2003'. Available from: www.elsevier.com/locate/system, accessed on 1 September 2005.

Celce-Murcia, M. and Olshtain, E. (2000) *Discourse and Context and Language Teaching: A Guide for Language Teachers.* Cambridge: Cambridge University Press.

Chamot, A. J. and O'Malley, J. M. (1987) 'The Cognitive Academic Language *Learning* Approach: a bridge to the mainstream', *TESOL Quarterly*, 21: 227–49.

Chamot, A. J., O'Malley, J. M., Küpper, L. and Impink-Hernandez, M. V. (1987) *A Study of Learning Strategies in Foreign Language Instruction: First Year Report*. Washington, DC: InterAmerica Research Associates.

Chamot, A. U. (1987) 'The power of learning strategies', *Ohio Bilingual-Multicultural Update*, March: 6–11.

Chamot, A. U., Barnhardt, S. and El-Dinary, P. B. (1996) 'Teaching strategies to develop effective language learners (final report)', unpublished manuscript.

Chamot, A. U., Barnhardt, S., El-Dinary, P. B. and Robbins, J. (1999) *The Learning Strategies Handbook*. New York: Longman.

Chamot, A. U. and El-Dinary, P. B. (1999) 'Children's learning strategies in language immersion classrooms', *Modern Language Journal*, 83: 319–38.

Chamot, A. U., Küpper, L., Thompson, I., Barruetta, M. and Toth, S. (1990) *Learning Strategies in the Foreign Language Classroom: Resource Guides for Listening Comprehension, Reading Comprehension, Speaking, and Writing*. McLean, VA: Interstate Research Associates.

Chamot, A. U. and O'Malley, J. M. (1994) *The CALLA Handbook: Implementing the Cognitive Academic Language Learning Approach*. New York: Addison-Wesley.

Chamot, A. U. and Rubin, J. (1994) 'Comments on Janie Rees-Miller's "A critical appraisal of learner training: theoretical bases and teaching applications"'. *TESOL Quarterly*, 27: 771–6.

Cheater, C. and Farren, A. (2001) *The Literacy Link*, London: CiLT.

Chesterfield, R. and Chesterfield, K. B. (1985) 'Natural order in children's use of second language learning strategies', *Applied Linguistics*, 6: 45–59.

Chomsky, N. (1959) 'A review of B. F. Skinner's *Verbal Behaviour*', *Language*, 35: 26–58.

Chomsky, N. (1965) *Aspects of the Theory of Syntax*. Cambridge, MA: MIT Press.

Chomsky, N. (1981) *Lectures on Government and Binding*. Dordrecht: Foris.

Chomsky, N. (1986) *Knowledge of Language: Its Nature, Origin, and Use*. New York: Praeger.

CiLT (1999) *Early Language Learning Bulletin*. Available from: www.cilt.org.uk/nacell/min2.htm, accessed on 8 February 2000.

CiLT (2002a) *The Early Language Learning Initiative Report on Phase 1 (1999–2001)*. London: Centre for Information on Language Teaching and Research.

CiLT (2002b) *Early Language Learning. Curricular Model*. London: National Centre for Language Learning.

CiLT and NACELL (2006) *Primary Languages Training Manual*. London: National Centre for Languages.

Cochran-Smith, M. (1984) *The Making of a Reader*. Norwood, NJ: Albex Publishing Corporation.

Cohen, A. D. (1998) *Strategies in Learning and Using a Second Language*. New York: Addison Wesley Longman.

Cohen, A. D., Weaver, S. J. and Li, Y. T. (1995) *The Impact on Strategies-based Instruction to Speaking a Foreign Language*. Minneapolis: National Language Resource Centre, Minnesota University.

Collier, V. P. (1989) 'How long? A synthesis of research on academic achievement in a second language', *TESOL Quarterly*, 23: 509–31.

Cook, V. (1997) *Inside Language*. London: Arnold.

Corder, P. (1967) 'The significance of learner errors', *International Review of Applied Linguistics*, 5: 161–70.

Cortazzi, M. and Jin, L. (1996) 'English teaching and learning in China', *Language Teaching*, 29: 61–80.

CotteralL, S. (1993) 'Reading strategy training in second language contexts: some caveats', *Aral*, 16: 71–82.

Council of Europe (2004) *European Language Portfolio, Principles and Guidelines*. Strasbourg: Language Policy Division.

Council of Europe and Council of Cultural Co-operation (1996) *Modern Languages: Learning, Teaching, Assessment. A Common European Framework of Reference.* Available from: http://www.coe.int/t/dg4/linguistic/CADRE_EN.asp, accessed on 11 January 2008.

Council of Europe and CILT (2006) *European Language Portfolio. Junior Version.* Revised edition. London: Central Books.

Coyle, D. (2000) 'Meeting the challenge: developing the 3Cs curriculum', in S. Green. (ed.), *New Perspectives on Teaching and Learning Modern Languages.* Clevedon, Avon: Multilingual Matters.

Crookes, G. and Schmidt, R. (1991) 'Reopening the research agenda', *Language Learning,* 41: 469–512.

Curtain, H. and Pesola, C. A. (1994) *Languages and Children. Making the Match.* New York: Longman.

Dam, L. (1995) *Learner Autonomy 3. From Theory to Classroom Practice.* Dublin: Authentik.

Deci, E. L. and Ryan, R. M. (1985) *Intrinsic Motivation and Self-Determination in Human Behaviour.* New York: Plenum Press.

De La Piedra, M. and Romo, H. D. (2003) 'Collaborative literacy in a Mexican immigrant household: the role of sibling mediators in the socialisation of pre-school learners', in R. Bayley, and S. R. Schecter (eds), *Language Socialisation in Bilingual and Multilingual Societies.* Clevedon, Avon: Multilingual Matters.

Department for Education and Employment (1990) *A Survey of Language Awareness and Foreign Language Taster Courses.* London: HMSO.

Department for Education and Employment (1999a) *The National Curriculum for England: The National Curriculum Handbook for Primary Teachers in England. Key Stages 1 and 2.* London: DfEE/QCA.

Department for Education and Employment (1999b) *Handbook for Primary Teachers in England, Key Stages 1 and 2: Guidelines for MFL at KS2 (non statutory).* London: DfEE/QCA.

Department for Education and Employment and Qualifications (1999c) *Modern Foreign Languages: The National Curriculum for England.* London: DfEE.

Department for Education and Skills (2002a) *Green Paper, 14–19: Extending Opportunities, Raising Standards.* London: DfES.

Department for Education and Skills (2002b) *Languages for All: Languages for Life: A Strategy for England.* London: DfES.

Department for Education and Skills (2003) *Framework for Teaching MFL: Years 7, 8 and 9.* Available from: http://publications.teachernet.gov.uk/default.aspx?PageFunction=productdetails&PageMode=publications&ProductId=DfES+0084+2003&, accessed on 11 January 2008.

Department for Education and Skills (2005a) *The Key Stage 2 Framework for Languages.* Nottingham: DfES Publications.

Department for Education and Skills (2005b) *The Languages Ladder, Steps for Success, Timetable for the Development of the Scheme.* Available from: www.dfes.gov.uk/languages/DSP_languagesladder_timetables.cfm, accessed on 11 January 2008.

Department for Education and Skills (2007) *Languages Review.* Nottingham: DfES Publications.

Dewey, J. (1916) *Democracy and Education.* New York: Macmillan.

Dewey, J. (1933) *How We Think: A Restatement of the Relation of Reflective Thinking to the Educative Press.* Chicago: Henry Regenery.

Díaz (1990) 'The social origins of self-regulation', in L. C. Moll (ed.), *Vygotsky and Education: Instructional Implications and Applications of Sociohistorical Psychology.* Cambridge: Cambridge University Press.

Dickinson, L. (1987) *Self-Instruction in Language Learning.* Cambridge: Cambridge University Press.

Dickinson, L. (1995) 'Autonomy and motivation: a literature review', *System,* 23: 165–74.

Donato, R. (2000) 'Sociocultural contributions to understanding the foreign and second language classroom', in J. P. Lantolf (ed.), *Sociocultural Theory and Second Language Learning*. Oxford: Oxford Applied Linguistics.

Donato, R. and McCormick, D. (1994) 'A sociocultural perspective on language learning strategies: the role of mediation', *The Modern Language Journal*, 78: 453–63.

Donmall, G. (ed.) (1985) *Language Awareness*. London: Longman.

Doyé, P. and Hurrell, A. (1997) *Foreign Language Learning in Primary Schools (age 5/6 to 10/11)*. Strasbourg: Council of Europe Publishing.

Driscoll, P. (1999a) 'Teacher expertise in the primary modern foreign languages classroom', in P. Driscoll and D. Frost (eds), *The Teaching of Modern Foreign Languages in the Primary School*. London: Routledge.

Driscoll, P. (1999b) 'MFL in the primary school: a fresh start', in P. Driscoll and D. Frost (eds), *The Teaching of Modern Foreign Languages in the Primary School*. London: Routledge.

Driscoll, P. and Frost, D. (eds) (1999) *The Teaching of Modern Foreign Languages in the Primary School*. London: Routledge.

Driscoll, P., Jones, J. and Macrory, G. (2004) *The Provision of Foreign Language Learning for Pupils at Key Stage 2*. London: Department for Education and Skills.

Drummond, M. J. (1993) *Assessing Children's Learning*, 1st edition. London: David Fulton Publishers.

Dulay, H. and Burt, M. (1974) 'Natural sequences in child second language learning', *Language Learning*, 24: 37–53.

Dulay, H., Burt, M. and Krashen, S. (1982) *Language Two*. Oxford: Oxford University Press.

Dyson, A. H. (1997) *What Difference Does Difference Make?* Berkeley, CA: University of California.

Edelenbos, P. and Johnstone, R. (1996) *Researching Languages at Primary School – Some European Perspectives*. London: Scottish CiLT.

Edelenbos, P., Johnstone, R. and Kubanek, A. (2006) *Pedagogical Principles Underlying the Teaching of Languages to Very Young Learners. Languages for the Children of Europe. Published Research, Good Practice and Main Principles*. Brussels: European Commission. Education and Culture, Culture and Communication.

Ehlers, G., Harder, K., Jävinen, H.-M., Brandford, V. and Materniak, M. (2006) *Storyline Approach in the Foreign Language Classroom. Berlin:* Comenius Project.

Ellis, R. (1984) 'Can syntax be taught? A study of the effects of formal instruction on the acquisition of Wh questions by children', *Applied Linguistics*, 5.

Ellis, R. (1994) *The Study of Second Language Acquistion*. Oxford: Oxford University Press.

Ellis, R. (1995) 'Implicit/Explicit knowledge and language pedagogy', *TESOL Quarterly*, 28.

Ellis, R. (1997) *Second Language Acquisition*. Oxford: Oxford University Press.

Ellis, R. (2003) *Task-based Language Learning and Teaching*. Oxford: Oxford University Press.

Ericsson, E. (1997) *Speech within Reach in Foreign Language Teaching*. Göteborg, Sweden: Utbildningstaden AB.

Erler, L. (2006) 'Developing strategies to process written French', paper presented at conference on 'Better learning: developing foreign language skills through strategy training', Oxford, 25 February.

Eurydice (2005) *Key Data on Teaching Languages at School in Europe,* Available from: www.eurydice.org/Documents/ KDLANG/2005/EN/FrameSet.htm, accessed on 18 September 2006.

Eurydice (2006) *National Summary Sheets on Education Systems in Europe and Ongoing Reforms*. Available from: www.eurydice.org/portal/page/portal/Eurydice/PubContents?pubid=047EN&country=null, accessed on 28 October 2007.

Farren, A. and Smith, R. (2003) *Bringing It Home. How Parents Can Support Children's Language Learning*. London: CiLT.

Fehse, K. and Kocher, D. (2002) 'Storyline projects in the foreign language classroom', in O. Kühn. and O. Mentz (eds), *Zwischen Kreativität, Konstruktion und Emotion: Der etwas andere Fremdsprachenunterricht.* Herbolzheim: Centaurus Verlag.

Felberbauer, M. and Heindler, D. (1995) *Foreign Language Education in Primary Schools,* Strasbourg: Council of Europe.

Fillmore, L. W. (1985) *Second Language Learning in Children: A Proposed Model. Issues in English Language Development.* Rosslyn, VA: National Clearing.

Firth, A. and Wagner, J. (1997) 'On discourse, communication and some fundamental concepts in SLA research', *Modern Languages Journal,* 81: 285–300.

Frost, R. (2005) *A Task-based Approach.* Available from: www.teachingenglish.org.uk/think/methodology/task_based. shtml, accessed on 14 December 2005.

Gagné, E. D. (1985) *The Cognitive Psychology of School Learning.* Boston: Little Brown.

Gagné, E. D., Yekovich, C. W. and Yekovich, F. R. (1993) *The Cognitive Psychology of School Learning.* New York: Harper Collins.

Gardner, R. C. (1988) 'The socio-educational model of second language learning: assumptions, findings and issues', *Language Learning,* 38: 101–26.

Gardner, R. C. and Lambert, W. E. (1972) *Attitudes and Motivation in Second Language Learning.* Rowley, MA: Newbury House.

Garner, R. (2007) 'Foreign languages to be compulsory from age seven', *The Independent, 13 March.*

Gass, S. (1988) 'Integrating research areas: a framework for second language acquisition studies', *Applied Linguistics,* 9: 198–217.

Gass, S. (1997) *Input, Interaction and the Second Language Learner.* Mahwah, NJ: Lawrence Erlbaum Associates.

Gattegno, C. (1972) *Teaching Foreign Languages in Schools: The Silent Way.* New York: Educational Solutions.

Genelot, S. and Tupin, F. (2001) 'Evaluation des pratiques pédagogiques: les atouts d'une approche méthodologique plurielle. Le cas du programme evlang', Quatrième congrès international d'actualité de la recherche en éducation et en formation, 5–8 September, Lille.

Gillette, B. (1994) 'The role of learner goals in L2 success', in J. P. Lantolf and G. Appel (eds), *Vygotskian Approaches to Second Language Research.* Norwood, NJ: Ablex Press.

Gouin, F. (1894) *The Art of Teaching and Studying Languages.* London: Philip.

Graham, B. (2006) *Foreign-Language Learning Promoted.* Available from: www.washingtonpost.com/wp-dyn/content/article/2006/01/05/AR2006010502199.html, accessed on 6 January 2006.

Graham, S. (1997) *Effective Language Learning. Positive Strategies for Advanced Level Language Learning.* Clevedon, Avon: Multilingual Matters.

Gregory, E. (1996) *Making Sense of a New World: Learning to Read in a Second Language.* London: Paul Chapman.

Gregory, E. (2008) *Learning to Read in a New Language: Making Sense of Words and Worlds.* London: Sage.

Gregory, E. and Williams, A. (1998) 'Family literacy history and children's learning strategies at home and at school', in A. Massey and G. Walford (eds), *Children Learning in Context. Studies in Educational Ethnography.* London: Jai Press.

Gregory, E., Williams, A. and Asghar, A. (2000) *Siblings as Mediators of Literacy in Two East London Communities.* London: ESRC Report R000222487.

Grenfell, M. (2000) 'Learning and teaching strategies', in S. Green (ed.), *New Perspectives on Teaching and Learning Modern Languages.* London: Multilingual Matters.

Grenfell, M. and Harris, V. (1993) 'How do pupils learn? (Part 1)'. *Language Learning Journal,* 8: 22–5.

Grenfell, M. and Harris, V. (1994) 'How do pupils learn? (Part 2)'. *Language Learning Journal,* 9: 7–11.

Grenfell, M. and Harris, V. (eds) (1999) *Modern Languages and Learning Strategies in Theory and Practice.* London and New York: Routledge.

Gretsch, G. (1992) *Computer im Schreibatelier*. Luxembourg: Ministère de l'Education Nationale.

Gu, Y. and Johnson, R. (1996) 'Vocabulary learning strategies and language learning outcomes', *Language Learning*, 46: 643–79.

Harambourre, F. (2007) 'De l'école au collège: quelles dynamiques, quelles continuités dans l'apprentissage des langues vivantes?', in F. Harambourre, M. Petit and C. Chambost (eds), *Enseigner les langues vivantes: enjeux contemporains*. Bordeaux: Bordeaux University Victor Segalen Bordeaux.

Harambourre, F. and Bonnet-Falandry, F. (2007) 'Lecture d'album en L2 et compétence interculturelle', *Les enjeux de la communication interculturelle*. Montpellier: University of Montpellier.

Harley, B. and Swain, M. (1984) 'The interlanguage of immersion students and its implications for second language teaching', in A. Davies, C. Criper, and A. Howatt, (eds), *Interlanguage*. Edinburgh: Edinburgh University Press.

Harris, V. (2003) 'Adapting classroom-based strategy instruction to a distance learning context', *TESL_Ej Teaching English as a Second or Foreign Language*. Available from: www.writing.berkeley.edu/TESL-EJ/ej26/a1.html, 7, accessed on 17 December 2003.

Harris, V., Burch, J., Jones, B. and Darcy, J. (2001) *Something to Say? Promoting Spontaneous Classroom Talk*. London: CiLT.

Hawkins, E. (1984) *Awareness of Language: An Introduction*. Cambridge: Cambridge University Press.

Hawkins, E. (1987) *Modern Languages in the Curriculum*. Cambridge: Cambridge University Press.

Hawkins, E. (ed.) (1999) *30 Years of Language Teaching*. London: CiLT.

Heath, S. B. (1983) *Ways with Words: Language, Life, and Work in Communities and Classrooms*. Cambridge: Cambridge University Press.

Hélot, C. and Young, A. (2005) 'The notion of diversity in language education: policy and practice at primary level in France', *Language, Culture and Curriculum*, 18: 242–57.

HMIE (2005) *Progress in Addressing the Recommendations of* Citizens of a Multilingual World. A report by HM Inspectorate for the Scottish Executive Education Department. Available from: www.hmie.gov.uk/documents/publication/hmiecoaml.html, accessed on 21 April 2006.

Hill, K., Davies, A., Oldfield, J. and Watson, N. (1997) 'Questioning an early start: the transition from primary to secondary foreign language learning', *Melbourne Papers in Language Testing*, 6: 21–35.

Holec, H. (1981) *Autonomy and Foreign Language Learning*. Oxford: Pergamon.

Holec, H. (1988) *Autonomy and self-directed Learning: Present Fields of Application,* Strasbourg: Council of Europe.

Holec, H. (1992) *Apprendre à apprendre les langues*. eric digest. ED368180. Available from: www.eric.ed.gov/ERICWeb Portal/recordDetail?accno=ED368180, accessed on 7 May 2000.

Holland, D. and Reeves, J. (1996) 'Activity Theory and the View from Somewhere: team perspectives on the intellectual work of programming', in B. Nardi (ed.), *Context and Consciousness: Activity Theory and Human-Computer Interaction*. Cambridge, MA: MIT Press.

Holt, R. D. (2003) *Introduction of National Security Language ACT.Congressional Record: 9 December 2003*. Available from: http://fas.org/irp/congress/2003_cr/hr3676.html. accessed on 7 May 2006.

Horwitz, E. K. (2006) *Becoming a Language Teacher: A Practical Guide to Second Language Learning and Teaching*. New York: Pearson.

Hsiao, T.-Y. and Oxford, R. (2002) 'Comparing theories of language learning strategies: a confirmatory factor analysis', *The Modern Language Journal*, 86: 368–83.

Hurrell, A. (1999) 'The four language skills: the whole works!', in P. Driscoll and D. Frost. (eds), *The Teaching of Modern Foreign Languages in the Primary School*. London: Routledge.

Huss-Kessler, R. (1997) 'Teacher perception of ethnic and linguistic minority parent involvement and its relationship to children's language and literacy learning: a case-study', *Teacher and Teacher Education*, 13: 171–82.

Hyltenstam, K. and Abrahamsson, N. (2001) 'Age and second language learning: the hazards of matching practical "implications" with theoretical "facts"', *TESOL Quarterly*, 35: 151–70.

Hymes, D. (1972) *On Communicative Competence*. Harmondsworth: Penguin Books.

IATEFL (2005) *A Brief History of English Teaching in China*. Available from: www.iatefl.org/content/newsletter/155.php, accessed on 5 June 2006.

Jenks, C. (1993) *Culture*. London: Routledge.

Johnson, K. (2001) *An Introduction to Foreign Language Learning and Teaching*. Harlow: Pearson Education Limited.

Johnson, M. (2004) *A Philosophy of Second Language Acquisition*. New Haven, and London: Yale University Press.

Johnstone, R. (1994) *Teaching Modern Languages at Primary School*. Edinburgh: Scottish Council for Research in Education Publication.

Johnstone, R., Cavani, J., Low, L. and McPake, J. (2000) *Assessing Modern Languages Achievement: a Scottish Pilot Study of Late Primary and Early Secondary Pupils*. Available from: www.cilt.org.uk/research/aap.htm, accessed on 3 March 2000.

Jones, B. (1995) *Exploring Otherness: An Approach to Cultural Awareness*. London: CiLT.

Jouannetaud, V. (2002) *Die Sprachmaus 3. Arbeitsblätter zum Sprachbuch für das dritte Schuljahr*. Luxembourg: Editions du Syndicat National des Enseignants.

Kasper, G. (1997) 'Can pragmatic competence be taught?', a *paper delivered at the 1997, TESOL Convention*. Available from: http://nflrc.hawaii.edu/NetWorks/NW06/default.html, accessed on 11 January 2008.

Kenner, C. (2000) 'Children writing in a multilingual nursery', in M. Martin-Jones and K. Jones (eds), *Multilingual Literacies*. Amsterdam: John Benjamins.

Kipp, S. (1996) 'How will learning French get me a job in Japan?', *Australian Language Matters*, 4: 16.

Kirsch, C. (1996) 'Es ist Osterhasenzeit', *Aeppelchen 3*. Luxembourg. MENFP/SCRIPT, DECOLAP.

Kirsch, C. (1997) 'Stratégies d'apprentissage du français en deuxième année. *DECOPRIM I/suite*. Luxembourg, MENFP/SCRIPT.

Kirsch, C. (2006a) 'English primary children learning foreign languages at home and at school: a sociocultural approach to the development of language learning strategies', Unpublished thesis, Goldsmiths College, London.

Kirsch, C. (2006b) 'Young children learning new languages out of school', *International Journal of Multilingualism*, 4: 258–80.

Klapper, J. (ed.) (2001) *Teaching Languages in Higher Education*. London: CiLT.

Klapper, J. (2003) 'Taking communication to task? A critical review of recent trends in language teaching', *Language Learning Journal*, 27: 33–44.

Klapper, J. (2006) *Understanding and Developing Good Practice. Language Teaching in Higher Education*. London: CiLT.

Kollwelter, S. (2007) *Immigration in Luxembourg: New Challenges for an Old Country*. Available from: www.migrationin-formation.org/Profiles/display.cfm?ID=587, accessed on 15 October 2007.

Krajnovic, M. and Mihaljevic Djigunovic, J. (2006). 'Razvoj samovrednovanje jezične kompetencije u dječjoj dobi' (The Development of Children's Self-assessment of Linguistic Competence), in *Dijete i jezik danas* (ed. Petrovic, E. *et al.*). Osijek: Sveuciliste Josipa Jurja Strassmayera u Osijeku.

Kramer, K. (2002) *Kramer.356*. Available from: http://sitemaker.umich.edu/kramer.356/foreign_language_study_in_other_countries, accessed on 11 January 2008.

Kramsch, C. (1993) *Context and Culture in Language Teaching*. Oxford: Oxford University Press.

Krashen, S. (1981) *Second Language Acquisition and Second Language Learning*. Oxford: Pergamon.

Krashen, S. (1982) *Principles and Practice in Second Language Acquisition*. Oxford: Pergamon.

Krashen, S. and Terrell, T. D. (1983) *The Natural Approach: Language Acquisition in the Classroom*. Hayward, CA: Hayward Press.

Kress, G. (1997) *Before Writing – Rethinking the Paths to Literacy*. London: Routledge.

Lado, R. (1957) *Linguistics across Cultures*. Ann Arbor, MI: University of Michigan Press.

Lam, A. S. L. (2005) *Language Education in China. Policy and Experience from 1949*. Hong Kong: Hong Kong University Press.

Lamarre, P. with Rossel Paredes, J. (2003) 'Growing up trilingual in Montreal: perceptions of college students', in R. Bayley, and S. R. Schecter (eds), *Language Socialisation in Bilingual and Multilingual Societies*. Clevedon, Avon: Multilingual Matters.

Lantolf, J. P. (1996) 'Second language theory building: letting all the flowers bloom', *Language Learning,* 46: 713–49.

Lantolf, J. P. (ed.) (2000) *Sociocultural Theory and Second Language Learning*. Oxford: Oxford Applied Linguistics.

Lantolf, J. P. and Appel, G. (eds) (1994) *Vygotskian Approaches to Second Language Research*. Norwood, NJ: Ablex.

Lantolf, J. P. and Pavlenko, A. (1995) 'Sociocultural theory and second language acquisition', *Annual Rreview of Applied Linguistics,* 15: 108–24.

Lantolf, J. P. and Thorne, S. L. (2006) *Sociocultural Theory and the Genesis of Second Language Development*. New York: Oxford University Press.

Larsen-Freeman, D. (2004) 'CA for SLA? It all depends', *Modern Language Journal,* 88: 603–7.

Lave, J. and Wenger, E. (1991) *Situated Learning: Legitimate Peripheral Participation*. Cambridge: Cambridge University Press.

Lenneberg, E. (1967) *Biological Foundations of Language*. New York: John Wiley and Sons.

Liddicoat, A. J., Scarino, A., Curnow, T. J., Kohler, M., Scrimgeour, A. and Morgan, A.-M. (2007) *An Investigation of the State and Nature of Languages in Australian Schools*. Prepared by the Research Centre for Languages and Cultures Education, University of South Australia. Canberra: Department of Education, Science and Training.

Lightbown, P. M. (1983) 'Acquiring English L2 in Quebec classrooms', in S. Felix and H., Wode (eds), *Language development at the crossroads*. Tübingen, Gunter Narr.

Lightbown, P. M. and Spada, N. (2003) *How Languages are Learned*. Oxford: Oxford University Press.

Lin, L. (2002) 'English education in present day China', *ABD,* 233(2): 8–9.

Littlewood, W. (1981) *Communicative Language Teaching*. Cambridge: Cambridge University Press.

Long, M. H. (1982) 'Native speaker/non-native speaker conversation in the second language classroom. TESOL: A book of readings', in M. Long and C. Richards (eds), *Methodology*. New York: Newbury House.

Long, M. H. (1983) 'Does Second Language Instruction make a difference? A review of research'. *TESOL Quarterly,* 17: 251–85.

Long, M. H. (1990) 'Maturational constraints on language development', *Studies in Second Language Acquisition,* 12: 251–85.

Long, M. H. (1996) 'The role of the linguistic environment in second language acquisition', in W. Richards and T. Bhatia (eds), *Handbook of Second Language Acquisition*. San Diego: Academic Press.

Long, M. H. (1997) *Focus on Form in Task-based Language Teaching*. Manoa: University of Hawaii.

Loschky, L. (1994) 'Comprehensible input and second language acquisition. What is the relationship?', *Studies in Second Language Acquisition,* 16: 303–23.

Low, L., Brown, S., Johnstone, R. and Pirrie, A. (1995) *Foreign Languages in Scottish Primary Schools – Evaluation of the Scottish Pilot Projects: Final Report to Scottish Office*. Stirling: Scottish CiLT.

Low, L., Duffield, J., Brown, S. and Johnstone, R. (1993) *Evaluating Foreign Languages in Scottish Primary Schools. Report to Scottish Office*. Stirling: Scottish CiLT.

Lozanov, G. (1978) *Suggestology and Outlines of Suggestopedy*. London: Gordon and Breach Science Publishers.

Lyster, R. and Ranta, L. (1997) 'Corrective feedback and learner uptake: negotiation of form in communicative classrooms, *Studies', in Second Language Acquisition,* 19: 37–61.

Macaro, E. (2003) *Teaching and Learning a Second Language: A Guide to Recent Research and Its Applications.* London: Continuum Publishing Group.

Macaro, E. (2006) 'Strategies for language learning and for language use: revising the theoretical framework', *Modern Language Journal,* 90: 320–37.

Mackey, A. (1999) 'Input, interaction and second language development', *Studies in Second Language Acquisition,* 21: 557–87.

McLaughlin, B. (1978) *Second-Language Acquisition in Childhood.* New York and London: Wiley.

McLaughlin, B. (1987) *Theories of Second Language Learning.* London: Edward Arnold.

McLaughlin, B., Rossman, T. and McLeod, B. (1983) 'Second language learning: an information processing perspective', *Language Learning,* 33: 135–58.

McNamee, G. D. and McLane, J. G. and Budwig, N. (1995) 'The adult-child dyad as a problem-solving system', *New Directions for Child and Adolescent Development,* 67: 41–4.

Mariani, L. (1992) 'Language awareness/Learning awareness in a communicative approach: a key to learner independence', *Perspectives, a Journal of TESOL– Italy,* Volume XVIII, December 1992.

Markee, N. (2000) *Conversation Analysis.* Mahwah, NJ: Erlbaum.

Markee, N. (2004) 'Zones of interactional transitions in ESL classes', *Modern Language Journal,* 88: 583–96.

Martin, C. (1995) *Games and Fun Activities.* London: CiLT.

Martin, C. (2000) *An Analysis of National and International Research on the Provision of Modern Foreign Languages in Primary Schools. A* report prepared for the Qualifications and Curriculum Authority. Available from: www.qca.org.uk/downloads/3809_cmartin_rpt_mfl_primaryschools.pdf, accessed on 12 August 2001.

Martin, C. (2002) *Rhythm and Rhyme. Developing Language in French and German.* London: CiLT.

Martin, C. and Cheater, C. (1998) *Let's Join In! Finger Rhymes and Action Rhymes.* London: CiLT.

MCEETYA (1999) *The Adelaide Declaration on National Goals for Schooling in the Twenty-First Century.* Available from: www.mceetya.edu.au/mceetya/nationalgoals/natgoals.htm, accessed on 17 April 2007.

MCEETYA (2003) *Review of Languages Education in Australian Schools.* Canberra: MCEETYA.

MCEETYA (2005) *National Statement for Languages Education in Australian Schools: National Plan for Languages Education in Australian Schools 2005–2008.* Adelaide: South Australian Department of Education and Children's Services.

MEN (1986) *Allo? Martine?* Luxembourg: Ministère de l'Education Nationale.

MENFPS (2003) *Mila.* Luxembourg: Ministère de l'Education Nationale, de la Formation Professionnelle et des Sports.

Michaels, S. (1986) 'Narrative presentations: an oral preparation for literacy with first graders', in J. Cook-Gumperz (ed.) *The Social Construction of Literacy.* Cambridge: Cambridge University Press.

Mitchell, R. (2003) 'Rethinking the concept of progression in the National Curriculum for Modern Foreign Languages: a research perspective', *Language Learning Journal,* 27: 15–23.

Mitchell, R. and Myles, F. (1998) *Second Language Acquisition Theories.* London: Arnold.

Mondada, L. and Pekarek Doehler, S. (2004) 'Second language acquisition as situated practice. Task accomplishment in the French second language classroom', *Modern Language Journal,* 88: 501–18.

Montgomery, C. and Eisenstein, M. (1985) 'Reality revisited: an experimental communicative course in ESL', *TESOL Quarterly,* 19: 317–34.

Muijs, D., Barnes, A. and Hunt, M. (2005) *Evaluation of the Key Stage 2 Language Learning Pathfinders.* Available from: www.dfes.gov.uk/research/programmeofresearch/projectinformation.cfm?projectId=14080andtype=5andresultspage=1, accessed on 12 August 2005.

Naiman, N., Fröhlich, H., Stern, H. H. and Todesco, A. (1978) *The Good Language Learner.* Ontario: The Ontario Institute for Studies in Education.

Nardi, B. (ed.) (1996) *Context and Consciousness: Activity Theory and Human-Computer Interaction.* Cambridge, MA: MIT Press.

Naysmith, J. (1999) 'Primary modern foreign language teaching: a picture of one country', *Language Learning Journal,* December: 15–19.

Nieto, S. (1999) *The Light in Their Eyes: Creating Multicultural Learning Communities.* New York: Teachers College Press.

Nisbet, J. and Shucksmith, J. (1986) *Learning strategies.* Boston: Routledge and Kegan Paul.

Nuffield Foundation (2000) *Languages: The Next Generation, The Final R*eport. London: Nuffield Foundation.

Nunan, D. (2004) *Task-based Language Teaching.* Cambridge: Cambridge University Press.

Nyikos, M. and Oxford, R. (1987) 'Strategies for foreign language learning and second language acquisition', paper presented at the Conference on Second Language Acquisition and Foreign Language Learning, University of Illinois, Champaign-Urbana.

OFSTED (2005) *Implementing Languages Entitlement in Primary Schools: An Evaluation of Progress in Ten Pathfinder LEAs.* Available from: www.ofsted.gov.uk/publications/index.cfm?fuseaction=pubs.summary&id=3948, accessed on 15 August 2006.

OFSTED (2007) *Cardwell Primary School. Inspection Report.* Available from: www.ofsted.gov.uk/reports/pdf/?inspection Number=307306&providerCategoryID=4096&fileName=\\school\\100\\s5_100155_20071122.pdf, accessed on 30 December 2007.

OFSTED (2007) *Portway Primary School. Inspection Report.* Available from: www.portway.newham.sch.uk/pdf.pdf, accessed on 24 July 2007.

O'Malley, J. M. and Chamot, A. J. (1990) *Learning Strategies in Second Language Acquisition.* Cambridge: Cambridge University Press.

O'Malley, J. M., Chamot, A. U. and Küpper, L. (1989) 'Listening comprehension strategies in second language acquisition', *Applied Linguistics,* 10: 418–35.

O'Malley, J. M., Chamot, A. U., Stewner-Manzanares, G., Küpper, L. and Russo, R. P. (1985) 'Learning strategies used by beginning and intermediate ESL students', *Language Learning,* 35: 21–46.

Oxford, R. L. (1990) *Language Learning Strategies, What Every Teacher Should Know.* Boston, MA: Heinle & Heinle Publishers.

Oxford, R. L. (1994) *Language Learning Strategies: An Update.* Available from: www.ericdigests.org/1995-2/update.htm, accessed on 23 April 1995.

Oxford, R. L., Lavine, R. Z., Felkins, G., Hollaway, M. E. and Saleh, A. (1996) 'Telling their stories: Language students use Diaries and recollection', in R. L. Oxford (ed.), *Language Learning Strategies around the World: Cross-cultural Perspectives. (Technical Report #13).* Honolulu: University of Hawaii, Second Language Teaching and Curriculum Center.

Oxford, R. L. and Leaver, B. L. (1996) 'A synthesis of strategy instruction for language', in Oxford R, L. (ed.), *Language Learning Strategies Around the World: Cross-cultural Perspectives (Technical Report #13).* Honolulu, University of Hawaii, Second Language Teaching and Curriculum Center.

Paley, V. G. (1992) *You Can't Say You Can't Play.* Cambridge, MA: Harvard University Press.

Palincsar, A. S. and Brown, A. L. (1984) 'Reciprocal teaching of comprehension-fostering and comprehension-monitoring activities', *Cognition and Instruction,* 1: 117–75.

Paribakht, T. and Wesche, W. (1997) 'Vocabulary enhancement activities and reading for meaning in second language vocabulary acquisition', in J. Coady and T. Huckin (eds), *Second Language Vocabulary Acquisition: A Rationale for Pedagogy*. New York: Cambridge University Press.

Penfield, W. and Roberts, J. (1959) *Speech and Brain Mechanisms*. Princeton, NJ: Princeton University Press.

Peschel, M. (2006) *Nikolaus. Kurze Gedichte für Weihnachten, zum Nikolaus und zum Advent*. Available from: www.fest-park.de/w000.html, accessed on 12 August 2006.

Peterson, L. R. (1975) *Learning*. Glenview, IL: Scott, Foresman.

Pica, T., Young, R. and Doughty, C. (1987) 'The impact of interaction on comprehension', *TESOL Quarterly*, 21: 737–58.

Pienemann, M., Kessler, J.-U. and Roos, E. (2006) *Englischerwerb in der Grundschule. Paderborn, Schöning*: UTB.

Platt, E. and Brooks, F. B. (1994) 'The "acquisition rich environment" revisited', *The Modern Language Journal*, 78: 497–511.

Pollard, A. with Filer, A. (1996) *The Social World of Children's Learning. Case Studies of Pupils from Four to Seven*. London: Cassell.

Powell, B., Wray, D., Rixon, S., Medwell, J., Barnes, A. and Hunt, M. (2000) 'Analysis and evaluation of the current situation relating to the teaching of Modern Foreign Languages at Key Stage 2 in England', Research report commissioned by the Qualifications and Curriculum Authority. Warwick, Language Centre Institute of Education Centre for Language Teacher Education (CELTE).

Powell *et al.* (2001) *QCA Project to Study the Feasibility of Introducing the Teaching of Modern Foreign Languages into the Statutory Curriculum at KS2*. Available from: www.qca.org.uk/downloads/3807_mfl_feas_ks2.pdf, accessed on 13 May 2002.

Prabhu, N. S. (1987) *Second Language Pedagogy*. Oxford: Oxford University Press.

Pressley, M. and McCormick, C. B. (1995) *Advanced Educational Psychology for Educators, Researchers and Policy-makers*. New York: Harper Collins.

Pufahl, I., Rhodes, N. and Christian, D. (2000) *Foreign Language Teaching: What the United States can learn from other countries*. Available from: www.cal.org/ericcll/countries.html, accessed on 3 November 2000.

Puren, C. (2002) 'Perspectives actionnelles et perspectives culturelles en didactique des langues: vers une perspective co-actionnelle co-culturelle', *Les Langues modernes*, 3: 55–71.

Puren, C. (2006) *Comment harmoniser le système d'évaluation français avec le cadre européen commun de référence? Conférence à l'Assemblée annuelle de la Régionale de Grenoble de l'APLV le 22 mars 2006*. Available from: www.aplv-languesmodernes.org, accessed on 28 October 2006.

QCA (2000) *Modern Foreign Languages: a Scheme of Work for Key Stage 2*. Available from: www.standards.dfes.gov.uk/schemes/primary_mfl/?view=get, accessed on 28 July 2000.

QCA (2005) *Characteristics of AfL*. Available from: www.qca.org.uk/qca_4337.aspx, accessed on 25 September 2005.

QCA (2007) *New Key Stage 2 Schemes of Work QCA 2007*. Available from: www.qca.org.uk/qca_11752.aspx#French, accessed on 26 April 2007.

Qiang, N. and Wolff, M. (2005) *English as a Foreign Language: The Modern Day Trojan Horse?* Available from: www.usingenglish.com/esl-in-china/trojan-horse.pdf., accessed on 12 May 2007.

Qiang, W. (2002) 'Primary school English teaching in China. New developments', *ELTED*, 7, 99–108.

Quicke, J. and Winter, C. (1994) 'Teaching the language of learning: towards a metacognitive approach to pupil empowerment', *British Educational Research Journal*, 20: 429–45.

Reinfried, M. (1999) 'Handlungsorientierung, Lernerzentrierung, Ganzheitlichkeit: Neuere Tendenzen in der Französischmethodik', *Französisch heute*, 3.

Rixon, S. (1992) 'English and other languages for younger children: practice and theory in rapidly changing world', *Language Teaching,* 25: 73–93.

Roberts, J. T. (1998) 'Humanistic approaches', in K. Johnson and H. Johnson (eds), *Encyclopedic Dictionary of Applied Linguistics.* Oxford: Blackwell.

Rogoff, B. (1990) *Apprenticeship in Thinking. Cognitive Development in Social Context.* Oxford and New York: Oxford University Press.

Rogoff, B. (2003) *The Cultural Nature of Human Development.* Oxford: Oxford University Press.

Rosenshine, B. and Meister, C. (1994) 'Reciprocal teaching: a review of the research', *Review of Educational Research,* 64: 479–531.

Rubin, J. (1975) 'What the "good language learner" can teach us', *TESOL Quarterly,* 9: 41–51.

Rumley, G. (1999) Games and songs for teaching modern foreign languages to young children', in P. Driscoll and D. Frost (eds), *The Teaching of Modern Foreign Languages in the Primary School.* London: Routledge.

Rumley, G. and Sharpe, K. (1999) *pilote plus.* Kent Council County.

Satchwell, P. (1997) *Keep Talking. Teaching in the Foreign Language.* London: CiLT.

Satchwell, P. and De Silva, J. (1995) *A Flying Start.* London: CiLT.

Sauer, H. (1992) 'Begegnung mit Sprachen in der Grundschule. Kritische Anmerkungen zum nord-rheinwestfälischen Begegnungssprachenkonzept, *Englisch,* 4: 128–31.

Savignon, S. (1972) *Communicative Competence: An Experiment in Foreign Language Teaching.* Philadelphia, PA: Center for Curriculum Development.

Savignon, S. and Berns, M. S. (eds) (1984) *Initiatives in Communicative Language Teaching.* Reading, PA: Addison-Wesley.

Savignon, S. J. (ed.) (2002) *Interpreting Communicative Language Teaching: Contexts and Concerns in Teacher Education.* New Haven, CT: Yale University Press.

Scarcella, R. C. and Oxford, R. (1992) *The Tapestry of Language Learning: The Individual in the Communicative Classroom.* Boston: Heinle.

Schieffelin, B. (1991) *The Give and Take of Everyday Life: Language Socialization of Kaluli Children.* New York: Cambridge University Press.

Schieffelin, B. and Ochs, E. (eds) (1986) *Language Socialization across Cultures.* Cambridge: Cambridge University Press.

Scollon, R. and Scollon, S. (1981) *Narrative, Literacy and Face in Interethnic Communication.* Norwood, NJ: Ablex.

Scottish Executive (2000) *Citizens of a Multilingual World, Ministerial Action Group on Languages.* Edinburgh: Tacita Solutions.

Searle, J. (1984) *Minds, Brains and Science.* Cambridge, MA: Harvard University Press.

Seedhouse, P. (1997) 'The case of the missing "No": The relationship between pedagogy and interaction', *Language Learning,* 47: 547–83.

Seedhouse, P. (2005) 'Task as a research construct', *Language Learning,* 55: 533–70.

Selinker, L. (1972) 'Interlanguage', *International Review of Applied Linguistics,* 10: 209–31.

Sharpe, K. (2001) *Modern Foreign Languages in the Primary School: the What, Why and How of Early Modern Foreign Languages Teaching.* London: Kogan Paul.

Singleton, D. (1989) *Language Aquisition and the Age Factor.* Clevedon, Avon: Multilingual Matters.

Skarbek, C. (1998) *First Steps to Reading and Writing.* London: CiLT.

Skehan, P. (1989) *Individual Differences in Second-Language Learning.* London: Edward Arnold.

Skinner, B. F. (1957) *Verbal Behaviour.* Englewood Cliffs, NJ: Prentice Hall.

Smithers, R. and Whitford, B. (2006) '"Free fall" fears as pupils abandon languages', *Education Guardian*, 25 August.

SNE (2002a) *Français écrit 3*. Luxemburg: Syndicat National des Enseignants.

SNE (2002b) *Français écrit 4*, Luxemburg: Syndicat National des Enseignants.

SNE (2002c) *Français écrit 5*, Luxemburg: Syndicat National des Enseignants.

Snow, C. E. and Hofnagel-Höhle, M. (1978) 'The critical period for language acquisition: evidence from second language learning', *Child Development*, 49: 1114–28.

Spada, N. (1997) Form-focussed instruction and second language acquisition: a review of classroom and laboratory research, *Language Teaching*: 73–87.

Spielmann, C. (2000) 'Fremdsprachenlernen mit allen Sinnen', in H. Sarter. (ed.), *Studienbrief und Materialienreihe: Fremdsprachen in Grund- und Hauptschulen, Fachdidaktik*. Koblenz: University of Koblenz, Landau.

Stein, B. (2000a) 'Lernerautonomie und Progression', in H. Sarter (ed.), *Lehrerfortbildung in NRW. Fremdsprachen in Grund- und Hauptschulen. Englisch in der Grundschule*. Koblenz: University of Koblenz, Landau.

Stein, B. (2000b) 'Spiel als Methode im Fremdsprachenunterricht (Unter Berücksitchitgung von Reimen, Gedichten und Liedern)', in H. Sarter (ed.), *Lehrerfortbildung in NRW. Fremdsprachen in Grund- und Hauptschulen. Englisch in der Grundschule*. Koblenz: University of Koblenz, Landau.

Steinbach, N. (2004) *Education report.Foreign Language Learning in the United States.VOA Special English Education Report*. Available from: www.voanews.com/specialenglish/archive/2004-04/a-2004-04-21-3-1.cfm, accessed on 22 April 2005.

Stern, H. H. (1975) 'What can we learn from the Good Language Learner?' *Canadian Modern Language Review*, 31: 304–18.

Stevick, E. W. (1976) *Memory, Meaning and Method*. Newbury: Newbury House Publishers.

Stewart, J. H. (2005) 'Foreign language study in elementary schools: benefits and implications for achievement in reading and writing', *Early Childhood Education Journal*, 33: 11–16.

Swain, M. (1985) 'Communicative competence: some roles of comprehensive input and comprehensible output in its development', in S. M. Gass and C. Madden (eds), *Input in Second Language Acquisition*. Cambridge, MA: Newbury House Publishers.

Swain, M. (1991) 'French immersion and its offshoots: getting two for one', in B. Freed, (ed.), *Foreign Language Acquisition: Research and the Classroom*. Lexington, MA: Heath.

Swain, M. (2000) 'The output hypothesis and beyond: mediating acquisition through collaborative dialogue', in J. P. Lantolf (ed.) *Sociocultural Theory and Second Language Learning*. Oxford: Oxford Applied Linguistics.

Taylor, D. (1994), 'Family literacy: conservation and change in the transmission of literacy styles and values', in J. Maybin (ed.), *Language and Literacy in Social Practice*. London: Multilingual Matters and Open University Press.

Taylor, H. (1981) 'Learning to listen in English', *TESOL Quarterly*, 15: 41–50.

Training and Development Agency (2007) *Primary Languages in Initial Teacher Training*. Available from: http://www.tda.gov.uk/upload/resources/pdf/t/tda0223.pdf, accessed on 22 March 2007.

Thorndike, E. (1932) *The Fundamentals of Learning*. New York: Teachers College Press.

Tierney, D. and Hope, M. (1998) *Making the Link*. London: CiLT.

Tierney, D. and Dobson, P. (1995) *Are You Sitting Comfortably?* London: CiLT.

Tsagari, C. (2005) 'Portfolio assessment with young EFL learners in Greek state schools', in P. Pavlou and K. Smith (eds) *Serving TEA to Young Learners: Proceedings of the Conference on Testing Young Learners organized by the University of Cyprus, IATEFL and CyTEA*. Israel: ORANIM – Academic College of Education, pp. 74–90.

US Department of State (2006) *National Security Language Initiative. Fact Sheet. Office of the Spokesman*. Washington, DC. 5 January 2006. Available from: www.state.gov/r/pa/prs/ps/2006/58733.htm, accessed on 31 October 2007.

Vilke, M. (1988) 'Some psychological aspects of early second-language acquisition', *Journal of Multilingual and Multicultural Development*, 9: 115–28.

Vincent, C. (1996) *Parents and Teachers: Power and Participation*. London: Falmer.

Vygotsky, L. (1962) *Thought and Language*. Cambridge, MA and London: MIT Press.

Vygotsky, L. S. (1978) *Mind in Society: The Development of Higher Psychological Processes*. Cambridge, MA: Harvard University Press.

Ward, M. C. (1971) *Them Children: A Study in Language Learning*. New York: Holt, Rinehart & Winston.

Wardhaugh, R. (1970) 'The Contrastive Analysis Hypothesis', *TESOL Quarterly*, 2: 123–30.

Wells, G. (1987) *The Meaning Makers: Children Learning Language and Using Language to Learn*. London: Hodder and Stoughton.

Welsh Language Board (2003) *Increase in number of Welsh speakers*. Available from: www.bwrdd-yr-iaith.org.uk/cynnwys. php?pID=241&langID=2&nID=174, accessed on 7 May 2007.

Wenden, A. L. and Rubin, J. (1987) *Learner Strategies in Language Learning*. Englewood Cliffs, NJ: Prentice Hall.

White, H. (1987) *The Content of the Form*. Baltimore, MD: Johns Hopkins Press.

Whitehead, M. (1996) *Materials and Methods 1966–1996 in 30 Years of Language Teaching*. London: CiLT.

Widdowson, H. G. (1978) *Teaching Language as Communication*. Oxford: Oxford University Press.

Willis, J. and Willis, D. (1996) *Challenge and Change in Language Education*. Oxford: Heinemann.

Wolff, D. (1999) 'Autonomes Lernen – ein Weg zur Mehrsprachigkeit', in H. Krechel, L. Diemo, M. Franzand J. Meißner (eds), *Kognition und neue Praxis im Französischunterricht. Akten des Französischlehrertages der Vereinigung für Französischlehrer*. Tübingen: Narr (Gießener Beiträge zur Fremdsprachendidaktik).

Wolff, D. and Rueschoff, B. (2000) 'Sprechen und Schreiben in der Fremdsprachenarbeit. Studienbrief Sprachwissenschaft Englisch', in H. Sarter (ed.), *Studienbrief- und Materialienreihe:Fremdsprachen in Grund- und Hauptschulen. Fernstudienprojekt Fremdsprachen in Grund- und Hauptschulen [CD-ROM]*. Koblenz: University of Koblenz-Landau.

Wood, D. (1998) *How Children Think and Learn*. MA: Blackwell Publishers.

Wood, D., Bruner, J. and Ross, G. (1976) 'The role of tutoring in problem-solving', *Journal of Child Psychology and Psychiatry*, 17: 89–100.

Yongqi, P. G., Hu, G. and Jun Zhang, L. (2005) 'Investigating language learner strategies among lower primary school pupils in Singapore', *Language and Education*, 19: 281–303.

Index

(whole chapter or section references in **bold**)